# THE
# PROMISE
# OF LIBERTY

## A PASSOVER HAGGADA

MAGGID

Stuart Halpern          Jacob Kupietzky

# THE PROMISE OF LIBERTY

## A PASSOVER HAGGADA

DESIGN BY
Suri Brand and Tani Bayer

Maggid Books

*The Promise of Liberty: A Passover Haggada*

First Edition, 2024

*Maggid Books*
*An imprint of Koren Publishers Jerusalem Ltd.*

POB 8531, New Milford, CT 06776-8531, USA
& POB 4044, Jerusalem 9104001, Israel

www.korenpub.com

The publication of this book was made possible through
the generous support of *The Jewish Book Trust.*

ISBN 978-1-59264-625-8, *hardcover*

Printed and bound in Turkey

# CONTENTS

## ESSAYS

# INTRODUCTION

In Philadelphia, on New Year's Day, 1808, Absalom Jones knew freedom had not yet been fully achieved. But there was still much to be grateful for.

Born into slavery in 1746, Jones was freed on the cusp of middle age, at age 38. Pursuing a career as a priest, he was the first African American ordained by the Episcopal Church in 1802.

Addressing his congregation on the day in which Congress's law prohibiting the importation of slaves, passed the year prior, finally took effect, Jones recalled another moment in which the promise of liberty began to shine forth. "The history of the world shows us," he thundered, "that the deliverance of the children of Israel from their bondage is not the only instance in which it has pleased God to appear in behalf of oppressed and distressed nations as the deliverer of the innocent and of those who call upon his name." Like in ancient times, "He has seen the anguish which has taken place, when parents have been torn from their children, and children from their parents, and conveyed, with their hands and feet bound in fetters." Jones himself had lived through such horrors. Earlier in his life, his master had sold his mother and siblings, but kept him.

But now was a time, Jones reassured his listeners in this "Thanksgiving Sermon," to recognize that Divine salvation was at hand. Once again, God has "heard the prayers that have ascended from the hearts of his people; and he has, as in the case of his ancient and chosen people the Jews, come down to deliver our suffering countrymen from the hands of their oppressors." Now was an occasion, he concluded, to "give thanks unto the Lord: let us call upon his name, and make known his deeds among the people. Let us sing psalms unto him and talk of all his wondrous works."

Every year at the Passover Seder, the Jewish story of liberation from Egypt – a tale which inspired Absalom Jones and countless others – is retold. Children, parents, and often grandparents sit together. Psalms of thanksgiving are sung to God in gratitude for His liberation of the oppressed millennia ago and in the hope of the ultimate future deliverance. We read of tyrants defeated, discuss the replacement of enslavement by revelation, and we set our sights on the Promised Land.

In *The Promise of Liberty: A Passover Haggada* you will find, alongside the traditional Haggada text, how American abolitionists and artists, Pilgrims and presidents, rabbis and revolutionaries, jazz critics and generals found inspiration in the Exodus story. From Sojourner Truth to the struggle to free Soviet Jewry, Harriet Tubman to Harry Truman, Mark Twain to Martin Luther King Jr., the Jewish story of redemption has inspired Americans of all backgrounds, from the country's inception to today.

◄ In his

In his journal entry dated December 17, 1773, the day after the Boston Tea Party, John Adams wrote in his diary that if the colonists were to resign themselves to taxation without representation, they would be "subjecting ourselves and our Posterity forever to Egyptian Taskmasters." Even the British press lamented King George III's mistreatment of his subjects across the pond, with one paper warning that if England did not make peace with the colonists, she would face the wrath of the "God of Battles" who "overthrew Pharaoh and his host in the Red Sea."

Amidst the harshness of the Revolutionary War, the physician and educator Benjamin Rush wrote to his friend the attorney Patrick Henry in 1778 lamenting that while they had successfully passed through the Red Sea, "A dreary wilderness is still before us, and unless a Moses or a Joshua are raised up in our behalf, we perish before we reach the promised land."

Of course, America found its Moses and Joshua in the form of General George Washington.

Washington himself reflected the impact of not only Jewish ideas, but of Jews themselves, on the American project. As president, he wrote to the Hebrew Congregation in Savannah, Georgia, with the invocation, "May the same wonder-working Deity, who long since delivering the Hebrews from their Egyptian Oppressors planted them in the promised land – whose providential agency has lately been conspicuous in establishing these United States as an independent nation – still continue to water them with the dews of Heaven and to make the inhabitants of every denomination participate in the temporal and spiritual blessings of that people…"

Through the subsequent development of America, the Passover story has always been present. The abolitionist poet Elizabeth Margaret Chandler wondered, "Are slavery and oppression aught more just/ Than in the days of Moses?" One of Martin Luther King Jr.'s final wishes was to "take a mental flight by Egypt" and watch a fractious group of slaves transform into a unified nation. George W. Bush spoke of "the truths of Sinai" that sustain our national life. To Barack Obama, the "story of perseverance amidst persecution, and faith in God and the Torah" has inspired generations of people forced to "weather poverty and persecution, while holding on to the hope that a better day was on the horizon."

*The Promise of Liberty* presents the Passover Seder's themes, images, ideas and ideals as the wellspring of the American founding and first 250 years and a source of wisdom for envisioning its brighter future.

As *The New York Times*'s David Brooks has written, the story can continue to serve as an organizing national tale, particularly amidst our currently fractious times. "It welcomes in each new group and gives it a template for how it fits into the common move from oppression to dignity. The book of Exodus is full of social justice – care for the vulnerable, the equality of all souls. It emphasizes that the moral and material journeys are intertwined and that for a nation to succeed materially, there has to be an invisible moral constitution and a fervent effort toward character education. It

◀ suggests that

suggests that history is in the shape of an upward spiral."

*The Promise of Liberty* seeks to inspire Jewish Americans, and all who might find themselves at a Passover Seder, by demonstrating how the ancient Israelites' songs of thanksgiving sung upon their Exodus from Egypt have long provided America with its own moral lyrics of liberty.

Following the text of the Haggada, leading contemporary Jewish American thinkers provide short reflections on the text within the Passover story that most resonates with them as American Jews. We invite you to consider your own favorite part of the Seder, as a Jew and as an American.

Thank you to research assistant Baruch-Lev Kelman and the team at Maggid Books for their incredible efforts in producing this book. Particularly enthusiastic gratitude is expressed to Matthew Miller, Reuven Ziegler, Caryn Meltz, Suri Brand, Aryeh Grossman, Tani Bayer, Atara Suna, and Rachel Miskin.

Wishing you a redemptive Passover!

Stuart Halpern and Jacob Kupietzky

# SEARCH FOR ḤAMETZ

On the night before Pesaḥ (Thursday night if Pesaḥ falls on Saturday night), a search for *ḥametz* is made in the house, customarily by candlelight. Before beginning the search, make the following blessing:

**Blessed are You, LORD our God, King of the Universe, who has made us holy through His commandments, and has commanded us about the removal of leaven.**

After the search, say:

**May** all *ḥametz* or leaven that is in my possession which I have not seen or removed, be annulled and deemed like the dust of the earth.

On the following morning, after burning the *ḥametz*, say:

**May** all *ḥametz* or leaven that is in my possession, whether I have seen it or not, whether I have removed it or not, be annulled and deemed like the dust of the earth.

# ERUV TAVSHILIN

It is not permitted to cook for Shabbat when a Yom Tov falls on Thursday or Friday unless an *Eruv Tavshilin* has been made prior to the Yom Tov. This is done by taking a piece of matza together with a boiled egg or some cooked food to be used on Shabbat. While holding them, say the following:

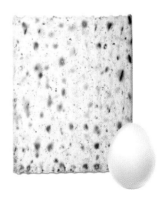

**Blessed are You, LORD our God, King of the Universe, who has made us holy through His commandments, and has commanded us about the mitzva of Eruv.**

**By** this Eruv may we be permitted to bake, cook, insulate food, light a flame and do everything necessary on the festival for the sake of the Sabbath, for us and for all Jews living in this city.

# בְּדִיקַת חָמֵץ

On the night before Pesaḥ (Thursday night if פסח falls on שבת מוצאי שבת), a search for חמץ is made in the house, customarily by candlelight. Before beginning the search, make the following blessing:

בָּרוּךְ אַתָּה יהוה אֱלֹהֵינוּ מֶלֶךְ הָעוֹלָם
אֲשֶׁר קִדְּשָׁנוּ בְּמִצְוֹתָיו וְצִוָּנוּ עַל בִּעוּר חָמֵץ.

After the search, say:

כָּל חֲמִירָא וַחֲמִיעָא דְּאִכָּא בִרְשׁוּתִי, דְּלָא חֲמִתֵּהּ
וּדְלָא בִעַרְתֵּהּ, לִבְטִיל וְלֶהֱוֵי הֶפְקֵר, כְּעַפְרָא דְאַרְעָא.

On the following morning, after burning the ḥametz, say:

כָּל חֲמִירָא וַחֲמִיעָא דְּאִכָּא בִרְשׁוּתִי, דַּחֲמִתֵּהּ וּדְלָא
חֲמִתֵּהּ, דְּבִעַרְתֵּהּ וּדְלָא בִעַרְתֵּהּ, לִבְטִיל וְלֶהֱוֵי
הֶפְקֵר, כְּעַפְרָא דְאַרְעָא.

# עֵירוּב תַּבְשִׁילִין

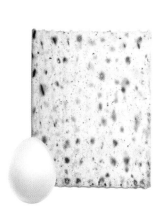

It is not permitted to cook for שבת when a יום טוב falls on Thursday or Friday unless an עֵירוּב תַּבְשִׁילִין has been made prior to the יום טוב. This is done by taking a piece of מצה together with a boiled egg or some cooked food to be used on שבת. While holding them, say the following:

בָּרוּךְ אַתָּה יהוה אֱלֹהֵינוּ מֶלֶךְ הָעוֹלָם
אֲשֶׁר קִדְּשָׁנוּ בְּמִצְוֹתָיו וְצִוָּנוּ עַל מִצְוַת עֵרוּב.

בְּדֵן עֵרוּבָא יְהֵא שָׁרֵא לָנָא לְמֵיפָא וּלְבַשָּׁלָא,
וּלְאַטְמָנָא וּלְאַדְלָקָא שְׁרָגָא וּלְמֶעְבַּד כָּל צָרְכָּנָא,
מִיּוֹמָא טָבָא לְשַׁבַּתָּא, לָנוּ וּלְכָל יִשְׂרָאֵל הַדָּרִים
בָּעִיר הַזֹּאת.

# הגדה של פסח

## THE PASSOVER HAGGADA

The first cup of wine is poured. Lift the cup with the right hand and say the following:

On Shabbat add:
And it was evening, and it was morning –

**The sixth day.** Then the heavens and the earth were completed, and all their array. With the seventh day, God completed the work He had done. He ceased on the seventh day from all the work He had done. God blessed the seventh day and declared it holy, because on it He ceased from all His work He had created to do.

On other evenings Kiddush starts here:

When saying Kiddush for others, add:
Please pay attention, my masters.

**Blessed are You, LORD our God, King of the Universe, who creates the fruit of the vine.**

On Shabbat, add the words in parentheses.

**Blessed** are You, LORD our God, King of the Universe, who has chosen us from among all peoples, raised us above all tongues, and made us holy through His commandments. You have given us, LORD our God, in love (Sabbaths for rest), festivals for rejoicing, holy days and seasons for joy, (this Sabbath day and) this day of the festival of matzot, the time of our freedom (with love), a holy assembly

# קדש

The first cup of wine is poured. Lift the cup with the right hand and say the following:

On שבת add:

וַיְהִי־עֶרֶב וַיְהִי־בֹקֶר

יוֹם הַשִּׁשִּׁי: וַיְכֻלּוּ הַשָּׁמַיִם וְהָאָרֶץ וְכָל־צְבָאָם: וַיְכַל
אֱלֹהִים בַּיּוֹם הַשְּׁבִיעִי מְלַאכְתּוֹ אֲשֶׁר עָשָׂה וַיִּשְׁבֹּת
בַּיּוֹם הַשְּׁבִיעִי מִכָּל־מְלַאכְתּוֹ אֲשֶׁר עָשָׂה: וַיְבָרֶךְ
אֱלֹהִים אֶת־יוֹם הַשְּׁבִיעִי, וַיְקַדֵּשׁ אֹתוֹ כִּי בוֹ שָׁבַת
מִכָּל־מְלַאכְתּוֹ, אֲשֶׁר־בָּרָא אֱלֹהִים, לַעֲשׂוֹת:

On other evenings קידוש starts here:

When saying קידוש for others, add:

סַבְרִי מָרָנָן:

בָּרוּךְ אַתָּה יהוה אֱלֹהֵינוּ מֶלֶךְ הָעוֹלָם
בּוֹרֵא פְּרִי הַגָּפֶן.

On שבת, add the words in parentheses.

בָּרוּךְ אַתָּה יהוה אֱלֹהֵינוּ מֶלֶךְ הָעוֹלָם, אֲשֶׁר בָּחַר
בָּנוּ מִכָּל עָם, וְרוֹמְמָנוּ מִכָּל לָשׁוֹן, וְקִדְּשָׁנוּ בְּמִצְוֹתָיו.
וַתִּתֶּן לָנוּ יהוה אֱלֹהֵינוּ בְּאַהֲבָה (שַׁבָּתוֹת לִמְנוּחָה
וּ)מוֹעֲדִים לְשִׂמְחָה, חַגִּים וּזְמַנִּים לְשָׂשׂוֹן אֶת יוֹם
(הַשַּׁבָּת הַזֶּה וְאֶת יוֹם) חַג הַמַּצוֹת הַזֶּה, זְמַן חֵרוּתֵנוּ

in memory of the Exodus from Egypt. For You have chosen us and sanctified us above all peoples, and given us as our heritage (Your holy Sabbath in love and favor and) Your holy festivals for joy and gladness. Blessed are you, LORD, who sanctifies (the Sabbath,) Israel and the festivals.

On Saturday night, the following Havdala is added:

**Blessed are You, LORD our God King of the Universe, who creates the lights of fire.**

**Blessed** are You, LORD our God, King of the Universe, who distinguishes between sacred and secular, between light and darkness, between Israel and the nations, between the seventh day and the six days of work. You have made a distinction between the holiness of the Sabbath and the holiness of festivals, and have sanctified the seventh day above the six days of work. You have distinguished and sanctified Your people Israel with Your holiness. Blessed are You, LORD, who distinguishes between sacred and sacred.

**Blessed are You, LORD our God, King of the Universe, who has given us life, sustained us, and brought us to this time.**

*Drink while reclining to the left.*

(בְּאַהֲבָה) מִקְרָא קֹדֶשׁ, זֵכֶר לִיצִיאַת מִצְרָיִם. כִּי בָנוּ
בָחַרְתָּ וְאוֹתָנוּ קִדַּשְׁתָּ מִכָּל הָעַמִּים, (וְשַׁבָּת) וּמוֹעֲדֵי
קָדְשֶׁךָ (בְּאַהֲבָה וּבְרָצוֹן) בְּשִׂמְחָה וּבְשָׂשׂוֹן הִנְחַלְתָּנוּ.
בָּרוּךְ אַתָּה יהוה, מְקַדֵּשׁ (הַשַּׁבָּת וְ)יִשְׂרָאֵל וְהַזְּמַנִּים.

On מוצאי שבת, the following הבדלה is added:

בָּרוּךְ אַתָּה יהוה אֱלֹהֵינוּ מֶלֶךְ הָעוֹלָם
בּוֹרֵא מְאוֹרֵי הָאֵשׁ.

בָּרוּךְ אַתָּה יהוה אֱלֹהֵינוּ מֶלֶךְ הָעוֹלָם, הַמַּבְדִּיל
בֵּין קֹדֶשׁ לְחֹל, בֵּין אוֹר לְחֹשֶׁךְ, בֵּין יִשְׂרָאֵל לָעַמִּים,
בֵּין יוֹם הַשְּׁבִיעִי לְשֵׁשֶׁת יְמֵי הַמַּעֲשֶׂה, בֵּין קְדֻשַּׁת
שַׁבָּת לִקְדֻשַּׁת יוֹם טוֹב הִבְדַּלְתָּ, וְאֶת יוֹם הַשְּׁבִיעִי
מִשֵּׁשֶׁת יְמֵי הַמַּעֲשֶׂה קִדַּשְׁתָּ, הִבְדַּלְתָּ וְקִדַּשְׁתָּ אֶת
עַמְּךָ יִשְׂרָאֵל בִּקְדֻשָּׁתֶךָ. בָּרוּךְ אַתָּה יהוה הַמַּבְדִּיל
בֵּין קֹדֶשׁ לְקֹדֶשׁ.

בָּרוּךְ אַתָּה יהוה אֱלֹהֵינוּ מֶלֶךְ הָעוֹלָם
שֶׁהֶחֱיָנוּ וְקִיְּמָנוּ וְהִגִּיעָנוּ לַזְּמַן הַזֶּה.

*Kiddush is recited on the first cup of wine*

Drink while reclining to the left.

# WHEN ASTRONAUTS CITED GENESIS TO INSPIRE THE WORLD

*Photo taken by Apollo 8 while in orbit around the moon*

וַיְכֻלּ֛וּ הַשָּׁמַ֥יִם וְהָאָ֖רֶץ וְכָל־ צְבָאָֽם

וַיְהִי־עֶרֶב וַיְהִי־בֹקֶר יוֹם הַשִּׁשִּׁי: וַיְכֻלּוּ הַשָּׁמַיִם וְהָאָרֶץ וְכָל־צְבָאָם:
וַיְכַל אֱלֹהִים בַּיּוֹם הַשְּׁבִיעִי מִכָּל־מְלַאכְתּוֹ אֲשֶׁר עָשָׂה.

*"And it was evening and it was morning – the sixth day. Then the heavens and the earth were completed, and all their array. With the seventh day, God completed the work He had done."*

Throughout the rich history of the United States, the Hebrew Bible has articulated the moral language of not only ideologues and political philosophers, but of pioneers and explorers. In December 1968, the crew of Apollo 8 – three such explorers, Jim Lovell (future mission commander of Apollo 13), Frank Borman, and Bill Anders – became the first human beings to reach the moon. While in orbit, they read aloud the first ten verses of the Book of Genesis, detailing the creation of the world. The reading was broadcast around the globe; it is estimated that one in four people – approximately one billion people in sixty-four countries – listened to the broadcast.

*Left to right: Lovell, Anders, Borman*

*Apollo 8 liftoff*

"We are now approaching lunar sunrise, and for all the people back on Earth, the crew of Apollo 8 has a message that we would like to send to you:

In the beginning God created the heaven and the earth. And the earth was without form, and void; and darkness was upon the face of the deep. And the Spirit of God moved upon the face of the waters. And God said, Let there be light: and there was light. And God saw the light, that it was good: and God divided the light from the darkness…'"

Water is brought to the leader.
The participants wash their hands
but do not say a blessing.

# URḤATZ

A small quantity of radish, greens, or roots
of parsley is dipped in salt water.
Say the following over the *karpas*,
with the intent to include the *maror* in the blessing:

# KARPAS

**Blessed are You, LORD our God, King of the Universe, who creates the fruit of the ground.**

Eat without reclining.

The middle matza is broken in two. The bigger
portion is then hidden away to serve as the
*afikoman* with which the meal is later concluded. The
smaller portion is placed between the two whole matzot.

# YAḤATZ

During the recital of this paragraph the
Seder plate is held up and the middle matza
is displayed to the company.

# MAGGID

**This is the bread** of oppression our fathers ate in the land of Egypt. Let all who are hungry come in and eat; let all who are in need come and join us for the Pesaḥ. Now we are here; next year in the Land of Israel. Now – slaves; next year we shall be free.

 וּרְחַץ

Water is brought to the leader.
The participants wash their hands
but do not say a blessing.

 כַּרְפַּס

A small quantity of radish, greens, or roots
of parsley is dipped in salt water.
Say the following over the כרפס,
with the intent to include the מרור in the blessing:

בָּרוּךְ אַתָּה יהוה אֱלֹהֵינוּ מֶלֶךְ הָעוֹלָם
בּוֹרֵא פְּרִי הָאֲדָמָה.

Eat without reclining.

 יַחַץ

The middle מצה is broken in two. The bigger
portion is then hidden away to serve as the
אפיקומן with which the meal is later concluded. The
smaller portion is placed between the two whole מצות.

 מַגִּיד

During the recital of this paragraph the
קערה is held up and the middle מצה
is displayed to the company.

הָא לַחְמָא עַנְיָא דִּי אֲכַלוּ אַבְהָתָנָא בְּאַרְעָא
דְמִצְרָיִם. כָּל דִּכְפִין יֵיתֵי וְיֵכֹל, כָּל דִּצְרִיךְ יֵיתֵי
וְיִפְסַח, הָשַׁתָּא הָכָא לְשָׁנָה הַבָּאָה בְּאַרְעָא
דְיִשְׂרָאֵל, הָשַׁתָּא עַבְדֵּי לְשָׁנָה הַבָּאָה בְּנֵי
חוֹרִין.

# CELEBRATING ISRAEL'S FREEDOM AMIDST CIVIL WAR

כָּל דִּצְרִיךְ וְיֵתֵי וְיִפְסַח

*Wife of a soldier waving a flag during the Civil War*

הָא לַחְמָא עַנְיָא דִי אֲכָלוּ אֲבָהָתָנָא בְּאַרְעָא דְמִצְרַיִם, כָּל דִּכְפִין
יֵיתֵי וְיֵכֹל, כָּל דִּצְרִיךְ יֵיתֵי וְיִפְסַח.

*"This is the bread of oppression our fathers ate in the land of Egypt. Let all who are hungry come in and eat; let all who are in need come and join us for the Pesaḥ."*

*In the forest during the Civil War*

In the April 1866 issue of *The Jewish Messenger*, Private Joseph A. Joel of the 23rd Ohio Volunteer Regiment poignantly recounts a Seder held in 1862, the first Passover during the Civil War, in Fayette, West Virginia, when he was 19.

> Being apprised of the approaching Feast of Passover, twenty of my comrades and co-religionists belonging to the Regiment, united in a request to our commanding officer for relief from duty, in order that we might keep the holydays, which he readily acceded to…. We were anxiously awaiting to receive our matzos and about the middle of the morning of ערב פסח [Eve of Passover] a supply train arrived in camp, and to our delight seven barrels of Matzos. On opening them, we were surprised and pleased to find that our thoughtful sutler had enclosed two Hagedahs and prayer-books….
>
> There, in the wild woods of West Virginia, away from home and friends, we consecrated and offered up to the ever-loving God of Israel our prayers and sacrifice. I doubt whether the spirits of our forefathers, had they been looking down on us, standing there with our arms by our side ready for an attack, faithful to our God and our cause, would have imagined themselves amongst mortals, enacting this commemoration of the scene that transpired in Egypt.

# "We consecrated and offered up to the ever-loving God of Israel our prayers."

## הָשַׁתָּא הָכָא לְשָׁנָה הַבָּאָה בְּאַרְעָא דְּיִשְׂרָאֵל.

*"Now we are here; next year in the Land of Israel."*

Founding Father and former president John Adams had a cordial correspondence with the American Jewish diplomat and journalist Mordecai Manuel Noah (1785–1851). In an 1819 letter to Noah, Adams expressed his wish that Jews would one day return to inhabit the Land of Israel, led by Noah, who long dreamed of a Jewish national restoration. Adams wrote:

*The Old City of Jerusalem*

*Mordecai Manuel Noah*

I wish you had continued your travels into Syria Judea & Jerusalem. I should attend more to your [interesting] remarks upon those interesting countries than to those of any traveler I have yet read – If I were to let my imagination loose...I could find it in my heart to wish that you had been at the head of a hundred thousand Israelites indeed as well disciplin'd as a French army – & marching with them into Judea & making a conquest of that country & restoring your nation to the dominion of it – For I really wish the Jews again in Judea an independent nation.

לְשָׁנָה הַבָּאָה בְּאַרְעָא דְיִשְׂרָאֵל

JOHN ADAMS
WISHES FOR
THE JEWISH
RETURN
TO ISRAEL

The Seder plate and the matzot are now covered and the second cup of wine is poured. The youngest child asks the following questions:

**What makes this night** unlike all other nights?

**So that every other night** we eat either bread or matza, but tonight there is only matza.

**And that every other night** we eat many different greens, but tonight we will eat bitter herbs.

**And that every other night** we do not dip [our food] at all, but tonight we will dip it twice.

**And that every other night** some sit to eat and some recline, but tonight we are all reclining.

*UNLIKE ALL OTHER NIGHTS*

Grated horseradish,
a bitter herb

מַה נִּשְׁתַּנָּה הַלַּיְלָה הַזֶּה מִכָּל הַלֵּילוֹת?

שֶׁבְּכָל הַלֵּילוֹת אָנוּ אוֹכְלִין חָמֵץ וּמַצָּה,
הַלַּיְלָה הַזֶּה כֻּלּוֹ מַצָּה.

שֶׁבְּכָל הַלֵּילוֹת אָנוּ אוֹכְלִין שְׁאָר יְרָקוֹת,
הַלַּיְלָה הַזֶּה מָרוֹר.

שֶׁבְּכָל הַלֵּילוֹת אֵין אָנוּ מַטְבִּילִין אֲפִילוּ
פַּעַם אֶחָת, הַלַּיְלָה הַזֶּה שְׁתֵּי פְעָמִים.

שֶׁבְּכָל הַלֵּילוֹת אָנוּ אוֹכְלִין בֵּין יוֹשְׁבִין וּבֵין
מְסֻבִּין, הַלַּיְלָה הַזֶּה – כֻּלָּנוּ מְסֻבִּין.

**We were slaves** to Pharaoh in Egypt, and the LORD our God brought us out of there with a strong hand and an outstretched arm. And if the Holy One, blessed be He, had not brought our fathers out of Egypt – then we, and our children, and the children of our children, would still be enslaved to Pharaoh in Egypt. And even were we all wise, all intelligent, all aged and all knowledgeable in the Torah, still the command would be upon us to tell of the coming out of Egypt; and the more one tells of the coming out of Egypt, the more admirable it is.

WE WERE SLAVES

16

The קְעָרָה and the מַצּוֹת are uncovered.

עֲבָדִים הָיִינוּ לְפַרְעֹה בְּמִצְרַיִם וַיּוֹצִיאֵנוּ יהוה אֱלֹהֵינוּ מִשָּׁם בְּיָד חֲזָקָה וּבִזְרוֹעַ נְטוּיָה. וְאִלּוּ לֹא הוֹצִיא הַקָּדוֹשׁ בָּרוּךְ הוּא אֶת אֲבוֹתֵינוּ מִמִּצְרַיִם, הֲרֵי אָנוּ וּבָנֵינוּ וּבְנֵי בָנֵינוּ מְשֻׁעְבָּדִים הָיִינוּ לְפַרְעֹה בְּמִצְרָיִם. וַאֲפִלּוּ כֻּלָּנוּ חֲכָמִים, כֻּלָּנוּ נְבוֹנִים, כֻּלָּנוּ זְקֵנִים, כֻּלָּנוּ יוֹדְעִים אֶת הַתּוֹרָה, מִצְוָה עָלֵינוּ לְסַפֵּר בִּיצִיאַת מִצְרָיִם, וְכָל הַמַּרְבֶּה לְסַפֵּר בִּיצִיאַת מִצְרַיִם הֲרֵי זֶה מְשֻׁבָּח.

*The Sphinx in Egypt*

וְאִלּוּ לֹא
הוֹצִיא

# BATTLING EGYPTIAN TASKMASTERS AT THE BOSTON TEA PARTY

*The destruction of tea at Boston Harbor*

וְאִלּוּ לֹא הוֹצִיא הַקָּדוֹשׁ בָּרוּךְ הוּא אֶת אֲבוֹתֵינוּ מִמִּצְרַיִם, הֲרֵי
אָנוּ וּבָנֵינוּ וּבְנֵי בָנֵינוּ מְשֻׁעְבָּדִים הָיִינוּ לְפַרְעֹה בְּמִצְרָיִם.

*"And if the Holy One, blessed be He, had not brought our fathers
out of Egypt – then we, and our children, and the children of our
children, would still be enslaved to Pharaoh in Egypt."*

*John Adams,
second president
of the United States*

In his diary entry dated December 17,
1773, John Adams described the colonists'
protest against the British:

> Last Night 3 Cargoes of Bohea Tea were
> emptied into the Sea. This Morning a
> Man of War sails....

> The Question is whether the Destruc-
> tion of this Tea was necessary? I appre-
> hend it was absolutely and indispens-
> ably so.... To let it be landed, would be
> giving up the Principle of Taxation by
> Parliamentary Authority, against which
> the Continent have struggled for 10
> years, it was loosing all our labour for
> 10 years and subjecting ourselves and
> our Posterity forever to Egyptian Task-
> masters – to Burthens, Indignities, to
> Ignominy, Reproach and Contempt, to
> Desolation and Oppression, to Poverty
> and Servitude.

# "It was...subjecting ourselves and our Posterity forever to Egyptian Taskmasters."

וְכָל הַמַּרְבֶּה לְסַפֵּר בִּיצִיאַת מִצְרַיִם הֲרֵי זֶה מְשֻׁבָּח.

*"And the more one tells of the coming out of Egypt, the more admirable it is."*

In Jerusalem, on March 21, 2013, President Barack Obama recounted Passover's story of perseverance amidst persecution.

Just a few days from now, Jews here in Israel and around the world will sit with family and friends at the Seder table, and celebrate with songs, wine and symbolic foods. After enjoying Seders with family and friends in Chicago and on the campaign trail, I'm proud that I've now brought this tradition into the White House. I did so because I wanted my daughters to experience the Haggada, and the story at the center of Passover that makes this time of year so powerful.

It's a story of centuries of slavery, and years of wandering in the desert; a story of perseverance amidst persecution, and faith in God and the Torah. It's a story about finding freedom in your own land. And for the Jewish people,

*Celebrating the abolition of slavery*

*Passover Seder at the White House*

this story is central to who you've become. But it's also a story that holds within it the universal human experience, with all of its suffering, but also all of its salvation.... To African Americans, the story of the Exodus was perhaps the central story, the most powerful image about emerging from the grip of bondage to reach for liberty and human dignity – a tale that was carried from slavery through the Civil Rights Movement into today.

For generations, this promise helped people weather poverty and persecution, while holding on to the hope that a better day was on the horizon. For me, personally, growing up in far-flung parts of the world and without firm roots, the story spoke to a yearning within every human being for a home.

*Portrayal of Black slavery, c. 1841*

# PERSEVERANCE
# AMIDST
# PERSECUTION

**Once, Rabbi Eliezer** and Rabbi Yehoshua and Rabbi Elazar ben Azaria and Rabbi Akiva and Rabbi Tarfon reclined [for the Seder] in Bnei Brak. And they told of the Exodus from Egypt all that night; until their students came in and said, "Teachers – the time for saying the *Shema* of the morning has come."

**Rabbi Elazar ben Azaria said:** I am almost seventy years old, and never have I merited to find the command to speak of the Exodus from Egypt at night – until Ben Zoma interpreted: It is written, "so that you remember the day of your exodus from Egypt all the days of your life." "The days of your life" would mean in the days; "all the days of your life" includes the nights. But the sages say, "The days of your life" would mean only in this world; "all the days of your life" brings in the time of the Messiah.

AND THEY TOLD OF THE EXODUS

מַעֲשֶׂה בְּרַבִּי אֱלִיעֶזֶר וְרַבִּי יְהוֹשֻׁעַ וְרַבִּי אֶלְעָזָר בֶּן עֲזַרְיָה וְרַבִּי עֲקִיבָא וְרַבִּי טַרְפוֹן, שֶׁהָיוּ מְסֻבִּין בִּבְנֵי בְרַק, וְהָיוּ מְסַפְּרִים בִּיצִיאַת מִצְרַיִם כָּל אוֹתוֹ הַלַּיְלָה, עַד שֶׁבָּאוּ תַלְמִידֵיהֶם וְאָמְרוּ לָהֶם, רַבּוֹתֵינוּ, הִגִּיעַ זְמַן קְרִיאַת שְׁמַע שֶׁל שַׁחֲרִית.

אָמַר רַבִּי אֶלְעָזָר בֶּן עֲזַרְיָה, הֲרֵי אֲנִי כְּבֶן שִׁבְעִים שָׁנָה וְלֹא זָכִיתִי שֶׁתֵּאָמֵר יְצִיאַת מִצְרַיִם בַּלֵּילוֹת עַד שֶׁדְּרָשָׁהּ בֶּן זוֹמָא, שֶׁנֶּאֱמַר: לְמַעַן תִּזְכֹּר אֶת־יוֹם צֵאתְךָ מֵאֶרֶץ מִצְרַיִם כָּל יְמֵי חַיֶּיךָ: יְמֵי חַיֶּיךָ הַיָּמִים, כֹּל יְמֵי חַיֶּיךָ הַלֵּילוֹת. וַחֲכָמִים אוֹמְרִים, יְמֵי חַיֶּיךָ הָעוֹלָם הַזֶּה, כֹּל יְמֵי חַיֶּיךָ לְהָבִיא לִימוֹת הַמָּשִׁיחַ.

# ISRAEL'S COUNCIL OF ELDERS

*The Jewish people in the wilderness surrounding the Tabernacle*

*"Once, Rabbi Eliezer and Rabbi Yehoshua and Rabbi Elazar ben Azaria and Rabbi Akiva and Rabbi Tarfon reclined [for the Seder] in Bnei Brak."*

*Second Continental Congress*

The rabbinic leaders who reclined together in Bnei Brak were, like the ancient elders in the biblical wilderness, offering spiritual and judicial leadership to their people. In a 1778 sermon for the parish of New Hampshire entitled "The Republic of The Israelites An Example To The American States," Samuel Langdon (1723–1797), a Boston minister and revolutionary preacher, drew inspiration from this Jewish model.

When first the Israelites came out from the bondage of Egypt, they were a multitude without any other order than what had been kept up, very feebly, under the ancient patriarchal authority.... Therefore, upon the complaint of Moses that the burden of government was too heavy for him, God commanded him to bring seventy men, chosen from among the elders and officers, and present them at the tabernacle; and there he endured them with the same spirit which was in Moses, that they might bear the burden with him. Thus a senate was evidently constituted, as necessary for the future government of the nation, under a chief commander. And as to the choice of this senate, doubtless the people were consulted, who appear to have had a voice in all public affairs from time to time, the whole congregation being called together on all important occasions: the government therefore was a proper republic.

If I am not mistaken, instead of the twelve tribes of Israel, we may substitute the thirteen states of the American union....

# "Instead of the twelve tribes of Israel, we may substitute the thirteen states of the American union."

שֶׁנֶּאֱמַר: לְמַעַן תִּזְכֹּר אֶת־יוֹם צֵאתְךָ מֵאֶרֶץ מִצְרַיִם כֹּל יְמֵי חַיֶּיךָ:
יְמֵי חַיֶּיךָ הַיָּמִים, כֹּל יְמֵי חַיֶּיךָ הַלֵּילוֹת.

*"It is written, 'so that you remember the day of your exodus from Egypt all the days of your life.' 'The days of your life' would mean in the days; 'all the days of your life' includes the nights."*

Thomas Wentworth Higginson (1823–1911) was a white Unitarian minister, an abolitionist, and captain in the 51st Massachusetts Infantry during the Civil War. His memoir, *Army Life in a Black Regiment*, gives a glimpse into the biblically charged mentality of Black soldiers in the Union army who saw themselves as modern Israelites fighting to free their families from bondage, envisioning in a prior redemption a promise for a future emancipation.

*Thomas Wentworth Higginson*

One can hardly imagine a body of men more disconsolate than a regiment suddenly transferred from an adventurous life in the enemy's country to the quiet of a sheltered camp…. My dusky soldiers, who based their whole walk and conversation strictly on the ancient Israelites, felt that the prophecies were all set at naught, and that they were on the wrong side of the Red Sea; indeed, I

fear they regarded even me as a sort of reversed Moses, whose Pisgah fronted in the wrong direction. Had they foreseen how the next occupation of the Promised Land was destined to result, they might have acquiesced with more of their wonted cheerfulness….

During the services there was singing, the chaplain deaconing out the hymn in their favorite way. This ended, he announced his text, "This poor man cried, and the Lord heard him, and delivered him out of all his trouble." Instantly, to my great amazement, the cracked voice of the chorister was uplifted, intoning the text, as if it were the first verse of another hymn…. Their memories are a vast bewildered chaos of Jewish history and biography; and most of the great events of the past… they instinctively attribute to Moses.

*Soldiers of the 25th Infantry from Buffalo*

MAGGID 26

כֹּל יְמֵי חַיֶּיךָ הַלֵּילוֹת

**A VAST
BEWILDERED
CHAOS OF
JEWISH
HISTORY**

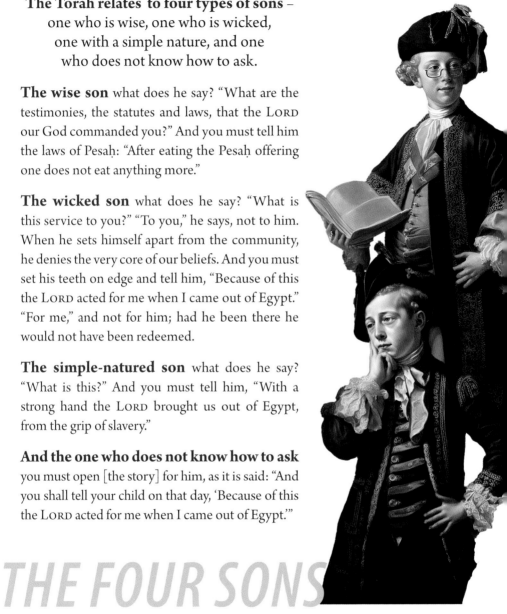

**Blessed is the One who gave His people Israel, the Torah – blessed is He.**

**The Torah relates to four types of sons –** one who is wise, one who is wicked, one with a simple nature, and one who does not know how to ask.

**The wise son** what does he say? "What are the testimonies, the statutes and laws, that the LORD our God commanded you?" And you must tell him the laws of Pesaḥ: "After eating the Pesaḥ offering one does not eat anything more."

**The wicked son** what does he say? "What is this service to you?" "To you," he says, not to him. When he sets himself apart from the community, he denies the very core of our beliefs. And you must set his teeth on edge and tell him, "Because of this the LORD acted for me when I came out of Egypt." "For me," and not for him; had he been there he would not have been redeemed.

**The simple-natured son** what does he say? "What is this?" And you must tell him, "With a strong hand the LORD brought us out of Egypt, from the grip of slavery."

**And the one who does not know how to ask** you must open [the story] for him, as it is said: "And you shall tell your child on that day, 'Because of this the LORD acted for me when I came out of Egypt.'"

*THE FOUR SONS*

בָּרוּךְ הַמָּקוֹם בָּרוּךְ הוּא, בָּרוּךְ שֶׁנָּתַן תּוֹרָה לְעַמּוֹ יִשְׂרָאֵל, בָּרוּךְ הוּא

כְּנֶגֶד אַרְבָּעָה בָנִים דִּבְּרָה תוֹרָה, אֶחָד חָכָם וְאֶחָד רָשָׁע וְאֶחָד תָּם וְאֶחָד שֶׁאֵינוֹ יוֹדֵעַ לִשְׁאֹל.

חָכָם מַה הוּא אוֹמֵר מָה הָעֵדֹת וְהַחֻקִּים וְהַמִּשְׁפָּטִים אֲשֶׁר צִוָּה יְהוָה אֱלֹהֵינוּ אֶתְכֶם: וְאַף אַתָּה אֱמָר לוֹ כְּהִלְכוֹת הַפֶּסַח אֵין מַפְטִירִין אַחַר הַפֶּסַח אֲפִיקוֹמָן.

רָשָׁע מַה הוּא אוֹמֵר, מָה הָעֲבֹדָה הַזֹּאת לָכֶם: לָכֶם וְלֹא לוֹ וּלְפִי שֶׁהוֹצִיא אֶת עַצְמוֹ מִן הַכְּלָל כָּפַר בָּעִקָּר, וְאַף אַתָּה הַקְהֵה אֶת שִׁנָּיו, וֶאֱמֹר לוֹ בַּעֲבוּר זֶה עָשָׂה יְהוָה לִי בְּצֵאתִי מִמִּצְרָיִם: לִי וְלֹא לוֹ אִלּוּ הָיָה שָׁם, לֹא הָיָה נִגְאָל.

תָּם מַה הוּא אוֹמֵר, מַה־זֹּאת, וְאָמַרְתָּ אֵלָיו בְּחֹזֶק יָד הוֹצִיאָנוּ יְהוָה מִמִּצְרַיִם מִבֵּית עֲבָדִים:

וְשֶׁאֵינוֹ יוֹדֵעַ לִשְׁאֹל אַתְּ פְּתַח לוֹ, שֶׁנֶּאֱמַר וְהִגַּדְתָּ לְבִנְךָ בַּיּוֹם הַהוּא לֵאמֹר בַּעֲבוּר זֶה עָשָׂה יְהוָה לִי בְּצֵאתִי מִמִּצְרָיִם:

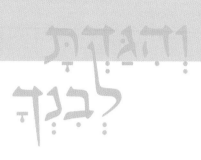

# A
# REVOLUTIONARY
# SEDER

וְהִגַּדְתָּ
לְבִנְךָ

וְהִגַּדְתָּ לְבִנְךָ בַּיּוֹם הַהוּא לֵאמֹר, בַּעֲבוּר זֶה עָשָׂה יהוה לִי בְּצֵאתִי מִמִּצְרָיִם.

*"And you shall tell your child on that day, 'Because of this the Lord acted for me when I came out of Egypt.'"*

During the Revolutionary era, Gershom Mendes Seixas was the *ḥazan* of Congregation Shearith Israel in New York, the oldest Jewish congregation in the United States. Seixas was an ardent supporter of the cause of independence. In August 1776, as the British army moved on to New York, Seixas delivered a revolutionary themed sermon in the synagogue, and then fled the city with the congregation's Torah scrolls, first to Stamford and then later on to Philadelphia. At the Revolutionary War's end, Seixas was asked to leave Philadelphia, presumably to return to his pulpit in New York. However, in a letter dated March 15, 1784, Seixas, reflecting the Haggada's emphasis on intergenerational

*Gershom Mendes Seixas*

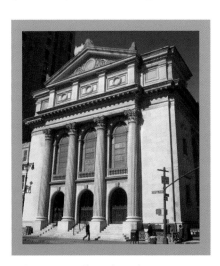

*Congregation Shearith Israel*

conversation, asked a certain Mr. Levy for permission to remain in Philadelphia during Passover so that he could celebrate the holiday with his family. He writes:

Dear & Worthy Sir,

Should the Prayer of the Letter (that I can stay in Philadelphia until the new month of Iyar) not be thought Eligible you will please let me know by Post – & I'll be with you for Shabbat Hagadol – & leave my Family till after Pesah – tho' – you must allow it to be a great Hardship for a Man to be without His Family on a Pesah.

Gershom Mendes Seixas

**One might have thought** that this meant from the beginning of the month. And so it says, "on that day." Had it said only "on that day," one might have thought [the obligation] applied during the day. And so it also says, "Because of this" – "because of this" can only be said when matza and bitter herbs are there before you.

**In the beginning,** our ancestors were idol worshippers. But now the Omnipresent has drawn us close in His service; as it is said: "Joshua said to all the people, 'This is what the LORD God of Israel has said: Beyond the river your ancestors always dwelled – Terah the father of Abraham, the father of Nahor – and they served other gods.'"

*The Luxor Temple in Egypt*

*Three ancient pagodas at the Wat Phra Si Sanphet Temple in Thailand*

*Ruins from the ancient Mayan civilization in Chichen Itza*

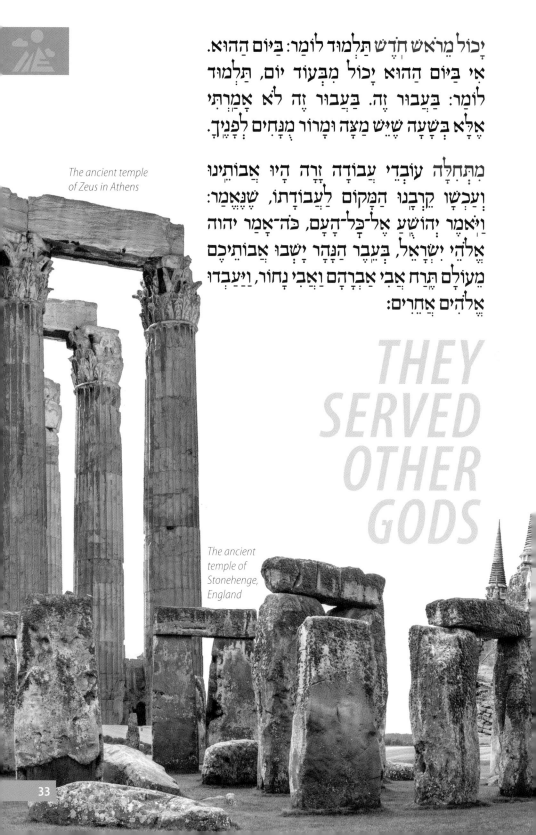

יָכוֹל מֵרֹאשׁ חֹדֶשׁ תַּלְמוּד לוֹמַר: בַּיּוֹם הַהוּא.
אִי בַּיּוֹם הַהוּא יָכוֹל מִבְּעוֹד יוֹם, תַּלְמוּד
לוֹמַר: בַּעֲבוּר זֶה. בַּעֲבוּר זֶה לֹא אָמַרְתִּי
אֶלָּא בְּשָׁעָה שֶׁיֵּשׁ מַצָּה וּמָרוֹר מֻנָּחִים לְפָנֶיךָ.

מִתְּחִלָּה עוֹבְדֵי עֲבוֹדָה זָרָה הָיוּ אֲבוֹתֵינוּ
וְעַכְשָׁו קֵרְבָנוּ הַמָּקוֹם לַעֲבוֹדָתוֹ, שֶׁנֶּאֱמַר:
וַיֹּאמֶר יְהוֹשֻׁעַ אֶל־כָּל־הָעָם, כֹּה־אָמַר יהוה
אֱלֹהֵי יִשְׂרָאֵל, בְּעֵבֶר הַנָּהָר יָשְׁבוּ אֲבוֹתֵיכֶם
מֵעוֹלָם תֶּרַח אֲבִי אַבְרָהָם וַאֲבִי נָחוֹר, וַיַּעַבְדוּ
אֱלֹהִים אֲחֵרִים:

*The ancient temple of Zeus in Athens*

*The ancient temple of Stonehenge, England*

THEY
SERVED
OTHER
GODS

# KING GEORGE III IS PHARAOH

*The Battle of Lexington,
April 1775*

מַתְחִיל
עוֹבְדִי
עֲבוֹדָה
זָרָה

מִתְּחִלָּה עוֹבְדֵי עֲבוֹדָה זָרָה הָיוּ אֲבוֹתֵינוּ, וְעַכְשָׁו קֵרְבָנוּ הַמָּקוֹם
לַעֲבוֹדָתוֹ.

*"In the beginning, our ancestors were idol worshippers. But now
the Omnipresent has drawn us close in His service."*

The political activist Thomas Paine, in his extremely influential 1776 pamphlet *Common Sense*, drew from the stories of the books of Exodus and Samuel to prove his assertion that monarchy was an evil that the Bible likened to idolatry.

> Government by kings was first introduced into the world by the Heathens, from whom the children of Israel copied the custom. It was the most prosperous invention the Devil ever set on foot for the promotion of idolatry.... How impious is the title of sacred Majesty applied to a worm, who in the midst of his splendor is crumbling into dust!

> As the exalting one man so greatly above the rest cannot be justified on the equal rights of nature, so neither

*Thomas Paine*

can it be defended on the authority of scripture; for the will of the Almighty as declared by Gideon, and the prophet Samuel, expressly disapproves of government by Kings.... Monarchy is ranked in scripture as one of the sins of the Jews, for which a curse in reserve is denounced against them....

No man was a warmer wisher for reconciliation than myself, before the fatal nineteenth of April 1775 [the battles of Lexington and Concord], but the moment the event of that day was made known, I rejected the hardened, sullen tempered Pharaoh of England for ever; and disdain the wretch, that with the pretended title of FATHER OF HIS PEOPLE, can unfeelingly hear of their slaughter, and composedly sleep with their blood upon his soul.

*King George III in coronation clothes*

וַיֹּאמֶר יְהוֹשֻׁעַ אֶל כָּל הָעָם, כֹּה אָמַר יהוה אֱלֹהֵי יִשְׂרָאֵל.

*"Joshua said to all the people, 'This is what the LORD God of Israel has said.'"*

The theologian, minister, president of Yale University and founder of Brown University Dr. Ezra Stiles had a deep affinity for the Hebrew Bible, which he shared with his beloved close friend Ḥakham Isaac Carigal. It was Stiles's love for the Bible which made him see the American cause for independence in biblical terms. In his 1783 sermon, "The United States Elevated to Honor and Glory," he compares the fledgling country to Israel and lauds General Washington as a new Joshua.

Ḥakham Isaac Carigal

> God be thanked, we have lived to see peace restored to this bleeding land, at least a general cessation of hostilities among the belligerent powers. And on this occasion does it not become us to reflect, how wonderful, how gracious, how glorious, has been the good hand of our God upon us, in carrying us thro'

so tremendous a warfare....

Congress put at the head of this spirited army, the only man, on whom the eyes of all Israel were placed. Posterity, I apprehend, and the world itself, inconsiderate and incredulous as they may be of the dominion of heaven, will yet do so much justice to the divine moral government, as to acknowledge, that this American Joshua was raised up by God, and *divinely formed* by a peculiar influence of the Sovereign of the Universe, for the great work of leading the armies of this American Joseph (now separated from his brethren) [the colonists], and conducting this people through the severe, the arduous conflict, to liberty and independence.

*Dr. Ezra Stiles*

וַיֹּאמֶר
יְהוֹשֻׁעַ
אֶל כָּל
הָעָם

*The Washington Monument
during the Cherry Blossom Festival*

GENERAL
GEORGE
WASHINGTON
IS
JOSHUA

"**But I took your father** Abraham from beyond the river, and I led him all the way across the land of Canaan, and I multiplied his offspring and gave him Isaac. And to Isaac I gave Jacob and Esau, and I gave Esau Mount Seir as an inheritance, while Jacob and his children went down to Egypt."

*BEYOND THE RIVER*

*Euphrates River, the river that Abraham crossed*

וָאֶקַּח אֶת־אֲבִיכֶם אֶת־אַבְרָהָם מֵעֵבֶר הַנָּהָר, וָאוֹלֵךְ אוֹתוֹ בְּכָל־אֶרֶץ כְּנָעַן, וָאַרְבֶּה אֶת־זַרְעוֹ, וָאֶתֶּן־לוֹ אֶת־יִצְחָק: וָאֶתֵּן לְיִצְחָק אֶת־יַעֲקֹב וְאֶת־עֵשָׂו, וָאֶתֵּן לְעֵשָׂו אֶת־הַר שֵׂעִיר לָרֶשֶׁת אוֹתוֹ, וְיַעֲקֹב וּבָנָיו יָרְדוּ מִצְרָיִם:

*Entrance to Petra, Jordan, the territory of the ancient Edomites, the descendants of Esau*

## HARRIET TUBMAN SINGS OF THE EXODUS

יָרְדוּ מִצְרָיִם

*Bust of Thutmose III*

So the God said: go down, Moses

Way down in Egypt land

Tell old Pharaohs to

Let my people go!

So Moses went to Egypt land

Let my people go!

He made old Pharaoh understand

Let my people go!

Yes the Lord said: go down, Moses

Way down in Egypt land

Tell old Pharaohs to

Let my people go!

Thus spoke the Lord, bold Moses said:

– let my people go!

if not I'll smite, your firstborn dead

– let my people go!

Cuz the Lord said: go down, Moses

Way down in Egypt land

Tell old Pharaohs to

Let my people go!

Tell old Pharaohs to

To let my people go.

וְיַעֲקֹב וּבָנָיו יָרְדוּ מִצְרָיִם.

*"Jacob and his children went down to Egypt."*

The Underground Railroad, the network of routes and safehouses used by enslaved African Americans to escape to freedom, was often described in biblical terms. Abolitionist journalist James Redpath said that "The Great Exodus of Slaves" in the Bible was "the first underground railroad that history ever mentions," while an imagined monologue of a slave printed in the African Methodist Episcopal Church's *Christian Recorder* asserted that the first track of the Railroad was laid in the Red Sea by the Lord Almighty with Moses and Aaron as its conductors.

*Harriet Tubman*

*The Underground Railroad was a network of clandestine routes and safehouses*

Agents of Harriet Tubman (1822–1913), the great heroine of the Railroad, sang gospel songs relating to the Exodus to secretly herald her arrival to slaves awaiting rescue. Tubman referred to the South as "the Land of Egypt" and was said to have sung an early version of Go Down Moses as she led slaves to freedom. The song was later popularized by Louis Armstrong in 1958:

*Go down Moses*

*Way down in Egypt land*

*Tell old Pharaoh to*

*Let my people go!*

*When Israel was in Egypt land*

*Let my people go!*

*Oppressed so hard they could not stand*

*Let my people go!*

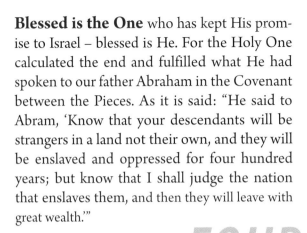

**Blessed is the One** who has kept His promise to Israel – blessed is He. For the Holy One calculated the end and fulfilled what He had spoken to our father Abraham in the Covenant between the Pieces. As it is said: "He said to Abram, 'Know that your descendants will be strangers in a land not their own, and they will be enslaved and oppressed for four hundred years; but know that I shall judge the nation that enslaves them, and then they will leave with great wealth.'"

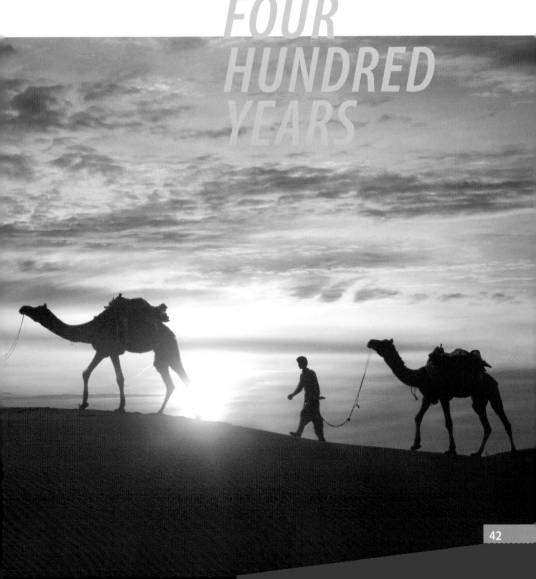

FOUR HUNDRED YEARS

בָּרוּךְ שׁוֹמֵר הַבְטָחָתוֹ לְיִשְׂרָאֵל בָּרוּךְ הוּא,
שֶׁהַקָּדוֹשׁ בָּרוּךְ הוּא חִשַּׁב אֶת הַקֵּץ לַעֲשׂוֹת,
כְּמָה שֶׁאָמַר לְאַבְרָהָם אָבִינוּ בִּבְרִית בֵּין
הַבְּתָרִים, שֶׁנֶּאֱמַר: וַיֹּאמֶר לְאַבְרָם, יָדֹעַ תֵּדַע כִּי־
גֵר יִהְיֶה זַרְעֲךָ בְּאֶרֶץ לֹא לָהֶם וַעֲבָדוּם וְעִנּוּ אֹתָם
אַרְבַּע מֵאוֹת שָׁנָה: וְגַם אֶת־הַגּוֹי אֲשֶׁר יַעֲבֹדוּ דָּן
אָנֹכִי, וְאַחֲרֵי־כֵן יֵצְאוּ בִּרְכֻשׁ גָּדוֹל:

# ABRAHAM LINCOLN'S COVENANT WITH GOD

was his duty to move forward in the cause of Emancipation.

On September 13, 1862, in what many would later call a miraculous turn of events, a Union officer discovered Confederate General Lee's strategy for the coming battle on a piece of paper wrapped around three cigars. Thanks to this new intelligence, the Union pulled off a narrow victory at Antietam that changed the course of the war.

*The Battle of Antietam*

לַעֲשׂוֹת כְּמָה שֶׁאָמַר לְאַבְרָהָם אָבִינוּ בִּבְרִית בֵּין הַבְּתָרִים.

*"and fulfilled what He had spoken to our father Abraham in the Covenant between the Pieces."*

*Abraham Lincoln and his son Willie*

The months leading up to the Battle of Antietam was a calamitous period for President Abraham Lincoln. His generals had repeatedly bungled battle after battle and for all its military might and superior organization the Union had failed to make much headway against the Confederacy. Tens of thousands of soldiers had already been killed in battle and closer to home Lincoln's beloved son Willie had died from typhoid fever in February. Overcome by grief, Lincoln began to question his commitment to winning the war. Specifically, Lincoln contemplated God's role in the war and in his personal life. In early September 1862, two weeks before the Battle of Antietam, Lincoln penned a private note on the subject which was later discovered by his secretary, John Hay. The note, now entitled "Meditation of the Divine Will," read:

The will of God prevails. In great contests each party claims to act in accordance with the will of God. Both *may* be, and one *must* be, wrong. God cannot be *for* and *against* the same thing at the same time. In the present civil war it is quite possible that God's purpose is something different from the purpose of either party – and yet the human instrumentalities, working just as they do, are of the best adaptation to effect His purpose. I am almost ready to say that this is probably true – that God wills this contest, and wills that it shall not end yet. By his mere great power, on the minds of the now contestants, He could have either *saved* or *destroyed* the Union without a human contest. Yet the contest began. And, having begun He could give the final victory to either side any day. Yet the contest proceeds.

Lincoln's uncertainty regarding the Divine plan for the outcome of the Civil War prompted him to follow the example of his biblical namesake, the Patriarch Abraham, and strike a bargain with God. Lincoln told his confidant, then Secretary of the Navy Gideon Welles, that he

had made a vow, a covenant, that if God gave us victory in the approaching battle, he would consider it an indication of the Divine Will, and that it

וְגַם אֶת־הַגּוֹי אֲשֶׁר יַעֲבֹדוּ דָּן אָנֹכִי, וְאַחֲרֵי־כֵן יֵצְאוּ בִּרְכֻשׁ גָּדוֹל.

*"But know that I shall judge the nation that enslaves them, and then they will leave with great wealth."*

Abolitionist and freed slave Sojourner Truth (1797–1883) saw herself as a modern fugitive from Egyptian bondage, but unlike the ancient Israelites, she took no property from her captors when she left the land of slavery. In an 1853 encounter with abolitionist writer Harriet Beecher Stowe, author of *Uncle Tom's Cabin*, Truth explained why she abandoned all trappings of her life as a slave, including her name. Stowe recounted the interaction with a literary flair in *The Atlantic Monthly*, giving Truth, who in fact spoke with a Dutch accent, a Southern speaking style:

*Sojourner Truth*

"My name was Isabella; but when I left the house of bondage, I left everything behind. I wa'n't goin' to keep nothin' of Egypt on me, an' so I went to the Lord an' asked Him to give me a new name. And the Lord gave me Sojourner, because I was to travel up an' down the land, showin' the people their sins, an' bein' a sign unto them. Afterwards I told the Lord I wanted another name, 'cause everybody else had two names; and the Lord gave me Truth, because I was to declare the truth to the people.

"Ye see some ladies have given me a white satin banner," she said, pulling out of her pocket and unfolding a white banner, printed with many texts, such as "Proclaim liberty throughout all the land unto all the inhabitants thereof," and others of like nature. "Well," she said, "I journeys round to camp-meetins, an' wherever folks is, an' I sets up my banner, an' then I sings, an' then folks always comes up round me, an' then I preaches to 'em."

## "When I left the house of bondage, I left everything behind."

King Tutankhamun's
coffin made of solid gold

וְאַחֲרֵי
כֵן יָצְאוּ
בִּרְכֻשׁ
גָּדוֹל

SOJOURNER
TRUTH
WASN'T GOING
TO KEEP
NOTHIN' OF
EGYPT ON HER

The matzot are covered and the wine cup is raised.

**And this [promise] is what has stood by** our ancestors and us; for it was not only one man who rose up to destroy us: in every single generation people rise up to destroy us – but the Holy One, blessed is He, saves us from their hands.

The wine cup is put down
and the matzot are uncovered.

*Depiction
of Crusaders
attacking
a village*

48

וְהִיא שֶׁעָמְדָה לַאֲבוֹתֵינוּ וְלָנוּ, שֶׁלֹּא אֶחָד בִּלְבָד עָמַד עָלֵינוּ לְכַלּוֹתֵנוּ, אֶלָּא שֶׁבְּכָל דּוֹר וָדוֹר עוֹמְדִים עָלֵינוּ לְכַלּוֹתֵנוּ, וְהַקָּדוֹשׁ בָּרוּךְ הוּא מַצִּילֵנוּ מִיָּדָם.

The wine cup is put down
and the מַצּוֹת are uncovered.

# PEOPLE RISE UP TO DESTROY US

# HARRY TRUMAN AND THE TEN COMMANDMENTS

וְהִיא שֶׁעָמְדָה

The Revelation at Mount Sinai

moral principles, for which the United Nations fight, must survive. Ultimately, all people must be led out of bondage....

It is sad to realize that the tragic world conflict still raging around the globe was started by a man whose hatred for race became such an obsession that he refused to treat people as human beings. Not satisfied with persecution and discrimination, Hitler, according to his own bitter words, finally sought to exterminate the entire Jewish race. To pave the way for his plans of world domination, the German dictator deliberately sought to make a scapegoat of the Jewish people. Little did he reckon with the courage and endurance of a race hardened by centuries of oppression, and strengthened by a firm faith that ultimately another Moses must come to lead them out of their modern bondage and into the Promised Land.

וְהִיא שֶׁעָמְדָה לַאֲבוֹתֵינוּ וְלָנוּ, שֶׁלֹּא אֶחָד בִּלְבָד עָמַד עָלֵינוּ
לְכַלּוֹתֵנוּ.

*"And this [promise] is what has stood by our ancestors and us; for
it was not only one man who rose up to destroy us."*

On March 26, 1945, during World War II, Vice President Harry S. Truman addressed the annual Passover service at the Jewish Welfare Board in Washington, D.C. The speech, which praised Jewish survival over the generations, was broadcast "to the Jewish men and women" in the Armed Forces.

*President Harry S. Truman*

Since biblical times, people of the Jewish faith have made great contributions to the moral code of mankind. From the revelation of the Ten Commandments by Moses to the philosophical teachings of modern Jewish scholars, there has been a constant search for a better way of life for the benefit of all. It was the Hebrews who first fought the worship of pagan idols in the western world and who preached eternal faith in one God – the God in whom we all put our trust.

This evening, as Passover begins, all God-fearing people can well join with those of the Jewish faith to thank the Almighty for many blessings received. Already millions of people, recently held in bondage in Europe, Asia, and Africa, have been liberated by the forces of freedom. Although this tragic worldwide conflict still continues to demand a heavy toll in lives and wealth, gratifying progress has been made toward the all-essential goal - complete victory!

In view of the evil objectives of our enemies, it is especially fortunate that righteousness will triumph. Today the Angel of Death is again passing over the house of the modern tyrants. If the dignity of every man is preserved, the

*U.S. Army soldiers of the 42nd Infantry Division celebrating Passover in Dahn, Germany, 1945*

אֶלָּא שֶׁבְּכָל דּוֹר וָדוֹר עוֹמְדִים עָלֵינוּ לְכַלּוֹתֵנוּ, וְהַקָּדוֹשׁ בָּרוּךְ
הוּא מַצִּילֵנוּ מִיָּדָם.

*"In every single generation people rise up to destroy us – but the
Holy One, blessed is He, saves us from their hands."*

During the American Revolution, Connecticut pastor Nicholas Street galvanized his parishioners into supporting the cause of independence by likening American colonists to the Israelites and the British to notorious enemies who sought to torment the Jews. In an April 1777 sermon titled, "The American states acting over the part of the children of Israel in the wilderness, and thereby impeding their entrance into Canaan's rest: or, The human heart discovering itself under trials," he preached:

*Nicholas Street*

Thus we are acting over the like sins with the children of Israel in the wilderness, under the conduct of Moses and Aaron, who was leading them out of a state of bondage into a land of liberty and plenty in Canaan. Again, we are ready to marvel at the unreasonable vileness and cruelty of the British tyrant and his ministry, in endeavouring to oppress, enslave and destroy these American States, who have been some of his most peaceable and profitable subjects; and yet we find the same wicked temper and disposition operating in Pharaoh king of Egypt above 3000 years ago.... But some may be ready to wonder, that since we are gone off from Great-Britain, and have declared ourselves independent States, and insist upon standing by ourselves, that they don't let us alone.... But we find the same disposition in the adversaries of Judah and Benjamin, who troubled them in building, and hired counsellors against them to frustrate their purposes.... And Great-Britain is now acting over just the same part towards us in these American States.... Great men are generally proud, ambitious and aspiring, disdainful of inferiors, and apt to resent the least indignities: We see this in Haman, an aspiring courtier, who when he saw that Mordecai bowed not nor did him reverence, was full of wrath; wherefore Haman sought to destroy all the Jews that were thro'out the whole kingdom of Ahasuerus.... And the British ministry have been acting over the same wicked, mischievous plot against the American States...and we have reason to hope that they will meet with the like fate.

עוֹמְדִים עָלֵינוּ לְכַלּוֹתֵנוּ

**AMERICANS FIGHT FOR INDEPENDENCE AGAINST BIBLICAL VILLAINY**

*The surrender of the British forces under the command of Major General Charles Cornwallis after the siege of Yorktown*

**Go and learn** what Laban the Aramean sought to do to our father Jacob: Pharaoh condemned only the boys to death, but Laban sought to uproot everything, as it is written:

**"An Aramean sought my father's death,
and he went down to Egypt and
resided there, just a handful of souls;
and there he became a nation –
large, mighty, and great."**

**"And he went down to Egypt"** – Compelled by what had been spoken.

**"And resided there"** – From this, learn that our father Jacob went down not to be absorbed into Egypt, but only to reside there for a time. As it is said: "They said to Pharaoh, 'We have come to reside in this land, for there is no pasture for your servants' flocks, for the famine is heavy in the land of Canaan; and now, if you please, let your servants dwell in the land of Goshen.'"

**"Just a handful of souls"** – As it is said: "Your ancestors were but seventy souls when they went down to Egypt – and now the LORD has made you as many as the sky has stars."

AS
MANY
AS THE
SKY HAS
STARS

A
NATION
LARGE
MIGHTY
AND
GREAT

צֵא וּלְמַד מַה בִּקֵשׁ לָבָן הָאֲרַמִּי לַעֲשׂוֹת
לְיַעֲקֹב אָבִינוּ, שֶׁפַּרְעֹה לֹא גָזַר אֶלָּא עַל הַזְּכָרִים,
וְלָבָן בִּקֵשׁ לַעֲקֹר אֶת הַכֹּל, שֶׁנֶּאֱמַר:

אֲרַמִּי אֹבֵד אָבִי וַיֵּרֶד מִצְרַיְמָה
וַיָּגָר שָׁם בִּמְתֵי מְעָט וַיְהִי־שָׁם
לְגוֹי גָּדוֹל עָצוּם וָרָב:

וַיֵּרֶד מִצְרַיְמָה אָנוּס עַל פִּי הַדִּבּוּר

וַיָּגָר שָׁם מְלַמֵּד שֶׁלֹּא יָרַד יַעֲקֹב אָבִינוּ לְהִשְׁתַּקֵּעַ
בְּמִצְרַיִם, אֶלָּא לָגוּר שָׁם, שֶׁנֶּאֱמַר: וַיֹּאמְרוּ אֶל־פַּרְעֹה,
לָגוּר בָּאָרֶץ בָּאנוּ כִּי־אֵין מִרְעֶה לַצֹּאן אֲשֶׁר לַעֲבָדֶיךָ,
כִּי־כָבֵד הָרָעָב בְּאֶרֶץ כְּנָעַן, וְעַתָּה יֵשְׁבוּ־נָא עֲבָדֶיךָ
בְּאֶרֶץ גֹּשֶׁן:

בִּמְתֵי מְעָט כְּמָה שֶׁנֶּאֱמַר: בְּשִׁבְעִים נֶפֶשׁ יָרְדוּ
אֲבֹתֶיךָ מִצְרַיְמָה, וְעַתָּה שָׂמְךָ יהוה אֱלֹהֶיךָ כְּכוֹכְבֵי
הַשָּׁמַיִם לָרֹב:

55

וּלְבֵן בִּקֵּשׁ לַעֲקֹר אֶת הַכֹּל

## SOVIET JEWRY AND THE CALL TO "LET MY PEOPLE GO!"

*Soviet Jewry protest in Washington, DC, December 6, 1987*

צֵא וּלְמַד... שֶׁפַּרְעֹה לֹא גָזַר אֶלָּא עַל הַזְּכָרִים, וְלָבָן בִּקֵשׁ לַעֲקֹר אֶת הַכֹּל.

*"Go and learn...Pharaoh condemned only the boys to death, but Laban sought to uproot everything."*

*Prime Minister Shimon Peres welcoming released prisoner Natan Sharansky in 1986*

Traditional Jewish commentaries distinguish between the persecution of Pharaoh and that of Laban, asserting that while Pharaoh sought to eradicate the Israelite people, Laban sought to crush their spirit. While many regimes throughout history followed Pharaoh's example, the Soviet regime, like Laban, targeted Jewish culture and tradition, through the cold arms of Yevsektsiya (a Jewish section of the Communist Party) and the KGB.

Similar to the patriarch Jacob, whom the commentator Rashi has proudly asserting: "I have dwelt with Laban, even so I have observed the 613 commandments," many Soviet Jews sought to maintain their Jewish identity. Thousands of Americans took to the streets on behalf of these Refuseniks, and on December 6, 1987, 250,000 people from across the country assembled at the National Mall for the Freedom Sunday for Soviet Jews. Their battle cry was "Let My People Go."

## "Let My People Go!"

וַיֹּאמְרוּ אֶל פַּרְעֹה, לָגוּר בָּאָרֶץ בָּאנוּ כִּי אֵין מִרְעֶה לַצֹּאן אֲשֶׁר
לַעֲבָדֶיךָ.

*"They said to Pharaoh, 'We have come to reside in this land, for there is no pasture for your servants' flocks.'"*

In Washington, D.C., on April 29, 1964, President Lyndon B. Johnson invited civil rights leaders to band together as was done in biblical times.

> Archbishop O'Boyle, Reverend Blake, Rabbi Miller, and Bishop Smith.... A hundred years ago Lincoln freed the slaves of their chains, but he did not free the country of its bigotry. A hundred years ago Lincoln signed the Emancipation Proclamation, but until education is unaware of race, until employment is blind to color, emancipation will be a proclamation, but it will not be a fact....

> It is your job as prophets in our time to direct the immense power of religion in shaping the conduct and the thoughts of men toward their

*President Lyndon B. Johnson*

> brothers in a manner consistent with compassion and love. So help us in this hour.... Inspire us with renewed faith.... Inspire and challenge us to put our principles into action. For the future of our faith is at stake, and the future of this Nation is at stake. As the Old Testament pleads, "Let there be no strife, I pray, between you and me, and between my herdmen and your herdmen, because we are brothers." So do we plead today.

> Yes, we are all brothers, and brothers together must build this great Nation into a great family, so that a hundred years from now in this house every man and woman present today will have their name pointed to with pride because in the hour of our greatest trial, we were willing to answer the roll and to stand up and be counted for morality and right.

*A civil rights protest, c. 1950s*

אֵין
מַרְעֶה
לַצֹּאן

PRESIDENT
LYNDON B.
JOHNSON
HEARKENS
TO BIBLICAL
SHEPHERDS

**"And there he became a nation"** – From this, learn that Israel was distinct there.

**"Large, mighty"** – As it is said: "And the children of Israel were fertile, and they swarmed, and grew more and more numerous and strong, and the land was filled with them."

**"And great"** – As it is said: "I let you grow wild like meadow plants, and you grew and matured and came forth in all your glory, your breasts full and your hair grown, and you were naked and exposed."

Some add:

"And I passed by you and saw you wallowing in your own blood – and I said to you, 'In your blood, live!' and I said, 'In your blood, live!'"

*IN YOUR BLOOD, LIVE!*

*"In your blood, live!" – in the merit of the blood of the Paschal lamb (Pirkei deRabbi Eliezer 29:12)*

וַיְהִי־שָׁם לְגוֹי מְלַמֵּד שֶׁהָיוּ יִשְׂרָאֵל מְצֻיָּנִים שָׁם.

גָּדוֹל עָצוּם כְּמָה שֶׁנֶּאֱמַר: וּבְנֵי יִשְׂרָאֵל פָּרוּ וַיִּשְׁרְצוּ
וַיִּרְבּוּ וַיַּעַצְמוּ בִּמְאֹד מְאֹד וַתִּמָּלֵא הָאָרֶץ אֹתָם:

וָרָב כְּמָה שֶׁנֶּאֱמַר: רְבָבָה כְּצֶמַח הַשָּׂדֶה נְתַתִּיךְ
וַתִּרְבִּי וַתִּגְדְּלִי, וַתָּבֹאִי בַּעֲדִי עֲדָיִים שָׁדַיִם נָכֹנוּ
וּשְׂעָרֵךְ צִמֵּחַ, וְאַתְּ עֵרֹם וְעֶרְיָה:

Some add:

וָאֶעֱבֹר עָלַיִךְ וָאֶרְאֵךְ מִתְבּוֹסֶסֶת בְּדָמָיִךְ, וָאֹמַר לָךְ
בְּדָמַיִךְ חֲיִי, וָאֹמַר לָךְ בְּדָמַיִךְ חֲיִי:

*"In your blood, live!" –
in the merit of the
blood of circumcision*

# JAZZ ICON ALBERT MURRAY'S FASCINATION WITH JOSEPH

וַיְהִי
יִשְׂרָאֵל
מְעֻנִּים
שָׁם

*Joseph forgives
the brothers*

וַיְהִי שָׁם לְגוֹי מְלַמֵּד שֶׁהָיוּ יִשְׂרָאֵל מְצֻיָּנִים שָׁם.

*"'And there he became a nation' – From this, learn that Israel was distinct there."*

*Albert Murray, New York, 2000*

Ever since his youth, the music critic Albert Murray (1916–2013) was fascinated by the biblical patriarch Joseph. He was especially taken with the character's depiction in Thomas Mann's *Joseph and his Brothers*, so much so that, upon enlisting in 1943, Murray expressed a desire to "live long enough for Thomas Mann to finish the last volume of *Joseph and His Brothers*." In his book, *The Hero and the Blues*, Murray explores the diverging characters of Joseph and Moses. He sees in Joseph elements of the archetypal epic hero of the blues musical tradition, overcoming hardships in exile to succeed in a corrupt society:

Indeed, Afro-Americans will find that Joseph shares fundamental qualities with the epic hero of the blues tradition, that uniquely American context of antagonistic cooperation. Joseph goes beyond his failures in a typically blues singing process of acknowledging them and admitting to himself how bad conditions are. Thus, his heroic optimism is informed by the facts of life. It is also geared to his knowledge of strategy and his skill with such tools and weapons as happen to be available. These are the qualities which enable him to turn misfortune into natural benefits. At any rate, he proceeds as if each setback were really a recoil action for a greater leap forward, as if each downfall were a deliberately designed crouch for higher elevation.

Those who follow Moses are forever talking about going back home; but to Joseph, for whom being at home was as much a matter of the spirit as of real estate, anywhere he is can become the Land of Great Promise. No one can deny Moses, great emancipator that he was, the position of epic hero of the anti-slavery movements. But neither should anyone overlook what Joseph, the riff-style improviser, did to slavery; he transcended it.

וָאֹמַר לָךְ בְּדָמַיִךְ חֲיִי, וָאֹמַר לָךְ בְּדָמַיִךְ חֲיִי.

*"And I said to you, 'In your blood, live!' and I said, 'In your blood, live!'"*

"A Time for Choosing," also known as "The Speech," was delivered in Los Angeles on October 27 during the 1964 U.S. presidential election campaign by future president Ronald Reagan on behalf of Republican candidate Barry Goldwater. The speech, which hearkened to the harsh conditions from which a revived Israel emerged, launched Reagan into national prominence in politics.

*Ronald Reagan with Barry Goldwater delivering "The Speech"*

You and I know and do not believe that life is so dear and peace so sweet as to be purchased at the price of chains and slavery. If nothing in life is worth dying for, when did this begin – just in the face of this enemy? Or should Moses have told the children of Israel to live in slavery under the pharaohs…should the patriots at Concord Bridge have thrown down their guns and refused to fire the shot heard 'round the world? The martyrs of history were not fools, and our honored dead who gave their lives to stop the advance of the Nazis didn't die in vain. Where, then, is the road to peace? Well it's a simple answer after all.

You and I have the courage to say to our enemies, "There is a price we will not pay." "There is a point beyond which they must not advance…." Winston Churchill said, "The destiny of man is not measured by material computations. When great forces are on the move in the world, we learn we're spirits – not animals." And he said, "There's something going on in time and space, and beyond time and space, which, whether we like it or not, spells duty."

You and I have a rendezvous with destiny. We'll preserve for our children this, the last best hope of man on earth, or we'll sentence them to take the last step into a thousand years of darkness.

## "Should Moses have told the children of Israel to live in slavery under the pharaohs?"

בְּדָמַיִךְ
חֲיִי

The "Shot Heard 'Round the World" – battle at Concord Bridge, Massachusetts, April 19, 1775

RONALD
REAGAN
URGES AN
AMERICAN
REVIVAL

> "And the Egyptians dealt cruelly
> with us and oppressed us, and
> imposed hard labor on us."

## THE EGYPTIANS DEALT CRUELLY WITH US

**"The Egyptians dealt cruelly with us"** –
As it is said: "We must act wisely against [this
people], in case it grows great, and when we are
called to war they may join our enemies, fight
against us, and rise up to leave the land."

וַיָּרֵעוּ אֹתָנוּ הַמִּצְרִים וַיְעַנּוּנוּ
וַיִּתְּנוּ עָלֵינוּ עֲבֹדָה קָשָׁה:

וַיָּרֵעוּ אֹתָנוּ הַמִּצְרִים כְּמָה שֶׁנֶּאֱמַר, הָבָה
נִתְחַכְּמָה לוֹ פֶּן־יִרְבֶּה, וְהָיָה כִּי־תִקְרֶאנָה מִלְחָמָה,
וְנוֹסַף גַּם־הוּא עַל־שֹׂנְאֵינוּ, וְנִלְחַם־בָּנוּ וְעָלָה מִן־
הָאָרֶץ:

*Colossal sculptures of the deified Pharaoh Ramesses II from the Great Temple at Abu Simbel*

# HERMAN MELVILLE AND COMMODORE LEVY COMBAT CORPORAL PUNISHMENT

וַיִּתְּנוּ
עָלֵינוּ
עֲבֹדָה
קָשָׁה

USS United States, the frigate on which Melville based the fictional Neversink, defeating the HMS Macedonian in battle during the War of 1812

וַיָּרֵעוּ אֹתָנוּ הַמִּצְרִים וַיְעַנּוּנוּ, וַיִּתְּנוּ עָלֵינוּ עֲבֹדָה קָשָׁה.

*"And the Egyptians dealt cruelly with us and oppressed us, and imposed hard labor on us."*

*Herman Melville*

Ancient Israel and modern Jews have long inspired the American fight against oppression. Herman Melville, known for his maritime novels including *Moby Dick*, drew from his fourteen months' experience as a sailor in the U.S. Navy to write *White-Jacket* (1850), the story of the crew of the frigate USS *Neversink*. The novel recalled the horrors of flogging, a common form of corporal punishment in the navy at the time, in vivid and bloody detail. *White-Jacket* was distributed to members of Congress and proved instrumental in abolishing flogging in the U.S. Navy. In the book, Melville asserted that the foundling nation of America, like Israel of old, had a responsibility to introduce new values of justice and liberty to the world:

> Escaped from the house of bondage, Israel of old did not follow after the ways of the Egyptians. To her was given an express dispensation; to her were given new things under the sun. And we Americans are the peculiar, chosen people – the Israel of our time; we bear the ark of the liberties of the world.... God has predestinated, mankind expects, great things from our race; and great things we feel in our souls. The rest of the nations must soon be in our rear. We are the pioneers of the world; the advance-guard, sent on through the wilderness of untried things, to break a new path in the New World that is ours. In our youth is our strength; in our inexperience, our wisdom.

The success of *White-Jacket* in abolishing flogging was compounded by the efforts of the U.S. Navy's first Jewish commodore, Uriah Phillips Levy. At the age of ten, Levy set off to sea for the rest of his life, only returning home briefly on his thirteenth birthday to celebrate his bar mitzva in Philadelphia. Levy was an outspoken critic of corporal punishment and rallied congressmen to ban the practice in 1850. According to a popular legend, while commanding the USS *Vandalia* in the 1840s, Levy was dismissed from service for refusing to flog a young sailor. President John Tyler intervened to reinstate Levy, who made it his life's mission to ban corporal punishment.

וְהָיָה כִּי־תִקְרֶאנָה מִלְחָמָה, וְנוֹסַף גַּם־הוּא עַל־שֹׂנְאֵינוּ, וְנִלְחַם־
בָּנוּ וְעָלָה מִן־הָאָרֶץ.

*"And when we are called to war they may join our enemies, fight against us, and rise up to leave the land."*

In Memphis, Tennessee on April 3, 1968, the night before he was assassinated, Reverend Martin Luther King Jr. spoke to striking sanitation workers of the trek from enslavement to the Promised Land.

Something is happening in Memphis; something is happening in our world. And you know, if I were standing at the beginning of time, with the possibility of taking a kind of general and panoramic view of the whole of human history up to now, and the Almighty said to me, 'Martin Luther King, which age would you like to live in?' I would take my mental flight by Egypt and I would watch God's children in their magnificent trek from the dark dungeons of Egypt through, or rather across the Red Sea, through the wilderness on toward the Promised Land.…

You know, whenever Pharaoh wanted to prolong the period of slavery in Egypt, he had a favorite, favorite formula for doing it. What was that? He kept the slaves fighting among themselves. But whenever the slaves get together, something happens in Pharaoh's court, and he cannot hold the slaves in slavery. When the slaves get together, that's the beginning of getting out of slavery. Now let us maintain unity.…

*Martin Luther King Jr.*

Well, I don't know what will happen now. We've got some difficult days ahead. But it doesn't matter with me now. Because I've been to the mountaintop. And I don't mind. Like anybody, I would like to live a long life. Longevity has its place. But I'm not concerned about that now. I just want to do God's will. And He's allowed me to go up to the mountain. And I've looked over. And I've seen the Promised Land. I may not get there with you. But I want you to know tonight, that we, as a people, will get to the Promised Land.

וַיַּעַל מִן
הָאָרֶץ

The Jewish people
enter the
Promised Land

**MARTIN
LUTHER
KING JR.'S
MENTAL
FLIGHT
BY EGYPT**

**"And oppressed us"** – As it is said: "They placed taskmasters over [the people] to oppress them under their burdens; they built store cities for Pharaoh: Pithom and Raamses."

**"And imposed hard labor on us"** – As it is said: "The Egyptians enslaved the children of Israel with heavy labor."

THEY
BUILT
STORE
CITIES

וַיְעַנּוּנוּ כְּמָה שֶׁנֶּאֱמַר, וַיָּשִׂימוּ עָלָיו שָׂרֵי מִסִּים
לְמַעַן עַנֹּתוֹ בְּסִבְלֹתָם, וַיִּבֶן עָרֵי מִסְכְּנוֹת לְפַרְעֹה
אֶת־פִּתֹם וְאֶת־רַעַמְסֵס:

וַיִּתְּנוּ עָלֵינוּ עֲבֹדָה קָשָׁה כְּמָה שֶׁנֶּאֱמַר,
וַיַּעֲבִדוּ מִצְרַיִם אֶת־בְּנֵי יִשְׂרָאֵל בְּפָרֶךְ:

*The Israelites building
Pithom and Raamses*

# RABBI DAVID EINHORN'S MORAL INDIGNATION

Depiction of Moses and
Aaron with the Ten
Commandments by
Dutch Jewish artist
Aron de Chaves in 1675

וַיָּשִׂימוּ עָלָיו שָׂרֵי מִסִּים לְמַעַן עַנֹּתוֹ בְּסִבְלֹתָם.

*"They placed taskmasters over [the people] to oppress them under their burdens."*

*Rabbi David Einhorn*

In response to Rabbi Morris Jacob Raphall's claim that the Bible endorsed slavery, Rabbi David Einhorn of Baltimore (1809–1879) dedicated an 1861 article in his German-language monthly magazine *Sinai* to refuting Raphall's claim. In the course of his article, Einhorn argued that:

A book which sets up this principle and at the same time says that all human beings are descended from the same human parents, can never approve of slavery and have it find favor in the sight of God. A law, which recognizes slavery, in its present day meaning, *neither according to the conception of the institution of it, nor in its literal sense*, and prescribes that the Hebrew, who after six years will not cease from serving as a slave, must as a sign of shame, submit to having his ear pierced, considers no human being to be property. A religion which spares the feeling of the animal mother as the order regarding the bird's nest proves, certainly objects to having the human mother forcibly deprived of her child. The Ten Commandments, the first of which is: "I am the Lord, thy God, who brought thee out of the land of Egypt, out of the house of bondage" can by no means want to place slavery of any human-being under divine sanction, it being furthermore true, what all our prophets have proclaimed and around which Israel's fondest hopes center, that all human beings on the wide globe are entitled to admittance to the service of God.

# "All human beings on the wide globe are entitled...to the service of God."

**"And we cried out to the Lord,
God of our ancestors, and the
Lord heard our voice, and He saw
our oppression and our labor
and slavery."**

**"And we cried out to the Lord, God
of our ancestors"** – As it is said: "It came
to be, as a long time passed, that the king of
Egypt died, and the children of Israel groaned
under the burden of work, and they cried
out, and their plea rose to God from amid the
work."

**"And the Lord heard our voice"** – As it
is said: "And God heard their groans, and God
remembered His covenant with Abraham,
Isaac, and Jacob."

**"And He saw our oppression"** – The separation of husband from wife, as it is said:
"And God saw the children of Israel, and God
knew."

**"And our labor"** – [The killing of] the sons,
as it is said: "Throw every boy who is born into
the river, and the girls let live."

**"And slavery"** – The forced labor that was
pressed down on them, as it is said: "I have
seen the slavery that Egypt forced upon you."

וַנִּצְעַק אֶל־יהוה אֱלֹהֵי אֲבֹתֵינוּ
וַיִּשְׁמַע יהוה אֶת־קֹלֵנוּ וַיַּרְא אֶת־עָנְיֵנוּ
וְאֶת־עֲמָלֵנוּ וְאֶת־לַחֲצֵנוּ:

וַנִּצְעַק אֶל־יהוה אֱלֹהֵי אֲבֹתֵינוּ כְּמָה שֶׁנֶּאֱמַר,
וַיְהִי בַיָּמִים הָרַבִּים הָהֵם וַיָּמָת מֶלֶךְ מִצְרַיִם
וַיֵּאָנְחוּ בְנֵי־יִשְׂרָאֵל מִן־הָעֲבֹדָה, וַיִּזְעָקוּ, וַתַּעַל
שַׁוְעָתָם אֶל־הָאֱלֹהִים מִן־הָעֲבֹדָה:

וַיִּשְׁמַע יהוה אֶת־קֹלֵנוּ כְּמָה שֶׁנֶּאֱמַר, וַיִּשְׁמַע
אֱלֹהִים אֶת־נַאֲקָתָם, וַיִּזְכֹּר אֱלֹהִים אֶת־בְּרִיתוֹ
אֶת־אַבְרָהָם אֶת־יִצְחָק וְאֶת־יַעֲקֹב:

וַיַּרְא אֶת־עָנְיֵנוּ זוֹ פְּרִישׁוּת דֶּרֶךְ אֶרֶץ כְּמָה
שֶׁנֶּאֱמַר, וַיַּרְא אֱלֹהִים אֶת־בְּנֵי יִשְׂרָאֵל וַיֵּדַע
אֱלֹהִים:

וְאֶת־עֲמָלֵנוּ אֵלּוּ הַבָּנִים כְּמָה שֶׁנֶּאֱמַר, כָּל־הַבֵּן
הַיִּלּוֹד, הַיְאֹרָה תַּשְׁלִיכֻהוּ, וְכָל־הַבַּת תְּחַיּוּן:

וְאֶת־לַחֲצֵנוּ זֶה הַדְּחַק כְּמָה שֶׁנֶּאֱמַר, וְגַם־רָאִיתִי
אֶת־הַלַּחַץ אֲשֶׁר מִצְרַיִם לֹחֲצִים אֹתָם:

THE
LORD
HEARD
OUR
VOICE

אֶתֶן עֲמָלֵנוּ׃
וְאֶת לַחֲצֵנוּ׃

**GO
SOUND
THE
JUBILEE**

*Slaves working in the sugarcane fields*

וַנִּצְעַק אֶל־יהוה אֱלֹהֵי אֲבֹתֵינוּ, וַיִּשְׁמַע יהוה אֶת־קֹלֵנוּ וַיַּרְא אֶת־
עָנְיֵנוּ וְאֶת־עֲמָלֵנוּ וְאֶת־לַחֲצֵנוּ.

*"And we cried out to the Lord, God of our ancestors, and the Lord heard our voice, and He saw our oppression and our labor and slavery."*

*The Fisk Jubilee Singers, c. 1876*

The nineteenth-century slave spiritual "Go Sound the Jubilee" refers to the biblical commandment to release slaves from bondage in the Jubilee year, to "proclaim Liberty throughout the Land to all the inhabitants thereof." The song was said to be sung by slaves as they were chained in gangs bound for the deep South. It echoes the cries of the enslaved Israelites in Egypt.

*See these poor souls from Africa,*

*Transported to America;*

*We are stolen, and sold to Georgia, will you go along with me?*

*We are stolen and sold to*

*Georgia, go sound the jubilee,*

*See wives and husbands sold apart,*

*The children's screams! – it breaks my heart;*

*There's a better day a coming, will you go along with me?*

*There's a better day a coming, go sound the jubilee.*

*O gracious Lord! when shall it be,*

*That we poor souls shall all be free?*

*Lord, break them Slavery powers – will you go along with me?*

*Lord, break them Slavery powers, go sound the jubilee.*

*Dear Lord! dear Lord! when Slavery'll cease,*

*Then we poor souls can have our peace;*

*There's a better day a coming, will you go along with me?*

*There's a better day a coming, go sound the jubilee.*

*Main deck of a slave ship, 18th century*

*"'And our labor' – [The killing of] the sons, as it is said: 'Throw*
*every boy who is born into the river, and the girls let live.'"*

In April 1775, the Revolutionary Reverend David Jones became pastor of Great Valley Church in Chester County, Pennsylvania. That year, he delivered a sermon to soldiers of the Continental Army where he cited the story of the biblical midwives, Shiphra and Puah, as an example of justified civil disobedience in the face of tyranny:

> Call to mind also, that in the days of Pharaoh, King of Egypt, he enjoined it as a law to all the midwives, that they should kill all the male children of the Jews. Did they obey or not? The text informs us that the fear of God prevented them, believing that no law can make that just, which in its own nature is unrighteous…. Certain it is, that the people must be the judges whether the laws are good or not – and I think it must be acknowledged by all, that laws are not good, except they secure every man's liberty and property, and defend the subject against the arbitrary power of kings, or any body of men whatsoever.

*Angelina Grimké*

Decades later, in an appeal to her fellow Southern women to advocate against slavery, the abolitionist Angelina Grimké wondered, "Can you not, my friends, understand the signs of the times; do you not see the sword of retributive justice hanging over the South, or are you still slumbering at your posts? Are there no Shiphras, no Puahs among you?"

# "Are there no Shiphras, no Puahs among you?"

וְאֶת
עֲמָלֵ֫נ֫וּ
אֵלּ֫וּ
הַבָּנִ֫

"Pharaoh and
the Midwives,"
by James Jacques
Tissot

## THE CIVIL
## DISOBEDIENCE
## OF SHIPHRA
## AND PUAH

> "And the Lord brought us out
> of Egypt with a strong hand
> and an outstretched arm,
> in an awesome happening,
> with signs and with wonders."

**"And the Lord brought us out of Egypt"** – Not through an angel, not through a seraph, not through any emissary. No, it was the Holy One, His glory, His own presence. As it is said: "I shall pass through the land of Egypt on that night; I shall kill every firstborn son in the land of Egypt, man and beast, and I shall pass judgment on all the gods of Egypt. I am the Lord."

"I shall pass through the land of Egypt on that night" – I and no angel. "I shall kill every firstborn son in the land of Egypt" – I and no seraph. "And I shall pass judgment on all the gods of Egypt" – I and no emissary. "I am the Lord" – It is I and no other.

**"With a strong hand"** – This refers to the pestilence, as it is said: "You shall see the hand of the Lord among your cattle in the field, among your horses and donkeys and camels, in the herd and in the flock, bringing harsh, heavy pestilence."

**"And an outstretched arm"** – This refers to the sword, as it is said: "And His sword was drawn in His hand, stretched out over Jerusalem."

*I SHALL KILL EVERY FIRST BORN*

וַיּוֹצִאֵנוּ יהוה מִמִּצְרַיִם
בְּיָד חֲזָקָה וּבִזְרֹעַ נְטוּיָה
וּבְמֹרָא גָּדֹל וּבְאֹתוֹת וּבְמֹפְתִים:

וַיּוֹצִאֵנוּ יהוה מִמִּצְרַיִם לֹא עַל יְדֵי מַלְאָךְ וְלֹא
עַל יְדֵי שָׂרָף וְלֹא עַל יְדֵי שָׁלִיחַ, אֶלָּא הַקָּדוֹשׁ
בָּרוּךְ הוּא בִּכְבוֹדוֹ וּבְעַצְמוֹ, שֶׁנֶּאֱמַר: וְעָבַרְתִּי
בְאֶרֶץ־מִצְרַיִם בַּלַּיְלָה הַזֶּה וְהִכֵּיתִי כָל־בְּכוֹר
בְּאֶרֶץ מִצְרַיִם מֵאָדָם וְעַד־בְּהֵמָה, וּבְכָל־אֱלֹהֵי
מִצְרַיִם אֶעֱשֶׂה שְׁפָטִים אֲנִי יהוה:

וְעָבַרְתִּי בְאֶרֶץ־מִצְרַיִם אֲנִי וְלֹא מַלְאָךְ, וְהִכֵּיתִי
כָל־בְּכוֹר אֲנִי וְלֹא שָׂרָף, וּבְכָל־אֱלֹהֵי מִצְרַיִם
אֶעֱשֶׂה שְׁפָטִים אֲנִי וְלֹא הַשָּׁלִיחַ, אֲנִי יהוה אֲנִי
הוּא וְלֹא אַחֵר.

בְּיָד חֲזָקָה זוֹ הַדֶּבֶר, כְּמָה שֶׁנֶּאֱמַר: הִנֵּה יַד־יהוה
הוֹיָה בְּמִקְנְךָ אֲשֶׁר בַּשָּׂדֶה בַּסּוּסִים בַּחֲמֹרִים
בַּגְּמַלִּים בַּבָּקָר וּבַצֹּאן דֶּבֶר כָּבֵד מְאֹד:

וּבִזְרֹעַ נְטוּיָה זוֹ הַחֶרֶב, כְּמָה שֶׁנֶּאֱמַר: וְחַרְבּוֹ
שְׁלוּפָה בְּיָדוֹ נְטוּיָה עַל־יְרוּשָׁלָיִם:

*Painting a sign on the doorpost so that the firstborn son will be spared*

# GOD WOULD STRETCH FORTH HIS ARM TO SAVE THE SLAVES

*"The Israelites Leaving Egypt," by David Roberts, c. 1830*

וּבְיָד
חֲזָקָה

וַיּוֹצִאֵנוּ יהוה מִמִּצְרַיִם בְּיָד חֲזָקָה וּבִזְרֹעַ נְטוּיָה וּבְמֹרָא גָּדֹל
וּבְאֹתוֹת וּבְמֹפְתִים.

*"And the* Lord *brought us out of Egypt with a strong hand and an outstretched arm, in an awesome happening, with signs and with wonders."*

*Thomas Wentworth Higginson*

In addition to his service in the Civil War, Thomas Wentworth Higginson furthered the abolitionist cause in his many writings. In "Gabriel's Defeat" printed in *The Atlantic Monthly*, Higginson recounted the story of Gabriel's Rebellion, a failed slave revolt led by escaped slave Gabriel Prosser. Higginson chronicled how Gabriel and his brother Martin saw God's outstretched hand reaching over America, poised to end slavery.

> Early in September, 1800, as a certain Mr. Moseley Sheppard of Henrico County in Virginia was one day sitting in his counting-room, two negroes knocked at the door and were let in. They shut the door themselves, and began to unfold an insurrectionary plot....
>
> Presently a man named Martin, Gabriel's brother, proposed religious services, caused the company to be duly seated, and began an impassioned exposition of Scripture, bearing upon the perilous theme. The Israelites were glowingly portrayed as a type of successful resistance to tyranny; and it was argued that now, as then, God would stretch forth His arm to save, and would strengthen a hundred to overthrow a thousand. Thus passed, the witness stated, this preparatory meeting.

*Gabriel Prosser*

**"In an awesome happening"** – This refers to the revelation of His Presence, as it is said: "Has any god ever tried to come and take a nation out of the midst of another, with trials and with signs and wonders, in war and with a strong hand, with an outstretched arm, inspiring great awe, as the LORD your God has done all this for you in Egypt, before your eyes?"

**"With signs"** – This refers to the staff, as it is said: "Take this staff in your hand, and with it you shall perform the signs."

**"And with wonders"** – This refers to the blood, as it is said: "I shall make wonders in the sky and on the earth."

A drop of wine is spilled from the cup as each wonder is mentioned:

## Blood, and fire, and pillars of smoke.

**Another interpretation:** "With a strong hand" – two. "And an outstretched arm" – two. "In an awesome happening" – two. "With signs" – two. "And with wonders" – two.

*Taking the staff to perform signs*

וּבְמֹרָא גָּדֹל זֶה גִּלּוּי שְׁכִינָה, כְּמָה שֶׁנֶּאֱמַר: אוֹ הֲנִסָּה אֱלֹהִים לָבוֹא לָקַחַת לוֹ גוֹי מִקֶּרֶב גּוֹי בְּמַסֹּת בְּאֹתֹת וּבְמוֹפְתִים וּבְמִלְחָמָה וּבְיָד חֲזָקָה, וּבִזְרוֹעַ נְטוּיָה וּבְמוֹרָאִים גְּדֹלִים, כְּכֹל אֲשֶׁר־עָשָׂה לָכֶם יהוה אֱלֹהֵיכֶם בְּמִצְרַיִם לְעֵינֶיךָ:

וּבְאֹתוֹת זֶה הַמַּטֶּה, כְּמָה שֶׁנֶּאֱמַר: וְאֶת־הַמַּטֶּה הַזֶּה תִּקַּח בְּיָדֶךָ אֲשֶׁר תַּעֲשֶׂה־בּוֹ אֶת־הָאֹתֹת:

וּבְמוֹפְתִים זֶה הַדָּם, כְּמָה שֶׁנֶּאֱמַר: וְנָתַתִּי מוֹפְתִים בַּשָּׁמַיִם וּבָאָרֶץ

A drop of wine is spilled from the cup
as each wonder is mentioned:

# דָּם וָאֵשׁ וְתִימְרוֹת עָשָׁן:

דָּבָר אַחֵר בְּיָד חֲזָקָה שְׁתַּיִם, וּבִזְרוֹעַ נְטוּיָה שְׁתַּיִם, וּבְמֹרָא גָּדֹל שְׁתַּיִם, וּבְאֹתוֹת שְׁתַּיִם, וּבְמוֹפְתִים שְׁתַּיִם.

# WASHINGTON'S "WONDER-WORKING DEITY"

בְּמַסֹּת
בְּאֹתֹת
וּבְמוֹפְתִים

וּבְמֹרָא גָּדֹל זֶה גִּלּוּי שְׁכִינָה, כְּמָה שֶׁנֶּאֱמַר: אוֹ הֲנִסָּה אֱלֹהִים לָבוֹא לָקַחַת לוֹ גוֹי מִקֶּרֶב גּוֹי בְּמַסֹּת בְּאֹתֹת וּבְמוֹפְתִים.

*"'In an awesome happening' – This refers to the revelation of His Presence, as it is said: "Has any god ever tried to come and take a nation out of the midst of another, with trials and with signs and wonders."*

*George Washington*

In George Washington's 1790 letter to the Jewish Congregation of Savannah, the president asks the congregants to join him in praying for God's help in advancing the nascent America, the same God who brought the Israelites out of Egypt.

Gentlemen,

I thank you with great sincerity for your congratulations on my appointment to the office, which I have the honor to hold by the unanimous choice of my fellow-citizens: and especially for the expressions which you are pleased to use in testifying the confidence that is reposed in me by your congrega-

tion.… I rejoice that a spirit of liberality and philanthropy is much more prevalent than it formerly was among the enlightened nations of the earth; and that your brethren will benefit thereby in proportion as it shall become still more extensive. Happily the people of the United States of America have, in many instances, exhibited examples worthy of imitation – the salutary influence of which will doubtless extend much farther, if gratefully enjoying those blessings of peace which (under favor of Heaven) have been obtained by fortitude in war, they shall conduct themselves with reverence to the Deity, and charity towards their fellow-creatures.

May the same wonder-working Deity, who long since delivering the Hebrews from their Egyptian Oppressors planted them in the promised land – whose providential agency has lately been conspicuous in establishing these United States as an independent nation – still continue to water them with the dews of Heaven and to make the inhabitants of every denomination participate in the temporal and spiritual blessings of that people whose God is Jehovah.

G. Washington

**These were the ten plagues** that the Holy One brought upon Egypt, and these are they –

A drop of wine is spilled from the cup as each plague, and each of the acronyms, *DeTzaKh*, *ADaSh*, and *Be'AḥaV*, is mentioned:

### Blood    Frogs    Lice
### Wild Animals    Pestilence    Boils
### Hail    Locusts    Darkness
### the Striking Down of the Firstborn.

Rabbi Yehuda grouped these under acronyms –

### DeTzaKh, ADaSh, Be'AḥaV.

*The plague of darkness*

אֵלּוּ עֶשֶׂר מַכּוֹת שֶׁהֵבִיא הַקָּדוֹשׁ בָּרוּךְ הוּא
עַל הַמִּצְרִים בְּמִצְרַיִם, וְאֵלּוּ הֵן:

A drop of wine is spilled from the cup
as each plague, and each of the acronyms,
דְּצַ"ךְ, עַדַ"שׁ, and בְּאַחַ"ב, is mentioned:

כִּנִּים    צְפַרְדֵּעַ    דָּם

שְׁחִין    דֶּבֶר    עָרוֹב

חֹשֶׁךְ    אַרְבֶּה    בָּרָד

מַכַּת בְּכוֹרוֹת.

רַבִּי יְהוּדָה הָיָה נוֹתֵן בָּהֶם סִימָנִים

דְּצַ"ךְ עַדַ"שׁ בְּאַחַ"ב

The plague of blood

THE TEN
PLAGUES

**Rabbi Yossei HaGelili says:** How can you know that the Egyptians were struck with ten plagues in Egypt and another fifty at the sea? For in Egypt it is said, "The astrologers said to Pharaoh, 'This is the finger of God,'" while at the sea it is said, "When Israel saw the great hand the LORD raised against the Egyptians, the people feared the LORD, and they believed in the LORD and in His servant Moses." If a finger struck them with ten plagues, conclude from this that they were struck with ten plagues in Egypt and with fifty plagues at the sea.

**Rabbi Eliezer says:** How can you know that each and every plague the Holy One brought upon the Egyptians in Egypt was in fact made up of four plagues? For it is said, "His fury was sent down upon them, great anger, rage, and distress, a company of messengers of destruction." "Great anger" – one, "rage" – two, "distress" – three, "a company of messengers of destruction" – four. Conclude from this that they were struck with forty plagues in Egypt and with two hundred plagues at the sea.

**Rabbi Akiva says:** How can you know that each and every plague the Holy One brought upon the Egyptians in Egypt was in fact made up of five plagues? For it is said, "His fury was sent down upon them, great anger, rage, and distress, a company of messengers of destruction." "His fury" – one, "great anger" – two, "rage" – three, "distress" – four, "a company of messengers of destruction" – five. Conclude from this that they were struck with fifty plagues in Egypt and with two hundred and fifty plagues at the sea.

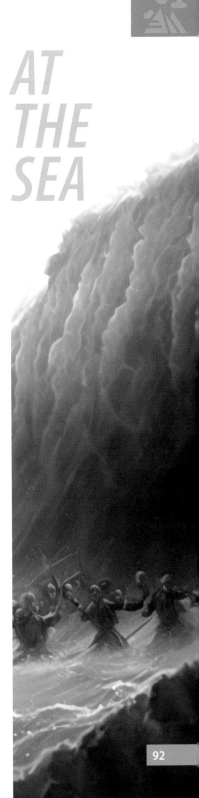

AT
THE
SEA

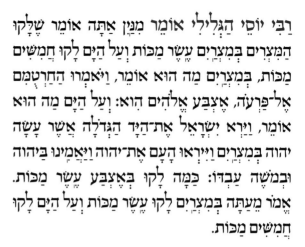

רַבִּי יוֹסֵי הַגְּלִילִי אוֹמֵר מִנַּיִן אַתָּה אוֹמֵר שֶׁלָּקוּ הַמִּצְרִים בְּמִצְרַיִם עֶשֶׂר מַכּוֹת וְעַל הַיָּם לָקוּ חֲמִשִּׁים מַכּוֹת, בְּמִצְרַיִם מַה הוּא אוֹמֵר, וַיֹּאמְרוּ הַחַרְטֻמִּם אֶל־פַּרְעֹה, אֶצְבַּע אֱלֹהִים הוּא: וְעַל הַיָּם מַה הוּא אוֹמֵר, וַיַּרְא יִשְׂרָאֵל אֶת־הַיָּד הַגְּדֹלָה אֲשֶׁר עָשָׂה יהוה בְּמִצְרַיִם וַיִּירְאוּ הָעָם אֶת־יהוה וַיַּאֲמִינוּ בַּיהוה וּבְמֹשֶׁה עַבְדּוֹ: כַּמָּה לָקוּ בְּאֶצְבַּע עֶשֶׂר מַכּוֹת. אֱמֹר מֵעַתָּה בְּמִצְרַיִם לָקוּ עֶשֶׂר מַכּוֹת וְעַל הַיָּם לָקוּ חֲמִשִּׁים מַכּוֹת.

רַבִּי אֱלִיעֶזֶר אוֹמֵר מִנַּיִן שֶׁכָּל מַכָּה וּמַכָּה שֶׁהֵבִיא הַקָּדוֹשׁ בָּרוּךְ הוּא עַל הַמִּצְרִים בְּמִצְרַיִם הָיְתָה שֶׁל אַרְבַּע מַכּוֹת, שֶׁנֶּאֱמַר: יְשַׁלַּח־בָּם חֲרוֹן אַפּוֹ עֶבְרָה וָזַעַם וְצָרָה, מִשְׁלַחַת מַלְאֲכֵי רָעִים: עֶבְרָה אַחַת וָזַעַם שְׁתַּיִם וְצָרָה שָׁלוֹשׁ מִשְׁלַחַת מַלְאֲכֵי רָעִים אַרְבַּע, אֱמֹר מֵעַתָּה, בְּמִצְרַיִם לָקוּ אַרְבָּעִים מַכּוֹת וְעַל הַיָּם לָקוּ מָאתַיִם מַכּוֹת.

רַבִּי עֲקִיבָא אוֹמֵר מִנַּיִן שֶׁכָּל מַכָּה וּמַכָּה שֶׁהֵבִיא הַקָּדוֹשׁ בָּרוּךְ הוּא עַל הַמִּצְרִים בְּמִצְרַיִם הָיְתָה שֶׁל חָמֵשׁ מַכּוֹת, שֶׁנֶּאֱמַר: יְשַׁלַּח־בָּם חֲרוֹן אַפּוֹ, עֶבְרָה וָזַעַם וְצָרָה, מִשְׁלַחַת מַלְאֲכֵי רָעִים: חֲרוֹן אַפּוֹ אַחַת עֶבְרָה שְׁתַּיִם וָזַעַם שָׁלוֹשׁ וְצָרָה אַרְבַּע מִשְׁלַחַת מַלְאֲכֵי רָעִים חָמֵשׁ, אֱמֹר מֵעַתָּה, בְּמִצְרַיִם לָקוּ חֲמִשִּׁים מַכּוֹת וְעַל הַיָּם לָקוּ חֲמִשִּׁים וּמָאתַיִם מַכּוֹת.

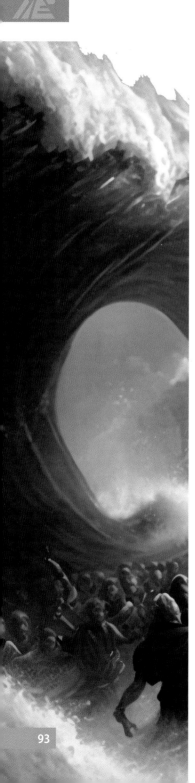

# ELIZABETH CHANDLER RAILS AGAINST THE VILE CAUSE OF SLAVERY

אֶצְבַּע

אֱלֹהִים

הוא

"Thus saith the Lord Jehovah, God Omnipotent!

Let thou this people go…"

But Pharaoh harden'd still his heart, till God,

With a high hand, brought out his chosen people,

And whelm'd the might of Egypt in the wave.

Oh ye! who still in cruel bondage, worse

Than e'en the Egyptian, hold the ill-starr'd slave,

Do ye not dread that God's long slumbering wrath

At length will pour its terrors upon you?

Are slavery and oppression aught more just

Than in the days of Moses?...

Symbols of the Zodiac

וַיֹּאמְרוּ הַחַרְטֻמִּם אֶל־פַּרְעֹה, אֶצְבַּע אֱלֹהִים הוּא.

*"The astrologers said to Pharaoh, 'This is the finger of God.'"*

*Elizabeth Margaret Chandler*

Elizabeth Margaret Chandler (1807–1834) was the first female writer to advance the abolitionist cause as her primary theme. She used the Bible to decry pro-slavery senators as hypocrites who celebrated the Exodus even as they promoted slavery themselves. Her poem, "Pharaoh," likens slave owners to the Egyptians and refers to slavery as a blotch like leprosy on the culture of America.

*Thus saith Jehovah! Let this people go!*

*The king was on his throne array'd all gorgeously,*

*In regal purple rich with fretted gold…*

*The nobles of his land were gather'd round,*

*Thronging the proud pavilion where he sate;*

*And the wise men, the Magi of the East,*

*The Priests, the Soothsayers, Astrologers,*

*And the most cunning sorcerers, were there.*

*And also, there, apart from all the rest,*

*Yet even at the foot of Pharaoh's throne,*

*Two men array'd in humble garments stood.*

*One spoke not, but with meekly folded arms,*

*Awaited silently the king's decree…*

## "Are slavery and oppression aught more just than in the days of Moses?"

וַיִּרְאוּ הָעָם אֶת־יהוה וַיַּאֲמִינוּ בַּיהוה וּבְמֹשֶׁה עַבְדּוֹ.

*"The people feared the Lord, and they believed in the Lord and in His servant Moses."*

When George Washington died in 1799, many speakers eulogized him as modern Moses. One such eulogy, delivered by Reverend Thaddeus Fiske of Cambridge, saw the death of Washington in the fledgling years of the new nation as akin to Moses's death at the edge of the Promised Land.

*George Washington on his deathbed*

[I]f the children of Israel had occasion to deplore the loss of Moses, well may America weep for the death of her WASHINGTON.… The life of Moses was continued useful and important to them even to its last hour; when he died his eye was not dim, nor his natural force abated. He was raised up, to be the instrument of their deliverance from Egyptian bondage, and the appointed medium of their blessings…and of their preservation as a nation. And as a General, Politician and Lawgiver, the world had never beheld his equal. With the enemies, they were called to encounter; in their unparalleled journey through the dreary desert; and in the administration of their laws and government, we see Moses at their head.…

[W]e see a striking resemblance to the part, which Washington has performed, in behalf of this American Israel.… And will it be too much for me to say, that the American nation, with their Washington, emancipated and made free and happy by him, shall be handed down to distant posterity, and perpetuated with

as much fame and glory, in the annals of profane history, as the Children of Israel, with their Moses, are celebrated in the sacred writings.…

WASHINGTON, as in his life, so in the hour of his death, somewhat resembled the celebrated leader of Israel. Like Moses, his eye was not dim, nor his natural force abated. His body and mind were unimpaired by service or by age; his life was important and useful to its last hour; and the Mount [Mount Vernon] to which he had retired, became the place of his death and burial.…

The Children of Israel mourned for their guide, they wept for Moses in the plains of Moab. And great was the loss which they deplored.… The Children of Columbia now weep for Washington in the plains of America.

MAGGID    96

וּבְמֹשֶׁה
עַבְדּוֹ

THE
MOSAIC
DELIVERER
OF AMERICA

*Leading the
Jewish people
to the Promised
Land*

**How much good, layer upon layer, the Omnipresent has done for us:**

Had He brought us out of Egypt
without bringing judgment upon [our oppressors],
    **that would have been enough for us.**

Had He brought judgment upon them
but not upon their gods,
    **that would have been enough for us.**

Had He brought judgment upon their gods
without killing their firstborn sons,
    **that would have been enough for us.**

Had He killed their firstborn sons
without giving us their wealth,
    **that would have been enough for us.**

Had He given us their wealth
without splitting the sea for us,
    **that would have been enough for us.**

Had He split the sea for us
but not brought us through it dry,
    **that would have been enough for us.**

Had He brought us through [the sea] dry
without drowning our enemies in it,
    **that would have been enough for us.**

Had He drowned our enemies in it
without providing for our needs
for forty years in the desert,
    **that would have been enough for us.**

Had He provided for our needs
for forty years in the desert,
without feeding us with manna,
    **that would have been enough for us.**

Had He fed us with manna
without giving us Shabbat,
    **that would have been enough for us.**

*THAT WOULD HAVE BEEN ENOUGH*

# כַּמָּה מַעֲלוֹת טוֹבוֹת
## לַמָּקוֹם עָלֵינוּ

אִלּוּ הוֹצִיאָנוּ מִמִּצְרַיִם
וְלֹא עָשָׂה בָהֶם שְׁפָטִים  דַּיֵּנוּ

אִלּוּ עָשָׂה בָהֶם שְׁפָטִים
וְלֹא עָשָׂה בֵאלֹהֵיהֶם  דַּיֵּנוּ

אִלּוּ עָשָׂה בֵאלֹהֵיהֶם
וְלֹא הָרַג אֶת בְּכוֹרֵיהֶם  דַּיֵּנוּ

אִלּוּ הָרַג אֶת בְּכוֹרֵיהֶם
וְלֹא נָתַן לָנוּ אֶת מָמוֹנָם  דַּיֵּנוּ

אִלּוּ נָתַן לָנוּ אֶת מָמוֹנָם
וְלֹא קָרַע לָנוּ אֶת הַיָּם  דַּיֵּנוּ

אִלּוּ קָרַע לָנוּ אֶת הַיָּם
וְלֹא הֶעֱבִירָנוּ בְתוֹכוֹ בֶּחָרָבָה  דַּיֵּנוּ

אִלּוּ הֶעֱבִירָנוּ בְתוֹכוֹ בֶּחָרָבָה
וְלֹא שִׁקַּע צָרֵינוּ בְתוֹכוֹ  דַּיֵּנוּ

אִלּוּ שִׁקַּע צָרֵינוּ בְתוֹכוֹ
וְלֹא סִפֵּק צָרְכֵּנוּ בַּמִּדְבָּר אַרְבָּעִים שָׁנָה  דַּיֵּנוּ

אִלּוּ סִפֵּק צָרְכֵּנוּ בַּמִּדְבָּר אַרְבָּעִים שָׁנָה
וְלֹא הֶאֱכִילָנוּ אֶת הַמָּן  דַּיֵּנוּ

אִלּוּ הֶאֱכִילָנוּ אֶת הַמָּן
וְלֹא נָתַן לָנוּ אֶת הַשַּׁבָּת  דַּיֵּנוּ

*Wandering through
the wilderness*

Had He given us Shabbat
without drawing us close around Mount Sinai,
**that would have been enough for us.**

Had He drawn us close around Mount Sinai
without giving us the Torah,
**that would have been enough for us.**

Had He given us the Torah
without bringing us to the Land of Israel,
**that would have been enough for us.**

Had He brought us to the Land of Israel
without building for us the House He chose,
**that would have been enough for us.**

## How many and manifold then, the Omnipresent's kindnesses are to us –

for He brought us out of Egypt and brought judgment upon [our oppressors] and upon their gods, and He killed their firstborn sons and gave us their wealth, and He split the sea for us and brought us through it on dry land and drowned our enemies there, and He provided for our needs for forty years in the desert and fed us manna, and He gave us Shabbat, and He drew us close around Mount Sinai and gave us the Torah, and He brought us to the Land of Israel and built for us the House He chose, so we could find atonement [there] for all our sins.

# THE HOUSE HE CHOSE

אִלּוּ נָתַן לָנוּ אֶת הַשַׁבָּת
וְלֹא קֵרְבָנוּ לִפְנֵי הַר סִינַי    דַּיֵּנוּ

אִלּוּ קֵרְבָנוּ לִפְנֵי הַר סִינַי
וְלֹא נָתַן לָנוּ אֶת הַתּוֹרָה    דַּיֵּנוּ

אִלּוּ נָתַן לָנוּ אֶת הַתּוֹרָה
וְלֹא הִכְנִיסָנוּ לְאֶרֶץ יִשְׂרָאֵל    דַּיֵּנוּ

אִלּוּ הִכְנִיסָנוּ לְאֶרֶץ יִשְׂרָאֵל
וְלֹא בָנָה לָנוּ אֶת בֵּית הַבְּחִירָה    דַּיֵּנוּ

עַל אַחַת כַּמָּה וְכַמָּה טוֹבָה
כְּפוּלָה וּמְכֻפֶּלֶת לַמָּקוֹם עָלֵינוּ

שֶׁהוֹצִיאָנוּ מִמִּצְרַיִם, וְעָשָׂה בָהֶם שְׁפָטִים, וְעָשָׂה
בֵאלֹהֵיהֶם, וְהָרַג בְּכוֹרֵיהֶם, וְנָתַן לָנוּ אֶת מָמוֹנָם,
וְקָרַע לָנוּ אֶת הַיָּם, וְהֶעֱבִירָנוּ בְתוֹכוֹ בֶּחָרָבָה,
וְשִׁקַּע צָרֵינוּ בְּתוֹכוֹ, וְסִפֵּק צָרְכֵּנוּ בַּמִּדְבָּר
אַרְבָּעִים שָׁנָה, וְהֶאֱכִילָנוּ אֶת הַמָּן, וְנָתַן לָנוּ
אֶת הַשַׁבָּת, וְקֵרְבָנוּ לִפְנֵי הַר סִינַי, וְנָתַן לָנוּ אֶת
הַתּוֹרָה, וְהִכְנִיסָנוּ לְאֶרֶץ יִשְׂרָאֵל, וּבָנָה לָנוּ אֶת
בֵּית הַבְּחִירָה לְכַפֵּר עַל כָּל עֲוֹנוֹתֵינוּ.

*Gathering the manna*

# BENJAMIN FRANKLIN'S SEAL OF THE SPLITTING OF THE SEA

*"Pharaoh's army engulfed by the Red Sea," oil on canvas, by Frederick Arthur Bridgman, 1900*

*Writing the Declaration of Independence*

In Philadelphia in 1776, as the Revolution began, delegates of the Continental Congress set about establishing the ensigns and symbols of the new nation they hoped to create. Benjamin Franklin proposed that America's Great Seal depict:

> Moses standing on the shore, and extending his Hand over the Sea, thereby causing the same to overwhelm Pharoah (*sic*) who is sitting his Chariot, a Crown on his head and a Sword in his Hand. Rays from a Pillar of Fire in the Cloud reaching to Moses, to express that he acts by the command of the Deity.

> Motto, Rebellion to Tyrants is Obedience to God.

(Centuries earlier, Christopher Columbus recalled that, in the stormy Atlantic, "the rising of the sea was very formidable to me as it happened formerly to Moses when he led the Jews from Egypt.")

The drawing of Franklin's proposed seal depicted below was made by Benson J. Lossing for *Harper's New Monthly Magazine* in July 1856.

Thomas Jefferson's suggestion for the Great Seal was the children of Israel in the wilderness, led by a cloud by day and a pillar of fire by night. Jefferson liked the motto "Rebellion to Tyrants is Obedience to God" so much that he used it on his personal seal.

*"And He provided for our needs for forty years in the desert."*

On June 16, 1978, in remarks delivered in Atlanta, Georgia to members of the Southern Baptist Brotherhood Commission, President Jimmy Carter described the Israelites' wilderness journey when he spoke of the dependence on God in ensuring national growth.

Thomas Jefferson

> A nation, like a person, has to continually be on an inward journey and an outward journey, and we grow stronger in the process. There's a relationship between personal leadership and a people.

Moses demonstrated this, as you know, when God called him to lead the Israelites out of Egypt. He was not ready to assume that responsibility until he had spent 40 years tending sheep, acquiring a family, discussing the problems with his father-in-law, Jethro. And he finally was able, reluctantly, to turn to God for help and support and a kind of a partnership, and then he was able to work with and sometimes against the people of Israel as they made their long, tortuous journey....

Thomas Jefferson, as he considered what the emblem of our Nation ought to be, the Seal of the United States, suggested that it be a picture of the people of Israel following a cloud and a column of fire, because he saw this inner journey and the outward journey interrelated, and also visualized, although he was not a very deeply religious man on the outside, he saw that dependence on God was good for his new Nation that he loved.

So, the great outward journey of the Israelites, of our own Nation, was based on an inward journey, where peace was derived from an inner strength and an awareness of the will of God and a willingness to carry this will out.

We cannot succeed without this. Moses couldn't. Lincoln couldn't. Lottie Moon [a Baptist missionary to China] couldn't. And neither can we as Baptists, Christians, or as Americans.

בְּמִדְבָּר
אַרְבָּעִים
שָׁנָה

A pillar of cloud
in the desert

# THE
# GREAT
# OUTWARD
# JOURNEY
# OF THE
# ISRAELITES

SUSTAINED
BY THE
TRUTHS
OF SINAI

וְקֵרְבָנוּ
לִפְנֵי
הַר סִינַי

*"And He drew us close around Mount Sinai."*

*President George W. Bush*

In his second Inaugural Address, delivered on January 20, 2005, President George W. Bush traced the American ideal of freedom to Mount Sinai:

> In America's ideal of freedom, the public interest depends on private character – on integrity, and tolerance toward others, and the rule of conscience in our own lives. Self-government relies, in the end, on the governing of the self. That edifice of character is built in families, supported by communities with standards, and sustained in our national life by the truths of Sinai.

# "The edifice of character is... sustained in our national life by the truths of Sinai."

## "And He brought us to the Land of Israel"

Founding Father Benjamin Rush was famously critical of the Continental Army's generals. A letter he penned to Patrick Henry in 1778 reveals that Rush's faith in the Revolution hinged not on the ability of its commanders, but on God. While most American revolutionaries were ecstatic with the recent defeat of the British in Saratoga and the promise of an alliance with France, Rush asserted that it was only due to God that the Revolution would succeed in producing the colonists' Promised Land:

*Benjamin Rush*

> We have only passed the Red Sea; a dreary wilderness is still before us, and unless a Moses or a Joshua is raised up on our behalf, we must perish before we reach the Promised Land. But

*The surrender of British General John Burgoyne at Saratoga on October 17, 1777*

is our case desperate? By no means. We have wisdom, virtue, and strength enough to save us, if they could be called into action. The Northern army has shown us what Americans are capable of doing with a general at their head. The spirit of the Southern army is no way inferior to that of the Northern. A Gates, Lee, or a Conway, would in a few weeks render them an irresistible body of men. The last of the above officers has accepted of the new office of inspector-general of our army, in order to reform abuses; but the remedy is only a palliative one. In one of his letters to a friend, he says, "a great and good God hath decreed America to be free, or the general and weak counselors would have ruined her long ago."

וְהִכְנִיסָנוּ
לְאֶרֶץ
יִשְׂרָאֵל

*An aerial view of
northern Israel*

## WISDOM
## IN THE
## WILDERNESS

**Rabban Gamliel** would say: Anyone who does not say these three things on Pesaḥ has not fulfilled his obligation, and these are they:

## Pesaḥ, Matza, and Bitter Herbs.

**The Pesaḥ** is what our ancestors would eat while the Temple stood: and what does it recall? It recalls the Holy One's passing over (*Pasaḥ*) the houses of our ancestors in Egypt, as it is said: "You shall say: 'It is a Pesaḥ offering for the Lord, for He passed over the houses of the children of Israel in Egypt while He struck the Egyptians, but saved those in our homes' – and the people bowed and prostrated themselves."

The matzot are now lifted:

**This Matza** that we eat: what does it recall? It recalls the dough of our ancestors, which did not have time to rise before the King, King of kings, the Holy One, blessed be He, revealed Himself and redeemed them,as it is said: "They baked the dough that they had brought out of Egypt into un-leavened cakes, for it had not risen, for they were cast out of Egypt and could not delay, and they made no provision for the way."

PESAH
MATZA
BITTER
HERBS

רַבָּן גַּמְלִיאֵל הָיָה אוֹמֵר, כָּל שֶׁלֹּא אָמַר שְׁלוֹשָׁה דְּבָרִים אֵלּוּ בַּפֶּסַח לֹא יָצָא יְדֵי חוֹבָתוֹ, וְאֵלּוּ הֵן

# פֶּסַח מַצָּה וּמָרוֹר

פֶּסַח שֶׁהָיוּ אֲבוֹתֵינוּ אוֹכְלִים בִּזְמַן שֶׁבֵּית הַמִּקְדָּשׁ הָיָה קַיָּם, עַל שׁוּם מָה, עַל שׁוּם שֶׁפָּסַח הַקָּדוֹשׁ בָּרוּךְ הוּא עַל בָּתֵּי אֲבוֹתֵינוּ בְּמִצְרַיִם, שֶׁנֶּאֱמַר: וַאֲמַרְתֶּם זֶבַח־פֶּסַח הוּא לַיהוה, אֲשֶׁר פָּסַח עַל־בָּתֵּי בְנֵי־יִשְׂרָאֵל בְּמִצְרַיִם בְּנָגְפּוֹ אֶת־מִצְרַיִם, וְאֶת־בָּתֵּינוּ הִצִּיל, וַיִּקֹּד הָעָם וַיִּשְׁתַּחֲווּ:

The מצות are now lifted:

מַצָּה זוֹ שֶׁאָנוּ אוֹכְלִים, עַל שׁוּם מָה, עַל שׁוּם שֶׁלֹּא הִסְפִּיק בְּצֵקָם שֶׁל אֲבוֹתֵינוּ לְהַחֲמִיץ עַד שֶׁנִּגְלָה עֲלֵיהֶם מֶלֶךְ מַלְכֵי הַמְּלָכִים הַקָּדוֹשׁ בָּרוּךְ הוּא, וּגְאָלָם, שֶׁנֶּאֱמַר: וַיֹּאפוּ אֶת־הַבָּצֵק אֲשֶׁר הוֹצִיאוּ מִמִּצְרַיִם עֻגֹת מַצּוֹת, כִּי לֹא חָמֵץ כִּי־גֹרְשׁוּ מִמִּצְרַיִם, וְלֹא יָכְלוּ לְהִתְמַהְמֵהַּ וְגַם־צֵדָה לֹא־עָשׂוּ לָהֶם:

THE
BREAD
HAS
BEGUN
TO RISE

מַצָּה זוּ
שֶׁאָנוּ אוֹכְלִים

מַצָּה זוֹ שֶׁאָנוּ אוֹכְלִים, עַל שׁוּם מָה, עַל שׁוּם שֶׁלֹא הִסְפִּיק
בְּצֵקָם שֶׁל אֲבוֹתֵינוּ לְהַחֲמִיץ.

*"This matza that we eat: what does it recall? It recalls the dough of our ancestors, which did not have time to rise."*

*Lieutenant General Mark W. Clark*

Lieutenant General Mark W. Clark was raised Episcopalian, although his mother was Jewish. The Allied lieutenant general had a special appreciation for the Passover Seder organized by soldiers of the United States Fifth Army in Naples at the height of the Second World War. At the April 1944 Seder in Naples, Italy, he wittily remarked:

> Tonight you are eating unleavened bread just as your forebears ate unleavened bread. Because the Exodus came so quickly the dough had no time to rise. There was a time of unleavened bread in this war. The time when it looked as though we might not have time to rise – time to raise an army and equip it, time to stop the onrush of a Germany that has already risen. But the bread has begun to rise. It started at Alamein. It was rising higher when the Fifth Army invaded Italy. It is reaching the top of the pan and soon the time will come when it will spread out…and the victory will be ours.

*Jewish servicemen holding a Seder, c. 1943*

# "There was a time of unleavened bread in this war."

**These bitter herbs** that we eat: what do they recall? They recall the bitterness that the Egyptians imposed on the lives of our ancestors in Egypt, as it is said: "They embittered their lives with hard labor, with clay and with bricks and with all field labors, with all the work with which they enslaved them – hard labor."

**Generation by generation,** each person must see himself as if he himself had come out of Egypt, as it is said: "And you shall tell your child on that day, 'Because of this the Lord acted for me when I came out of Egypt.'" It was not only our ancestors whom the Holy One redeemed; He redeemed us too along with them, as it is said: "He took us out of there, to bring us to the land He promised our ancestors and to give it to us."

מָרוֹר זֶה שֶׁאָנוּ אוֹכְלִים, עַל שׁוּם מָה, עַל שׁוּם שֶׁמֵּרְרוּ
הַמִּצְרִים אֶת חַיֵּי אֲבוֹתֵינוּ בְּמִצְרַיִם, שֶׁנֶּאֱמַר: וַיְמָרְרוּ
אֶת־חַיֵּיהֶם בַּעֲבֹדָה קָשָׁה, בְּחֹמֶר וּבִלְבֵנִים וּבְכָל־
עֲבֹדָה בַּשָּׂדֶה אֵת כָּל־עֲבֹדָתָם אֲשֶׁר־עָבְדוּ בָהֶם
בְּפָרֶךְ:

בְּכָל דּוֹר וָדוֹר חַיָּב אָדָם לִרְאוֹת אֶת עַצְמוֹ כְּאִלּוּ
הוּא יָצָא מִמִּצְרַיִם, שֶׁנֶּאֱמַר: וְהִגַּדְתָּ לְבִנְךָ בַּיּוֹם הַהוּא
לֵאמֹר, בַּעֲבוּר זֶה עָשָׂה יהוה לִי בְּצֵאתִי מִמִּצְרָיִם:
לֹא אֶת אֲבוֹתֵינוּ בִּלְבַד גָּאַל הַקָּדוֹשׁ בָּרוּךְ הוּא
אֶלָּא אַף אוֹתָנוּ גָּאַל עִמָּהֶם, שֶׁנֶּאֱמַר: וְאוֹתָנוּ הוֹצִיא
מִשָּׁם לְמַעַן הָבִיא אֹתָנוּ לָתֶת לָנוּ אֶת־הָאָרֶץ אֲשֶׁר
נִשְׁבַּע לַאֲבֹתֵינוּ:

AS IF
HE
HIMSELF
CAME
OUT OF
EGYPT

# FREDERICK DOUGLASS'S PASSOVER

Allow me to say, in conclusion, notwithstanding the dark picture I have this day presented of the state of the nation, I do not despair of this country. There are forces in operation, which must inevitably work the downfall of slavery. "The arm of the Lord is not shortened," and the doom of slavery is certain. I, therefore, leave off where I began, with hope.

בְּכָל דּוֹר וָדוֹר

בְּכָל דּוֹר וָדוֹר חַיָּב אָדָם לִרְאוֹת אֶת עַצְמוֹ כְּאִלּוּ הוּא יָצָא
מִמִּצְרָיִם.

*"Generation by generation, each person must see himself as if he himself had come out of Egypt."*

*Frederick Douglass*

In July 1852, Frederick Douglass shared his frustration with America's slow crawl towards abolition in a meeting of the Rochester Ladies Anti-Slavery Society. The speech, now called "What to the Slave is the Fourth of July?" likens the national holiday to a modern Passover, citing the hypocrisy of America's cause for independence in light of the institution of slavery.

Mr. President, Friends and Fellow Citizens…This, for the purpose of this celebration, is the 4th of July. It is the birthday of your National Independence, and of your political freedom. This, to you, is what the Passover was to the emancipated people of God. It carries your minds back to the day, and to the act of your great deliverance; and to the signs, and to the wonders, associated with that act, and that day…. As the sheet

anchor takes a firmer hold, when the ship is tossed by the storm, so did the cause of your fathers grow stronger, as it breasted the chilling blasts of kingly displeasure. The greatest and best of British statesmen admitted its justice, and the loftiest eloquence of the British Senate came to its support. But, with that blindness which seems to be the unvarying characteristic of tyrants, since Pharaoh and his hosts were drowned in the Red Sea, the British Government persisted in the exactions complained of.

[…]

What have I, or those I represent, to do with your national independence? Fellow-citizens, pardon me, allow me to ask, why am I called upon to speak here to-day? What have I, or those I represent, to do with your national independence? Are the great principles of political freedom and of natural justice, embodied in that Declaration of Independence, extended to us?…This Fourth [of] July is yours, not mine. You may rejoice, I must mourn. To drag a man in fetters into the grand illuminated temple of liberty, and call upon him to join you in joyous anthems, were inhuman mockery and sacrilegious irony. Do you mean, citizens, to mock me, by asking me to speak to-day?

[…]

**Therefore** it is our duty to thank, praise, laud, glorify, exalt, honor, bless, raise high, and acclaim the One who has performed all these miracles for our ancestors and for us; who has brought us out from slavery to freedom, from sorrow to joy, from grief to celebration; from darkness to great light and from enslavement to redemption; and so we shall sing a new song before Him. HALLELUYA!

The cup is put down.

**Halleluya!** Servants of the LORD, give praise; praise the name of the LORD. Blessed be the name of the LORD now and for evermore. From the rising of the sun to its setting, may the LORD's name be praised. High is the LORD above all nations; His glory is above the heavens. Who is like the LORD our God, who sits enthroned so high, yet turns so low to see the heavens and the earth? He raises the poor from the dust and the needy from the refuse heap, giving them a place alongside princes, the princes of His people. He makes the woman in a childless house a happy mother of children. HALLELUYA!

**When Israel came out** of Egypt, the house of Jacob from a people of foreign tongue, Judah became His sanctuary, Israel His dominion. The sea saw and fled; the Jordan turned back. The mountains skipped like rams, the hills like lambs. Why was it, sea, that you fled? Jordan, why did you turn back? Why, mountains, did you skip like rams, and you, hills, like lambs? It was at the presence of the LORD, Creator of the earth, at the presence of the God of Jacob, who turned the rock into a pool of water, flint into a flowing spring.

# SING A NEW SONG

The מצות are covered and the cup is raised.

לְפִיכָךְ אֲנַחְנוּ חַיָּבִים לְהוֹדוֹת, לְהַלֵּל, לְשַׁבֵּחַ, לְפָאֵר לְרוֹמֵם, לְהַדֵּר, לְבָרֵךְ, לְעַלֵּה וּלְקַלֵּס לְמִי שֶׁעָשָׂה לַאֲבוֹתֵינוּ וְלָנוּ אֶת כָּל הַנִּסִּים הָאֵלֶּה, הוֹצִיאָנוּ מֵעַבְדוּת לְחֵרוּת, מִיָּגוֹן לְשִׂמְחָה, מֵאֵבֶל לְיוֹם טוֹב וּמֵאֲפֵלָה לְאוֹר גָּדוֹל וּמִשִׁעְבּוּד לִגְאֻלָּה, וְנֹאמַר לְפָנָיו שִׁירָה חֲדָשָׁה הַלְלוּיָהּ.

The cup is put down.

הַלְלוּיָהּ הַלְלוּ עַבְדֵי יהוה, הַלְלוּ אֶת־שֵׁם יהוה: יְהִי שֵׁם יהוה מְבֹרָךְ, מֵעַתָּה וְעַד־עוֹלָם: מִמִּזְרַח־שֶׁמֶשׁ עַד־מְבוֹאוֹ, מְהֻלָּל שֵׁם יהוה: רָם עַל־כָּל־גּוֹיִם יהוה, עַל הַשָּׁמַיִם כְּבוֹדוֹ: מִי כַּיהוה אֱלֹהֵינוּ, הַמַּגְבִּיהִי לָשָׁבֶת: הַמַּשְׁפִּילִי לִרְאוֹת, בַּשָּׁמַיִם וּבָאָרֶץ: מְקִימִי מֵעָפָר דָּל, מֵאַשְׁפֹּת יָרִים אֶבְיוֹן: לְהוֹשִׁיבִי עִם־ נְדִיבִים, עִם נְדִיבֵי עַמּוֹ: מוֹשִׁיבִי עֲקֶרֶת הַבַּיִת, אֵם־ הַבָּנִים שְׂמֵחָה הַלְלוּיָהּ:

בְּצֵאת יִשְׂרָאֵל מִמִּצְרָיִם, בֵּית יַעֲקֹב מֵעַם לֹעֵז: הָיְתָה יְהוּדָה לְקָדְשׁוֹ, יִשְׂרָאֵל מַמְשְׁלוֹתָיו: הַיָּם רָאָה וַיָּנֹס, הַיַּרְדֵּן יִסֹּב לְאָחוֹר: הֶהָרִים רָקְדוּ כְאֵילִים, גְּבָעוֹת כִּבְנֵי־צֹאן: מַה־לְּךָ הַיָּם כִּי תָנוּס, הַיַּרְדֵּן תִּסֹּב לְאָחוֹר: הֶהָרִים תִּרְקְדוּ כְאֵילִים, גְּבָעוֹת כִּבְנֵי־צֹאן: מִלִּפְנֵי אָדוֹן חוּלִי אָרֶץ, מִלִּפְנֵי אֱלוֹהַּ יַעֲקֹב: הַהֹפְכִי הַצּוּר אֲגַם־מָיִם, חַלָּמִישׁ לְמַעְיְנוֹ־מָיִם:

לְפִיכָךְ אֲנַחְנוּ חַיָּבִים לְהוֹדוֹת, לְהַלֵּל, לְשַׁבֵּחַ, לְפָאֵר, לְרוֹמֵם,
לְהַדֵּר, לְבָרֵךְ, לְעַלֵּה וּלְקַלֵּס לְמִי שֶׁעָשָׂה לַאֲבוֹתֵינוּ וְלָנוּ אֶת כָּל
הַנִּסִּים הָאֵלֶה.

*"Therefore it is our duty to thank, praise, laud, glorify, exalt,
honor, bless, raise high, and acclaim the One who has performed
all these miracles."*

In November of 1620, Governor of Plymouth Colony William Bradford led the new arrivals fresh off the Mayflower in a reading of Psalm 107, thanking God for providing for their safe journey across the Atlantic.

Bradford and his fellow Puritans saw themselves as modern Israelites having escaped modern Egypt, the European continent. The pilgrim William Bradford likened his fellow Mayflower passengers' journey to "Moses and the Israelites when they went out of Egypt," and John Winthrop, one of the founders of Massachusetts Bay Colony, compared his own departure for New England to how the Lord "carried the Israelites into the wilderness and made them forget the fleshpots of Egypt."

Bradford's edition of the Psalms, published by Henry Ainsworth in 1612, included Ainsworth's *Annotations* to the Psalms. Ainsworth's comments to Psalm 107 read:

> And from this Psalme, and this verse of it, the Hebrues have this Canon; Foure must confess (unto God) The sick, when he is healed; the prisoner when he is released out of bonds; they that goe down to sea, when they are come up (to land); and wayfaring men, when they are come to the inhabited land.

*Colonel William Bradford*

And they must make confession before ten men, and two of them wise men, Ps. 107.32. And the manner of confessing and blessing is thus; He standeth among them and blesseth the Lord, the King eternal, that bounteously rewardeth good things unto sinners, etc. Maimony in Misn. Treat. Of Blessings, chap. 10, sect. 8.

As Nick Bunker notes in his *Making Haste from Babylon*, Ainsworth's citation from Maimonides refers to the four scenarios recorded in the Talmud that obligate a Jew to bring a Thanksgiving offering to the Temple. Thus, in Bunker's estimation, it is possible that Ainsworth's note regarding Jewish law may have inspired Bradford's prayers and the first American Thanksgiving.

חַיָּבִים לְהוֹדוֹת

*The first Thanksgiving*

# THE TALMUD
# AND THE
# FIRST
# THANKSGIVING

# THE SECOND CUP

**Blessed** are You, LORD our God, King of the Universe, who has redeemed us and redeemed our ancestors from Egypt, and brought us to this night to eat matza and bitter herbs. So may the LORD our God bring us in peace to other seasons and festivals that are coming to us, happy in the building of Your city and rejoicing in Your service; and there we shall eat of sacrifices and Pesaḥ offerings [On Motza'ei Shabbat: of Pesaḥ offerings and sacrifices], of which the blood will reach the side of Your altar to be accepted. And we shall thank You in a new song for our redemption and for our lives' salvation. Blessed are You, LORD, Redeemer of Israel.

**Blessed are You, LORD our God, King of the Universe, who creates the fruit of the vine.**

Drink while reclining to the left.

In preparation for the meal, all participants wash their hands and recite the blessing:

## RAḤTZA

**Blessed are You, LORD our God, King of the Universe, who has made us holy through His commandments and has commanded us about washing hands.**

בָּרוּךְ אַתָּה יהוה אֱלֹהֵינוּ מֶלֶךְ הָעוֹלָם, אֲשֶׁר
גְּאָלָנוּ, וְגָאַל אֶת אֲבוֹתֵינוּ מִמִּצְרַיִם, וְהִגִּיעָנוּ
הַלַּיְלָה הַזֶּה לֶאֱכָל בּוֹ מַצָּה וּמָרוֹר, כֵּן יהוה
אֱלֹהֵינוּ וֵאלֹהֵי אֲבוֹתֵינוּ יַגִּיעֵנוּ לְמוֹעֲדִים
וְלִרְגָלִים אֲחֵרִים, הַבָּאִים לִקְרָאתֵנוּ לְשָׁלוֹם,
שְׂמֵחִים בְּבִנְיַן עִירֶךָ וְשָׂשִׂים בַּעֲבוֹדָתֶךָ, וְנֹאכַל
שָׁם מִן הַזְּבָחִים וּמִן הַפְּסָחִים (מוצאי שבת: מִן
הַפְּסָחִים וּמִן הַזְּבָחִים) אֲשֶׁר יַגִּיעַ דָּמָם עַל קִיר
מִזְבַּחֲךָ לְרָצוֹן, וְנוֹדֶה לְךָ שִׁיר חָדָשׁ עַל גְּאֻלָּתֵנוּ
וְעַל פְּדוּת נַפְשֵׁנוּ, בָּרוּךְ אַתָּה יהוה, גָּאַל יִשְׂרָאֵל.

בָּרוּךְ אַתָּה יהוה אֱלֹהֵינוּ מֶלֶךְ הָעוֹלָם
בּוֹרֵא פְּרִי הַגָּפֶן.

Drink while reclining to the left.

 רחצה

In preparation for the meal,
all participants wash their hands
and recite the blessing:

בָּרוּךְ אַתָּה יהוה אֱלֹהֵינוּ מֶלֶךְ הָעוֹלָם
אֲשֶׁר קִדְּשָׁנוּ בְּמִצְוֹתָיו וְצִוָּנוּ עַל נְטִילַת יָדָיִם.

# MATZOT IN BUCHENWALD

Jewish prisoners upon being
liberated from the concentration
camp, April 1945

אֲשֶׁר גְּאָלָנוּ, וְגָאַל אֶת אֲבוֹתֵינוּ מִמִּצְרָיִם, וְהִגִּיעָנוּ הַלַּיְלָה הַזֶּה,
לֶאֱכָל בּוֹ מַצָּה וּמָרוֹר.

*"Who has redeemed us and redeemed our ancestors from Egypt,
and brought us to this night to eat matza and bitter herbs."*

*General George S. Patton*

Chaplain Herschel Schacter of the Third Army's VIII Corps was among the first allied officers to enter the camp on April 11th. Rabbi Schacter greeted them with *"Shalom aleikhem, Yidden – ihr zint frei!* You are free!" He immediately took it upon himself to see to the survivors' material and spiritual needs. One of his first acts was to distribute boxes of matza to the liberated prisoners, even though Passover had already concluded some days before. Like their ancestors some three thousand years earlier, the Jewish survivors of Buchenwald ate matza to commemorate their passage from slavery to freedom.

On April 11, 1945, General George S. Patton's Third Army entered the concentration camp Buchenwald. Upon their arrival, they came face to face with the appalling signs of the atrocity that had occurred there. Fearing that the German public would dismiss reports of Nazi brutality as allied propaganda, General Patton ordered a thousand civilians from the nearby city of Weimar to come to the camp and witness its horrors for themselves.

*Supervising the matza baking at the Manischewitz Matzo Bakery; left: D. Beryl Manischewitz, grandson of the founder*

# "Shalom aleikhem, Yidden –
# ihr zint frei! You are free!"

The leader holds all three matzot and recites:

# MOTZI MATZA

**Blessed are You, Lord our God, King of the Universe, who brings forth bread from the earth.**

The lowermost matza is replaced.
The leader recites the following blessing while holding the uppermost and middle matzot:

**Blessed are You, Lord our God, King of the Universe, who has made us holy through His commandments and has commanded us to eat matza.**

A piece of the uppermost matza, together with a piece of the middle matza, are given to each member of the company. Eat while reclining to the left.

The *maror* is dipped in the *ḥaroset* before it is eaten.

# MAROR

**Blessed are You, Lord our God, King of the Universe, who has made us holy through His commandments and has commanded us to eat bitter herbs.**

Bitter herbs are sandwiched between two pieces of matza taken from the lowermost matza.

# KOREKH

**In memory** of the Temple, in the tradition of Hillel. This is what Hillel would do when the Temple still stood: he would wrap [the Pesaḥ offering] up with matza and bitter herbs and eat them together, to fulfill what is said: "You shall eat it with matza and bitter herbs."

Eat while reclining to the left.

## מוֹצִיא מַצָּה

The leader holds all three מצות and recites:

בָּרוּךְ אַתָּה יהוה אֱלֹהֵינוּ מֶלֶךְ הָעוֹלָם
הַמּוֹצִיא לֶחֶם מִן הָאָרֶץ.

The lowermost מצה is replaced.
The leader recites the following blessing while
holding the uppermost and middle מצות:

בָּרוּךְ אַתָּה יהוה אֱלֹהֵינוּ מֶלֶךְ הָעוֹלָם
אֲשֶׁר קִדְּשָׁנוּ בְּמִצְוֹתָיו וְצִוָּנוּ עַל אֲכִילַת מַצָּה.

A piece of the uppermost מצה, together with
a piece of the middle מצה, are given to each member
of the company. Eat while reclining to the left.

## מָרוֹר

The מרור is dipped in the חרוסת before it is eaten.

בָּרוּךְ אַתָּה יהוה אֱלֹהֵינוּ מֶלֶךְ הָעוֹלָם
אֲשֶׁר קִדְּשָׁנוּ בְּמִצְוֹתָיו וְצִוָּנוּ עַל אֲכִילַת מָרוֹר.

## כּוֹרֵךְ

Bitter herbs are sandwiched between two pieces of
מצה taken from the lowermost מצה.

זֵכֶר לַמִּקְדָּשׁ כְּהִלֵּל. כֵּן עָשָׂה הִלֵּל בִּזְמַן שֶׁבֵּית
הַמִּקְדָּשׁ הָיָה קַיָּם, הָיָה כּוֹרֵךְ פֶּסַח, מַצָּה וּמָרוֹר,
וְאוֹכֵל בְּיַחַד, לְקַיֵּם מַה שֶּׁנֶּאֱמַר: עַל־מַצּוֹת וּמְרֹרִים
יֹאכְלֻהוּ:

Eat while reclining to the left.

אֲשֶׁר קִדְּשָׁנוּ בְּמִצְוֹתָיו וְצִוָּנוּ עַל אֲכִילַת מָרוֹר.

**"Who has made us holy through His commandments and has commanded us to eat bitter herbs."**

The Revolutionary era poet Mercy Otis Warren likened King George III to Pharaoh, demanding the Israelites make bricks (represented at the Seder by the ḥaroset in which the bitter herbs are dipped) without providing them with straw.

*On the best plan to save a sinking state;*

*The oratorial fair, as they inclin'd,*

*Freely discuss'd, and frankly spake their mind.*

*Lamira wish'd that freedom might succeed,*

*But to such terms what female ere agreed?*

*To British marts forbidden to repair,*

*(Where ev'ry lux'ry tempts the blooming fair,)*

*Equals the rigour of those ancient times*

*When Pharaoh, harden'd as a G – in crimes,*

*Plagu'd Israel's race, and tax'd them by a law,*

*Demanding brick, when destitute of straw;*

*Miraculously led from Egypt's port,*

*They lov'd the fashions of the tyrant's court;*

Mercy Otis Warren

*Sigh'd for the leeks, and waters of the Nile,*

*As we for gewgaws from Britannia's isle;*

*That haughty isle, whose mercenary hand,*

*Spreads wide confusion round this fertile land,*

*Destroys the concord, and breaks down the shrine,*

*By virtue rear'd, to harmony divine...*

עַל
אֲכִילַת
מָרוֹר

# FROM
# DESTITUTE
# OF STRAW
# TO HARMONY
# DIVINE

*Illustration depicting slaves producing mudbricks painted on the walls of the tomb of Rekhmire in Thebes*

The festive meal is now eaten.

# SHULḤAN OREKH

At the end of the meal, the remaining piece of the middle matza which had been hidden earlier (the *afikoman*), is eaten.

# TZAFUN

The third cup of wine is poured.

# BAREKH

**A song of ascents.** When the Lᴏʀᴅ brought back the exiles of Zion we were like people who dream. Then were our mouths filled with laughter, and our tongues with songs of joy. Then was it said among the nations, "The Lᴏʀᴅ has done great things for them." The Lᴏʀᴅ did do great things for us and we rejoiced. Bring back our exiles, Lᴏʀᴅ, like streams in a dry land. May those who sowed in tears, reap in joy. May one who goes out weeping, carrying a bag of seed, come back with songs of joy, carrying his sheaves.

Some say:

My mouth shall speak the praise of God, and all creatures shall bless His holy name for ever and all time. We will bless God now and for ever. Halleluya! Thank the Lᴏʀᴅ for He is good: His loving-kindness is for ever. Who can tell of the Lᴏʀᴅ's mighty acts and make all His praise be heard?

## שׁוּלְחָן עוֹרֵךְ

The festive meal is now eaten.

## צָפוּן

At the end of the meal, the remaining piece of the middle מצה which had been hidden earlier (the אפיקומן), is eaten.

## בָּרֵךְ

The third cup of wine is poured.

שִׁיר הַמַּעֲלוֹת בְּשׁוּב יהוה אֶת־שִׁיבַת צִיּוֹן, הָיִינוּ כְּחֹלְמִים: אָז יִמָּלֵא שְׂחוֹק פִּינוּ וּלְשׁוֹנֵנוּ רִנָּה, אָז יֹאמְרוּ בַגּוֹיִם, הִגְדִּיל יהוה לַעֲשׂוֹת עִם־אֵלֶּה: הִגְדִּיל יהוה לַעֲשׂוֹת עִמָּנוּ, הָיִינוּ שְׂמֵחִים: שׁוּבָה יהוה אֶת־שְׁבִיתֵנוּ, כַּאֲפִיקִים בַּנֶּגֶב: הַזֹּרְעִים בְּדִמְעָה, בְּרִנָּה יִקְצֹרוּ: הָלוֹךְ יֵלֵךְ וּבָכֹה נֹשֵׂא מֶשֶׁךְ־הַזָּרַע, בֹּא־יָבֹא בְרִנָּה נֹשֵׂא אֲלֻמֹּתָיו:

Some say:

תְּהִלַּת יהוה יְדַבֶּר פִּי, וִיבָרֵךְ כָּל־בָּשָׂר שֵׁם קָדְשׁוֹ לְעוֹלָם וָעֶד: וַאֲנַחְנוּ נְבָרֵךְ יָהּ מֵעַתָּה וְעַד־עוֹלָם, הַלְלוּיָהּ: הוֹדוּ לַיהוה כִּי־טוֹב, כִּי לְעוֹלָם חַסְדּוֹ: מִי יְמַלֵּל גְּבוּרוֹת יהוה, יַשְׁמִיעַ כָּל־תְּהִלָּתוֹ:

The festive meal is eaten

When three or more men say *Birkat HaMazon* together, the following *zimmun* is said. When three or more women say *Birkat HaMazon*, substitute "Friends" for "Gentlemen." The leader should ask permission from those with precedence to lead the *Birkat HaMazon*.

Leader: **Gentlemen, let us say grace.**

Others: May the name of the LORD be blessed from now and for ever.

Leader: May the name of the LORD be blessed from now and for ever. With your permission, (my father and teacher / my mother and teacher / the Kohanim present / our teacher the Rabbi / the master of this house / the mistress of this house) my masters and teachers, let us bless (in a minyan: our God,) the One from whose food we have eaten.

Others: Blessed be (in a minyan: our God,) the One from whose food we have eaten, and by whose goodness we live.

**Blessed** are You, LORD our God, King of the Universe, who in His goodness feeds the whole world with grace, kindness and compassion. He gives food to all living things, for His kindness is for ever. Because of His continual great goodness, we have never lacked food, nor may we ever lack it, for the sake of His great name. For He is God who feeds and sustains all, does good to all, and prepares food for all creatures He has created. Blessed are You, LORD, who feeds all.

*FEEDS THE WHOLE WORLD*

When three or more men say ברכת המזון together,
the following זימון is said. When three or more women
say ברכת המזון, substitute חֲבְרוֹתַי for רַבּוֹתַי.
The leader should ask permission from those
with precedence to lead the ברכת המזון.

*God feeds and sustains
all living things*

המזמן: רַבּוֹתַי, נְבָרֵךְ.

המסובים: יְהִי שֵׁם יהוה מְבֹרָךְ מֵעַתָּה וְעַד־עוֹלָם:

המזמן: יְהִי שֵׁם יהוה מְבֹרָךְ מֵעַתָּה וְעַד־עוֹלָם:
בִּרְשׁוּת (אָבִי מוֹרִי / אִמִּי מוֹרָתִי / כֹּהֲנִים / מוֹרֵנוּ הָרַב /
בַּעַל הַבַּיִת הַזֶּה / בַּעֲלַת הַבַּיִת הַזֶּה) מָרָנָן וְרַבָּנָן וְרַבּוֹתַי
נְבָרֵךְ (במניין: אֱלֹהֵינוּ) שֶׁאָכַלְנוּ מִשֶּׁלּוֹ.

המסובים: בָּרוּךְ (במניין: אֱלֹהֵינוּ) שֶׁאָכַלְנוּ מִשֶּׁלּוֹ
וּבְטוּבוֹ חָיִינוּ.

בָּרוּךְ אַתָּה יהוה אֱלֹהֵינוּ מֶלֶךְ הָעוֹלָם הַזָּן אֶת
הָעוֹלָם כֻּלּוֹ בְּטוּבוֹ בְּחֵן בְּחֶסֶד וּבְרַחֲמִים הוּא
נוֹתֵן לֶחֶם לְכָל בָּשָׂר כִּי לְעוֹלָם חַסְדּוֹ. וּבְטוּבוֹ
הַגָּדוֹל, תָּמִיד לֹא חָסַר לָנוּ וְאַל יֶחְסַר לָנוּ מָזוֹן
לְעוֹלָם וָעֶד בַּעֲבוּר שְׁמוֹ הַגָּדוֹל. כִּי הוּא אֵל
זָן וּמְפַרְנֵס לַכֹּל וּמֵטִיב לַכֹּל וּמֵכִין מָזוֹן לְכָל
בְּרִיּוֹתָיו אֲשֶׁר בָּרָא, בָּרוּךְ אַתָּה יהוה, הַזָּן אֶת
הַכֹּל.

**We thank You,** LORD our God, for having granted as a heritage to our ancestors a desirable, good
and spacious land; for bringing us out, LORD our
God, from the land of Egypt, freeing us from the
house of slavery; for Your covenant which You
sealed in our flesh; for Your Torah which You taught
us; for Your laws which You made known to us; for
the life, grace and kindness You have bestowed on
us; and for the food by which You continually feed
and sustain us, every day, every season, every hour.

**For all this,** LORD our God, we thank and bless
You. May Your name be blessed continually by the
mouth of all that lives, for ever and all time – for so
it is written: "You will eat and be satisfied, then you
shall bless the LORD your God for the good land
He has given you." Blessed are You, LORD, for the
land and for the food.

**Have compassion,** please, LORD our God, on
Israel Your people, on Jerusalem Your city, on Zion
the dwelling place of Your glory, on the royal house
of David Your anointed, and on the great and holy
House that bears Your name. Our God, our Father,
tend us, feed us, sustain us and support us, relieve
us and send us relief, LORD our God, swiftly from
all our troubles. Please, LORD our God, do not
make us dependent on the gifts or loans of other
people, but only on Your full, open, holy and generous hand so that we may suffer neither shame nor
humiliation for ever and all time.

Barley kernels, one of
the seven species of
the Land of Israel

On Shabbat say:

**Favor** and strengthen us, LORD our God, through
Your commandments, especially through the commandment of the seventh day, this great and holy
Sabbath. For it is, for You, a great and holy day. On
it we cease work and rest in love in accord with Your
will's commandment. May it be Your will, LORD

FOR
THE
GOOD
LAND

נוֹדֶה לְּךָ יהוה אֱלֹהֵינוּ עַל שֶׁהִנְחַלְתָּ לַאֲבוֹתֵינוּ אֶרֶץ
חֶמְדָּה טוֹבָה וּרְחָבָה, וְעַל שֶׁהוֹצֵאתָנוּ יהוה אֱלֹהֵינוּ
מֵאֶרֶץ מִצְרַיִם וּפְדִיתָנוּ מִבֵּית עֲבָדִים, וְעַל בְּרִיתְךָ
שֶׁחָתַמְתָּ בִּבְשָׂרֵנוּ, וְעַל תּוֹרָתְךָ שֶׁלִּמַּדְתָּנוּ, וְעַל
חֻקֶּיךָ שֶׁהוֹדַעְתָּנוּ, וְעַל חַיִּים חֵן וָחֶסֶד שֶׁחוֹנַנְתָּנוּ,
וְעַל אֲכִילַת מָזוֹן שָׁאַתָּה זָן וּמְפַרְנֵס אוֹתָנוּ תָּמִיד,
בְּכָל יוֹם וּבְכָל עֵת וּבְכָל שָׁעָה.

וְעַל הַכֹּל, יהוה אֱלֹהֵינוּ אֲנַחְנוּ מוֹדִים לָךְ, וּמְבָרְכִים
אוֹתָךְ, יִתְבָּרַךְ שִׁמְךָ בְּפִי כָּל חַי תָּמִיד לְעוֹלָם וָעֶד,
כַּכָּתוּב: וְאָכַלְתָּ וְשָׂבָעְתָּ, וּבֵרַכְתָּ אֶת־יהוה אֱלֹהֶיךָ
עַל־הָאָרֶץ הַטֹּבָה אֲשֶׁר נָתַן־לָךְ: בָּרוּךְ אַתָּה יהוה,
עַל הָאָרֶץ וְעַל הַמָּזוֹן.

רַחֶם נָא יהוה אֱלֹהֵינוּ עַל יִשְׂרָאֵל עַמֶּךָ, וְעַל
יְרוּשָׁלַיִם עִירֶךָ, וְעַל צִיּוֹן מִשְׁכַּן כְּבוֹדֶךָ, וְעַל מַלְכוּת
בֵּית דָּוִד מְשִׁיחֶךָ, וְעַל הַבַּיִת הַגָּדוֹל וְהַקָּדוֹשׁ שֶׁנִּקְרָא
שִׁמְךָ עָלָיו. אֱלֹהֵינוּ, אָבִינוּ, רְעֵנוּ, זוּנֵנוּ, פַּרְנְסֵנוּ
וְכַלְכְּלֵנוּ וְהַרְוִיחֵנוּ, וְהַרְוַח לָנוּ יהוה אֱלֹהֵינוּ מְהֵרָה
מִכָּל צָרוֹתֵינוּ. וְנָא אַל תַּצְרִיכֵנוּ, יהוה אֱלֹהֵינוּ, לֹא
לִידֵי מַתְּנַת בָּשָׂר וָדָם וְלֹא לִידֵי הַלְוָאָתָם, כִּי אִם
לְיָדְךָ הַמְּלֵאָה, הַפְּתוּחָה, הַקְּדוֹשָׁה וְהָרְחָבָה שֶׁלֹּא
נֵבוֹשׁ וְלֹא נִכָּלֵם לְעוֹלָם וָעֶד.

On Shabbat say:

רְצֵה וְהַחֲלִיצֵנוּ, יהוה אֱלֹהֵינוּ, בְּמִצְוֹתֶיךָ וּבְמִצְוַת יוֹם
הַשְּׁבִיעִי הַשַּׁבָּת הַגָּדוֹל וְהַקָּדוֹשׁ הַזֶּה, כִּי יוֹם זֶה גָּדוֹל
וְקָדוֹשׁ הוּא לְפָנֶיךָ, לִשְׁבָּת בּוֹ, וְלָנוּחַ בּוֹ בְּאַהֲבָה
כְּמִצְוַת רְצוֹנֶךָ, וּבִרְצוֹנְךָ הָנִיחַ לָנוּ, יהוה אֱלֹהֵינוּ,
שֶׁלֹּא תְהֵא צָרָה וְיָגוֹן וַאֲנָחָה בְּיוֹם מְנוּחָתֵנוּ, וְהַרְאֵנוּ,

our God, to grant us rest without distress, grief, or lament on our day of rest. May You show us the consolation of Zion Your city, and the rebuilding of Jerusalem Your holy city, for You are the Master of salvation and consolation.

**Our God** and God of our ancestors, may there rise, come, reach, appear, be favored, heard, regarded and remembered before You, our recollection and remembrance, as well as the remembrance of our ancestors, and of the Messiah son of David Your servant, and of Jerusalem Your holy city, and of all Your people the house of Israel – for deliverance and well-being, grace, loving-kindness and compassion, life and peace, on this day of the festival of matzot. On it remember us, LORD our God, for good; recollect us for blessing, and deliver us for life. In accord with Your promise of salvation and compassion, spare us and be gracious to us; have compassion on us and deliver us, for our eyes are turned to You because You are God, gracious and compassionate.

**And may Jerusalem** the holy city be rebuilt soon, in our time. Blessed are You, LORD, who in His compassion will rebuild Jerusalem. Amen.

**Blessed** are You, LORD our God, King of the Universe – God our Father, our King, our Sovereign, our Creator, our Redeemer, our Maker, our Holy One, the Holy One of Jacob. He is our Shepherd, Israel's Shepherd, the good King who does good to all. Every day He has done, is doing, and will do good to us. He has acted, is acting, and will always act kindly toward us for ever, granting us grace, kindness and compassion, relief and rescue, prosperity, blessing, redemption and comfort, sustenance and support, compassion, life, peace and all good things, and of all good things may He never let us lack.

# KING WHO DOES GOOD TO ALL

*A bowl of dried dates, one of the seven species of the Land of Israel*

יהוה אֱלֹהֵינוּ, בְּנֶחָמַת צִיּוֹן עִירֶךָ וּבְבִנְיַן יְרוּשָׁלַיִם עִיר קָדְשֶׁךָ, כִּי אַתָּה הוּא בַּעַל הַיְשׁוּעוֹת וּבַעַל הַנֶּחָמוֹת.

יַעֲלֶה וְיָבוֹא וְיַגִּיעַ וְיֵרָאֶה וְיֵרָצֶה וְיִשָּׁמַע וְיִפָּקֵד וְיִזָּכֵר זִכְרוֹנֵנוּ וּפִקְדּוֹנֵנוּ, וְזִכְרוֹן אֲבוֹתֵינוּ וְזִכְרוֹן מָשִׁיחַ בֶּן דָּוִד עַבְדֶּךָ, וְזִכְרוֹן יְרוּשָׁלַיִם עִיר קָדְשֶׁךָ, וְזִכְרוֹן כָּל עַמְּךָ בֵּית יִשְׂרָאֵל לְפָנֶיךָ, לִפְלֵיטָה לְטוֹבָה, לְחֵן וּלְחֶסֶד וּלְרַחֲמִים לְחַיִּים וּלְשָׁלוֹם בְּיוֹם חַג הַמַּצּוֹת הַזֶּה. זָכְרֵנוּ יהוה אֱלֹהֵינוּ בּוֹ לְטוֹבָה וּפָקְדֵנוּ בּוֹ לִבְרָכָה וְהוֹשִׁיעֵנוּ בּוֹ לְחַיִּים. וּבִדְבַר יְשׁוּעָה וְרַחֲמִים חוּס וְחָנֵּנוּ וְרַחֵם עָלֵינוּ, וְהוֹשִׁיעֵנוּ כִּי אֵלֶיךָ עֵינֵינוּ, כִּי אֵל חַנּוּן וְרַחוּם אָתָּה.

וּבְנֵה יְרוּשָׁלַיִם עִיר הַקֹּדֶשׁ בִּמְהֵרָה בְיָמֵינוּ. בָּרוּךְ אַתָּה יהוה, בּוֹנֵה בְרַחֲמָיו יְרוּשָׁלָיִם, אָמֵן.

בָּרוּךְ אַתָּה יהוה אֱלֹהֵינוּ מֶלֶךְ הָעוֹלָם, הָאֵל אָבִינוּ, מַלְכֵּנוּ, אַדִּירֵנוּ בּוֹרְאֵנוּ, גּוֹאֲלֵנוּ, יוֹצְרֵנוּ, קְדוֹשֵׁנוּ, קְדוֹשׁ יַעֲקֹב רוֹעֵנוּ, רוֹעֵה יִשְׂרָאֵל, הַמֶּלֶךְ הַטּוֹב וְהַמֵּטִיב לַכֹּל שֶׁבְּכָל יוֹם וָיוֹם הוּא הֵיטִיב, הוּא מֵטִיב, הוּא יֵיטִיב לָנוּ, הוּא גְמָלָנוּ, הוּא גוֹמְלֵנוּ, הוּא יִגְמְלֵנוּ לָעַד לְחֵן וּלְחֶסֶד וּלְרַחֲמִים, וּלְרֶוַח, הַצָּלָה וְהַצְלָחָה, בְּרָכָה וִישׁוּעָה, נֶחָמָה, פַּרְנָסָה וְכַלְכָּלָה וְרַחֲמִים וְחַיִּים וְשָׁלוֹם וְכָל טוֹב, וּמִכָּל טוּב לְעוֹלָם אַל יְחַסְּרֵנוּ.

*Sliced figs, one of the seven species of the Land of Israel*

May the Compassionate One reign over us for ever and all time.

May the Compassionate One be blessed in heaven and on earth.

May the Compassionate One be praised from generation to generation, be glorified by us to all eternity, and honored among us for ever and all time.

May the Compassionate One grant us an honorable livelihood.

May the Compassionate One break the yoke from our neck and lead us upright to our land.

May the Compassionate One send us many blessings to this house and this table at which we have eaten.

May the Compassionate One send us Elijah the Prophet – may he be remembered for good – to bring us good tidings of salvation and consolation.

May the Compassionate One bless the State of Israel, first flowering of our redemption.

May the Compassionate One bless the members of Israel's Defense Forces, who stand guard over our land.

*THIS HOUSE AND THIS TABLE*

A guest says:

May it be Your will that the master of this house shall not suffer shame in this world, nor humiliation in the World to Come. May all he owns prosper greatly, and may his and our possessions be successful and close to hand. Let not the Accuser hold sway over his deeds or ours, and may no thought of sin, iniquity or transgression enter him or us from now and for evermore.

*A bowl of olives, one of the seven species of the Land of Israel*

הָרַחֲמָן הוּא יִמְלֹךְ עָלֵינוּ לְעוֹלָם וָעֶד.

הָרַחֲמָן הוּא יִתְבָּרַךְ בַּשָּׁמַיִם וּבָאָרֶץ.

הָרַחֲמָן הוּא יִשְׁתַּבַּח לְדוֹר דּוֹרִים, וְיִתְפָּאַר בָּנוּ לָעַד וּלְנֵצַח נְצָחִים, וְיִתְהַדַּר בָּנוּ לָעַד וּלְעוֹלְמֵי עוֹלָמִים.

הָרַחֲמָן הוּא יְפַרְנְסֵנוּ בְּכָבוֹד.

הָרַחֲמָן הוּא יִשְׁבֹּר עֻלֵּנוּ מֵעַל צַוָּארֵנוּ וְהוּא יוֹלִיכֵנוּ קוֹמְמִיּוּת לְאַרְצֵנוּ.

הָרַחֲמָן הוּא יִשְׁלַח לָנוּ בְּרָכָה מְרֻבָּה בַּבַּיִת הַזֶּה וְעַל שֻׁלְחָן זֶה שֶׁאָכַלְנוּ עָלָיו.

הָרַחֲמָן הוּא יִשְׁלַח לָנוּ אֶת אֵלִיָּהוּ הַנָּבִיא זָכוּר לַטּוֹב וִיבַשֶּׂר לָנוּ בְּשׂוֹרוֹת טוֹבוֹת יְשׁוּעוֹת וְנֶחָמוֹת.

הָרַחֲמָן הוּא יְבָרֵךְ אֶת מְדִינַת יִשְׂרָאֵל רֵאשִׁית צְמִיחַת גְּאֻלָּתֵנוּ.

הָרַחֲמָן הוּא יְבָרֵךְ אֶת חַיָּלֵי צְבָא הַהֲגָנָה לְיִשְׂרָאֵל הָעוֹמְדִים עַל מִשְׁמַר אַרְצֵנוּ.

*Bless the members of Israel's Defense Forces*

A guest says:

יְהִי רָצוֹן שֶׁלֹּא יֵבוֹשׁ בַּעַל הַבַּיִת בָּעוֹלָם הַזֶּה, וְלֹא יִכָּלֵם לָעוֹלָם הַבָּא, וְיִצְלַח מְאֹד בְּכָל נְכָסָיו, וְיִהְיוּ נְכָסָיו וּנְכָסֵינוּ מֻצְלָחִים וּקְרוֹבִים לָעִיר, וְאַל יִשְׁלֹט שָׂטָן לֹא בְּמַעֲשֵׂה יָדָיו וְלֹא בְּמַעֲשֵׂה יָדֵינוּ. וְאַל יִזְדַּקֵּר לֹא לְפָנָיו וְלֹא לְפָנֵינוּ שׁוּם דְּבַר הִרְהוּר חֵטְא, עֲבֵירָה וְעָוֹן, מֵעַתָּה וְעַד עוֹלָם.

**May** the Compassionate One bless –

When eating at one's own table, say
(include the words in parentheses that apply):

me, (my wife / husband / my father, my teacher / my mother, my teacher / my children) and all that is mine,

A guest at someone else's table says
(include the words in parentheses that apply):

the master of this house, him (and his wife, the mistress of this house / and his children) and all that is his,

Children at their parents' table say
(include the words in parentheses that apply):

my father, my teacher (master of this house), and my mother, my teacher (mistress of this house), them, their household, their children, and all that is theirs.

For all other guests, add:

and all the diners here,

together with us and all that is ours. Just as our forefathers Abraham, Isaac and Jacob were blessed in all, from all, with all, so may He bless all of us together with a complete blessing, and let us say:

**On high,** may grace be invoked for them and for us, as a safeguard of peace. May we receive a blessing from the Lord and a just reward from the God of our salvation, and may we find grace and good favor in the eyes of God and man.

*Pomegranates, one of the seven species of the Land of Israel*

On Shabbat: May the Compassionate One let us inherit the time that will be entirely Shabbat and rest for life everlasting.

**May** the Compassionate One let us inherit the day that is all good.

## הָרַחֲמָן הוּא יְבָרֵךְ

When eating at one's own table, say
(include the words in parentheses that apply):

אוֹתִי (וְאֶת אִשְׁתִּי / וְאֶת בַּעֲלִי / וְאֶת אָבִי מוֹרִי / וְאֶת
אִמִּי מוֹרָתִי / וְאֶת זַרְעִי) וְאֶת כָּל אֲשֶׁר לִי.

A guest at someone else's table says
(include the words in parentheses that apply):

אֶת בַּעַל הַבַּיִת הַזֶּה, אוֹתוֹ (וְאֶת אִשְׁתּוֹ בַּעֲלַת הַבַּיִת
הַזֶּה / וְאֶת זַרְעוֹ) וְאֶת כָּל אֲשֶׁר לוֹ.

Children at their parents' table say
(include the words in parentheses that apply):

אֶת אָבִי מוֹרִי (בַּעַל הַבַּיִת הַזֶּה), וְאֶת אִמִּי מוֹרָתִי
(בַּעֲלַת הַבַּיִת הַזֶּה), אוֹתָם וְאֶת בֵּיתָם וְאֶת זַרְעָם וְאֶת
כָּל אֲשֶׁר לָהֶם

For all other guests, add:

וְאֶת כָּל הַמְסֻבִּין כָּאן

אוֹתָנוּ וְאֶת כָּל אֲשֶׁר לָנוּ, כְּמוֹ שֶׁנִּתְבָּרְכוּ אֲבוֹתֵינוּ
אַבְרָהָם יִצְחָק וְיַעֲקֹב, בַּכֹּל, מִכֹּל, כֹּל, כֵּן יְבָרֵךְ אוֹתָנוּ
כֻּלָּנוּ יַחַד בִּבְרָכָה שְׁלֵמָה, וְנֹאמַר אָמֵן.

בַּמָּרוֹם יְלַמְּדוּ עֲלֵיהֶם וְעָלֵינוּ זְכוּת שֶׁתְּהֵא
לְמִשְׁמֶרֶת שָׁלוֹם וְנִשָּׂא בְרָכָה מֵאֵת יהוה וּצְדָקָה
מֵאֱלֹהֵי יִשְׁעֵנוּ, וְנִמְצָא חֵן וְשֵׂכֶל טוֹב בְּעֵינֵי אֱלֹהִים
וְאָדָם.

בשבת: הָרַחֲמָן הוּא יַנְחִילֵנוּ יוֹם שֶׁכֻּלּוֹ שַׁבָּת וּמְנוּחָה לְחַיֵּי
הָעוֹלָמִים.

הָרַחֲמָן הוּא יַנְחִילֵנוּ יוֹם שֶׁכֻּלּוֹ טוֹב.

May the Compassionate One make us worthy of the messianic age and life in the World to Come. He is a tower of salvation to His king, showing kindness to His anointed, to David and his descendants for ever. He who makes peace in His high places, may He make peace for us and all Israel, and let us say: Amen.

Fear the Lord, you His holy ones; those who fear Him lack nothing. Young lions may grow weak and hungry, but those who seek the LORD lack no good thing. Thank the LORD for He is good: His loving-kindness is for ever. You open Your hand and satisfy the desire of every living thing. Blessed is the person who trusts in the LORD, whose trust is in the LORD alone. Once I was young, and now I am old, yet I have never watched a righteous man forsaken or his children begging for bread. The LORD will give His people strength. The LORD will bless His people with peace.

### Blessed are You, LORD our God, King of the Universe, who creates the fruit of the vine.

Drink while reclining to the left.

A cup of wine is now poured in honor of Elijah, and the door opened.

Pour out Your rage upon the nations that do not know You, and on regimes that have not called upon Your name. For Jacob is devoured; they have laid his places waste. Pour out Your great anger upon them, and let Your blazing fury overtake them. Pursue them in Your fury and destroy them from under the heavens of the LORD.

*THE THIRD CUP*

הָרַחֲמָן הוּא יְזַכֵּנוּ לִימוֹת הַמָּשִׁיחַ וּלְחַיֵּי
הָעוֹלָם הַבָּא, מִגְדּוֹל יְשׁוּעוֹת מַלְכּוֹ וְעֹשֶׂה־
חֶסֶד לִמְשִׁיחוֹ לְדָוִד וּלְזַרְעוֹ עַד־עוֹלָם: עֹשֶׂה
שָׁלוֹם, בִּמְרוֹמָיו, הוּא יַעֲשֶׂה שָׁלוֹם עָלֵינוּ וְעַל
כָּל יִשְׂרָאֵל, וְאִמְרוּ אָמֵן.

יְראוּ אֶת־יהוה קְדֹשָׁיו כִּי־אֵין מַחְסוֹר לִירֵאָיו:
כְּפִירִים רָשׁוּ וְרָעֵבוּ, וְדֹרְשֵׁי יהוה לֹא־יַחְסְרוּ
כָל־טוֹב: הוֹדוּ לַיהוה כִּי־טוֹב, כִּי לְעוֹלָם חַסְדּוֹ:
פּוֹתֵחַ אֶת־יָדֶךָ, וּמַשְׂבִּיעַ לְכָל־חַי רָצוֹן: בָּרוּךְ
הַגֶּבֶר אֲשֶׁר יִבְטַח בַּיהוה, וְהָיָה יהוה מִבְטַחוֹ:
נַעַר הָיִיתִי גַּם־זָקַנְתִּי, וְלֹא־רָאִיתִי צַדִּיק נֶעֱזָב
וְזַרְעוֹ מְבַקֶּשׁ־לָחֶם: יהוה עֹז לְעַמּוֹ יִתֵּן, יהוה
יְבָרֵךְ אֶת־עַמּוֹ בַשָּׁלוֹם:

בָּרוּךְ אַתָּה יהוה אֱלֹהֵינוּ מֶלֶךְ הָעוֹלָם
בּוֹרֵא פְּרִי הַגָּפֶן.

Drink while reclining to the left.

A cup of wine is now poured in honor of Elijah,
and the door opened.

שְׁפֹךְ חֲמָתְךָ אֶל־הַגּוֹיִם אֲשֶׁר לֹא־יְדָעוּךָ וְעַל
מַמְלָכוֹת אֲשֶׁר בְּשִׁמְךָ לֹא קָרָאוּ: כִּי אָכַל אֶת־
יַעֲקֹב, וְאֶת־נָוֵהוּ הֵשַׁמּוּ: שְׁפָךְ־עֲלֵיהֶם זַעְמֶךָ
וַחֲרוֹן אַפְּךָ יַשִּׂיגֵם: תִּרְדֹּף בְּאַף וְתַשְׁמִידֵם
מִתַּחַת שְׁמֵי יהוה:

THE
CUP OF
ELIJAH

## PASSOVER IN THE ARMY

*American soldiers eating a*
*Passover meal, c. 1945*

*Senator Charles McNary*

At a June 30, 1942 memorial service for a Jewish officer who lost his life at Pearl Harbor, Senator Charles McNary of Oregon hearkened to the history of Israel's constant battles against its enemies:

Jews have been fighting oppression and tyranny for centuries. They received their basic training in Egypt and became seasoned soldiers on the battlegrounds of Europe.... Wherever tyranny threatens, wherever the rights of man are in danger of being destroyed, there you will find the Jew, joining forces with others willing to fight and die for freedom.

# "Wherever tyranny threatens... there you will find the Jew."

The fourth cup of wine is poured,
and Hallel is completed.

**Not to us,** Lord, not to us, but to Your name give glory, for Your love, for Your faithfulness. Why should the nations say, "Where now is their God?" Our God is in heaven; whatever He wills He does. Their idols are silver and gold, made by human hands. They have mouths but cannot speak; eyes but cannot see. They have ears but cannot hear; noses but cannot smell. They have hands but cannot feel; feet but cannot walk. No sound comes from their throat. Those who make them become like them; so will all who trust in them. Israel, trust in the Lord – He is their Help and their Shield. House of Aaron, trust in the Lord – He is their Help and their Shield. You who fear the Lord, trust in the Lord – He is their Help and their Shield.

**The Lord remembers** us and will bless us. He will bless the house of Israel. He will bless the house of Aaron. He will bless those who fear the Lord, small and great alike. May the Lord give you increase: you and your children. May you be blessed by the Lord, Maker of heaven and earth. The heavens are the Lord's, but the earth He has given over to mankind. It is not the dead who praise the Lord, nor those who go down to the silent grave. But we will bless the Lord, now and for ever. HALLELUYA!

# הלל

The fourth cup of wine is poured,
and הלל is completed.

*TO*
*YOUR*
*NAME*
*GIVE*
*GLORY*

לֹא לָנוּ יהוה לֹא לָנוּ כִּי־לְשִׁמְךָ תֵּן כָּבוֹד עַל־
חַסְדְּךָ עַל־אֲמִתֶּךָ: לָמָּה יֹאמְרוּ הַגּוֹיִם אַיֵּה־נָא
אֱלֹהֵיהֶם: וֵאלֹהֵינוּ בַשָּׁמָיִם, כֹּל אֲשֶׁר־חָפֵץ עָשָׂה:
עֲצַבֵּיהֶם כֶּסֶף וְזָהָב, מַעֲשֵׂה יְדֵי אָדָם: פֶּה־לָהֶם
וְלֹא יְדַבֵּרוּ, עֵינַיִם לָהֶם וְלֹא יִרְאוּ: אָזְנַיִם לָהֶם וְלֹא
יִשְׁמָעוּ, אַף לָהֶם וְלֹא יְרִיחוּן: יְדֵיהֶם וְלֹא יְמִישׁוּן,
רַגְלֵיהֶם וְלֹא יְהַלֵּכוּ, לֹא־יֶהְגּוּ בִּגְרוֹנָם: כְּמוֹהֶם
יִהְיוּ עֹשֵׂיהֶם, כֹּל אֲשֶׁר־בֹּטֵחַ בָּהֶם: יִשְׂרָאֵל בְּטַח
בַּיהוה עֶזְרָם וּמָגִנָּם הוּא: בֵּית אַהֲרֹן בִּטְחוּ בַיהוה
עֶזְרָם וּמָגִנָּם הוּא: יִרְאֵי יהוה בִּטְחוּ בַיהוה עֶזְרָם
וּמָגִנָּם הוּא:

יהוה זְכָרָנוּ יְבָרֵךְ, יְבָרֵךְ אֶת־בֵּית יִשְׂרָאֵל, יְבָרֵךְ
אֶת־בֵּית אַהֲרֹן: יְבָרֵךְ יִרְאֵי יהוה, הַקְּטַנִּים עִם־
הַגְּדֹלִים: יֹסֵף יהוה עֲלֵיכֶם, עֲלֵיכֶם וְעַל־בְּנֵיכֶם:
בְּרוּכִים אַתֶּם לַיהוה, עֹשֵׂה שָׁמַיִם וָאָרֶץ: הַשָּׁמַיִם
שָׁמַיִם לַיהוה, וְהָאָרֶץ נָתַן לִבְנֵי־אָדָם: לֹא הַמֵּתִים
יְהַלְלוּ־יָהּ, וְלֹא כָּל־יֹרְדֵי דוּמָה: וַאֲנַחְנוּ נְבָרֵךְ יָהּ,
מֵעַתָּה וְעַד־עוֹלָם הַלְלוּיָהּ:

**I love the LORD,** for He hears my voice, my pleas. He turns His ear to me whenever I call. The bonds of death encompassed me, the anguish of the grave came upon me, I was overcome by trouble and sorrow. Then I called on the name of the LORD: "LORD, I pray, save my life." Gracious is the LORD, and righteous; our God is full of compassion. The LORD protects the simple hearted. When I was brought low, He saved me. My soul, be at peace once more, for the LORD has been good to you. For You have rescued me from death, my eyes from weeping, my feet from stumbling. I shall walk in the presence of the LORD in the land of the living. I had faith, even when I said, "I am greatly afflicted," even when I said rashly, "All men are liars."

**How can I repay** the LORD for all His goodness to me? I will lift the cup of salvation and call on the name of the LORD. I will fulfill my vows to the LORD in the presence of all His people. Grievous in the LORD's sight is the death of His devoted ones. Truly, LORD, I am Your servant; I am Your servant, the son of Your maidservant. You set me free from my chains. To You I shall bring a thanksgiving-offering and call on the LORD by name. I will fulfill my vows to the LORD in the presence of all His people, in the courts of the House of the LORD, in your midst, Jerusalem. HALLELUYA!

**Praise** the LORD, all nations; acclaim Him, all you peoples; for His loving-kindness to us is strong, and the LORD's faithfulness is everlasting. HALLELUYA!

Thank the LORD for He is good,
                        His loving-kindness is for ever.
Let Israel say
                        His loving-kindness is for ever.
Let the house of Aaron say
                        His loving-kindness is for ever.
Let those who fear the LORD say
                        His loving-kindness is for ever.

אָהַבְתִּי כִּי־יִשְׁמַע יהוה, אֶת־קוֹלִי תַּחֲנוּנָי: כִּי־
הִטָּה אָזְנוֹ לִי, וּבְיָמַי אֶקְרָא: אֲפָפוּנִי חֶבְלֵי־מָוֶת
וּמְצָרֵי שְׁאוֹל מְצָאוּנִי צָרָה וְיָגוֹן אֶמְצָא: וּבְשֵׁם־יהוה
אֶקְרָא, אָנָּה יהוה מַלְּטָה נַפְשִׁי: חַנּוּן יהוה וְצַדִּיק,
וֵאלֹהֵינוּ מְרַחֵם: שֹׁמֵר פְּתָאיִם יהוה, דַּלּוֹתִי וְלִי
יְהוֹשִׁיעַ: שׁוּבִי נַפְשִׁי לִמְנוּחָיְכִי, כִּי־יהוה גָּמַל עָלָיְכִי:
כִּי חִלַּצְתָּ נַפְשִׁי מִמָּוֶת, אֶת־עֵינִי מִן־דִּמְעָה, אֶת־רַגְלִי
מִדֶּחִי: אֶתְהַלֵּךְ לִפְנֵי יהוה, בְּאַרְצוֹת הַחַיִּים: הֶאֱמַנְתִּי
כִּי אֲדַבֵּר, אֲנִי עָנִיתִי מְאֹד: אֲנִי אָמַרְתִּי בְחָפְזִי, כָּל־
הָאָדָם כֹּזֵב:

מָה־אָשִׁיב לַיהוה, כָּל־תַּגְמוּלוֹהִי עָלָי: כּוֹס־יְשׁוּעוֹת
אֶשָּׂא, וּבְשֵׁם יהוה אֶקְרָא: נְדָרַי לַיהוה אֲשַׁלֵּם, נֶגְדָה־
נָּא לְכָל־עַמּוֹ: יָקָר בְּעֵינֵי יהוה, הַמָּוְתָה לַחֲסִידָיו: אָנָּה
יהוה כִּי־אֲנִי עַבְדֶּךָ, אֲנִי־עַבְדְּךָ בֶּן־אֲמָתֶךָ פִּתַּחְתָּ
לְמוֹסֵרָי: לְךָ־אֶזְבַּח זֶבַח תּוֹדָה, וּבְשֵׁם יהוה אֶקְרָא:
נְדָרַי לַיהוה אֲשַׁלֵּם, נֶגְדָה־נָא לְכָל־עַמּוֹ: בְּחַצְרוֹת
בֵּית יהוה, בְּתוֹכֵכִי יְרוּשָׁלִָם הַלְלוּיָהּ:

הַלְלוּ אֶת־יהוה כָּל־גּוֹיִם, שַׁבְּחוּהוּ כָּל־הָאֻמִּים: כִּי
גָבַר עָלֵינוּ חַסְדּוֹ, וֶאֱמֶת־יהוה לְעוֹלָם הַלְלוּיָהּ:

| הוֹדוּ לַיהוה כִּי־טוֹב | כִּי לְעוֹלָם חַסְדּוֹ: |
| יֹאמַר־נָא יִשְׂרָאֵל | כִּי לְעוֹלָם חַסְדּוֹ: |
| יֹאמְרוּ־נָא בֵית־אַהֲרֹן | כִּי לְעוֹלָם חַסְדּוֹ: |
| יֹאמְרוּ־נָא יִרְאֵי יהוה | כִּי לְעוֹלָם חַסְדּוֹ: |

# HALLELUYA!

149

**In my distress** I called on the Lord. The Lord answered me and set me free. The Lord is with me; I will not be afraid. What can man do to me? The Lord is with me. He is my Helper. I will see the downfall of my enemies. It is better to take refuge in the Lord than to trust in man. It is better to take refuge in the Lord than to trust in princes. The nations all surrounded me, but in the Lord's name I drove them off. They surrounded me on every side, but in the Lord's name I drove them off. They surrounded me like bees, they attacked me as fire attacks brushwood, but in the Lord's name I drove them off. They thrust so hard against me, I nearly fell, but the Lord came to my help. The Lord is my strength and my song; He has become my salvation. Sounds of song and salvation resound in the tents of the righteous: "The Lord's right hand has done mighty deeds. The Lord's right hand is lifted high. The Lord's right hand has done mighty deeds." I will not die but live, and tell what the Lord has done. The Lord has chastened me severely, but He has not given me over to death. Open for me the gates of righteousness that I may enter them and thank the Lord. This is the gateway to the Lord; through it, the righteous shall enter.

**I will thank You,** for You answered me, and became my salvation.

> I will thank You, for You answered me, and became my salvation.

**The stone** the builders rejected has become the main cornerstone.

> The stone the builders rejected has become the main cornerstone.

**This is** the Lord's doing. It is wondrous in our eyes.

> This is the Lord's doing. It is wondrous in our eyes.

**This is the day** the Lord has made. Let us rejoice and be glad in it.

> This is the day the Lord has made. Let us rejoice and be glad in it.

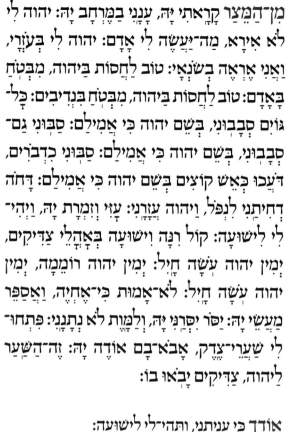

*I WILL THANK YOU*

מִן־הַמֵּצַר קָרָאתִי יָּהּ, עָנָנִי בַמֶּרְחָב יָהּ: יהוה לִי
לֹא אִירָא, מַה־יַּעֲשֶׂה לִי אָדָם: יהוה לִי בְּעֹזְרָי,
וַאֲנִי אֶרְאֶה בְשֹׂנְאָי: טוֹב לַחֲסוֹת בַּיהוה, מִבְּטֹחַ
בָּאָדָם: טוֹב לַחֲסוֹת בַּיהוה, מִבְּטֹחַ בִּנְדִיבִים: כָּל־
גּוֹיִם סְבָבוּנִי, בְּשֵׁם יהוה כִּי אֲמִילַם: סַבּוּנִי גַם־
סְבָבוּנִי, בְּשֵׁם יהוה כִּי אֲמִילַם: סַבּוּנִי כִדְבֹרִים,
דֹּעֲכוּ כְּאֵשׁ קוֹצִים בְּשֵׁם יהוה כִּי אֲמִילַם: דָּחֹה
דְחִיתַנִי לִנְפֹּל, וַיהוה עֲזָרָנִי: עָזִּי וְזִמְרָת יָהּ, וַיְהִי־
לִי לִישׁוּעָה: קוֹל רִנָּה וִישׁוּעָה בְּאָהֳלֵי צַדִּיקִים,
יְמִין יהוה עֹשָׂה חָיִל: יְמִין יהוה רוֹמֵמָה, יְמִין
יהוה עֹשָׂה חָיִל: לֹא־אָמוּת כִּי־אֶחְיֶה, וַאֲסַפֵּר
מַעֲשֵׂי יָהּ: יַסֹּר יִסְּרַנִּי יָּהּ, וְלַמָּוֶת לֹא נְתָנָנִי: פִּתְחוּ־
לִי שַׁעֲרֵי־צֶדֶק, אָבֹא־בָם אוֹדֶה יָהּ: זֶה־הַשַּׁעַר
לַיהוה, צַדִּיקִים יָבֹאוּ בוֹ:

אוֹדְךָ כִּי עֲנִיתָנִי, וַתְּהִי־לִי לִישׁוּעָה:
אוֹדְךָ כִּי עֲנִיתָנִי, וַתְּהִי־לִי לִישׁוּעָה:

אֶבֶן מָאֲסוּ הַבּוֹנִים, הָיְתָה לְרֹאשׁ פִּנָּה:
אֶבֶן מָאֲסוּ הַבּוֹנִים, הָיְתָה לְרֹאשׁ פִּנָּה:

מֵאֵת יהוה הָיְתָה זֹּאת, הִיא נִפְלָאת בְּעֵינֵינוּ:
מֵאֵת יהוה הָיְתָה זֹּאת, הִיא נִפְלָאת בְּעֵינֵינוּ:

זֶה־הַיּוֹם עָשָׂה יהוה, נָגִילָה וְנִשְׂמְחָה בוֹ:
זֶה־הַיּוֹם עָשָׂה יהוה, נָגִילָה וְנִשְׂמְחָה בוֹ:

*"Open for me the gates of righteousness that I may enter them and thank the LORD. This is the gateway to the LORD; through it, the righteous shall enter."*

Born to a Western Sephardic family in New York, Emma Lazarus mastered poetry at a young age. By the time she penned "The New Colossus" in 1883, Lazarus was a well-established and published poet. "The New Colossus" was written for an exhibition of art and literature organized to raise funds to erect the Statue of Liberty in New York Harbor. At the time, the poem received little attention. However, after her death, Lazarus's poem was cast in bronze and hung on the pedestal of the Statue of Liberty. Her words evoke the biblical image of gates opened with a spirit of righteousness.

*Emma Lazarus*

*Not like the brazen giant of Greek fame,*

*With conquering limbs astride from land to land;*

*Here at our sea-washed, sunset gates shall stand*

*A mighty woman with a torch, whose flame*

*Is the imprisoned lightning, and her name*

*Mother of Exiles. From her beacon-hand*

*Glows world-wide welcome; her mild eyes command*

*The air-bridged harbor that twin cities frame.*

*"Keep, ancient lands, your storied pomp!" cries she*

*With silent lips. "Give me your tired, your poor,*

*Your huddled masses yearning to breathe free,*

*The wretched refuse of your teeming shore.*

*Send these, the homeless, tempest-tost to me,*

*I lift my lamp beside the golden door!"*

פִּתְחוּ לִי שַׁעֲרֵי צֶדֶק

*The Statue of Liberty against the backdrop of the New York cityscape*

# EMMA LAZARUS'S LAMP

## THANKSGIVING HALLEL

נְגִילָה וְנִשְׂמְחָה בּוֹ

our fathers have gone through since the time of our first progenitor among the Patriarchs; for so soon as the promise of the holy land was made unto him he became a sojourner therein, and in the course of four hundred years his posterity had been sojourners and at last mere slaves to a people who knew not the Lord; they were cruelly oppressed in bondage until they cried unto the Lord, who heard them from his holy habitation and sent Moses and Aaron to redeem them…

From the foregoing, you will naturally observe the duties we owe our Creator…to support that government which is founded upon the strictest principles of equal liberty and justice. If to seek the peace and prosperity of the city wherin we dwell be a duty, even under bad governments, what must it be when we are situated under the best of constitutions?

To this day, Congregation Shearith Israel celebrates Thanksgiving with the recitation of Hallel.

זֶה־הַיּוֹם עָשָׂה יהוה, נָגִילָה וְנִשְׂמְחָה בּוֹ.

*"This is the day the LORD has made. Let us rejoice and be glad in it."*

*George Washington's inauguration as the first president on April 30, 1789*

In 1789, President Washington issued the following proclamation expressing national joy and gratitude and establishing the holiday of Thanksgiving:

Whereas it is the duty of all Nations to acknowledge the providence of Almighty God, to obey his will, to be grateful for his benefits, and humbly to implore his protection and favor – and whereas both Houses of Congress have by their joint Committee requested me "to recommend to the People of the United States a day of public thanksgiving and prayer to be observed by acknowledging with grateful hearts the many signal favors of Almighty God especially by affording them an opportunity peaceably to establish a form of government for their safety and happiness.

Now therefore I do recommend and assign Thursday the 26th day of November next to be devoted by the People of these States to the service of that great and glorious Being, who is the beneficent Author of all the good that was, that is, or that will be…

New York's Congregation Shearith Israel responded enthusiastically by hosting their own Thanksgiving celebration in which psalms were sung and Ḥazan Gershom Mendes Seixas delivered a poignant sermon in which he included the birth of the United States on a list of events for which the Jewish people are eternally grateful to God, including the Exodus.

…Let us only revolve in our minds the many different situations that we and

# "It is the duty of all Nations to acknowledge the providence of Almighty God."

**Lord, please, save us.**
**Lord, please, save us.**
**Lord, please, grant us success.**
**Lord, please, grant us success.**

**Blessed** is one who comes in the name of the Lord; we bless you from the House of the Lord.

Blessed is one who comes in the name of the Lord; we bless you from the House of the Lord.

**The Lord** is God; He has given us light. Bind the festival offering with thick cords [and bring it] to the horns of the altar.

The Lord is God; He has given us light. Bind the festival offering with thick cords [and bring it] to the horns of the altar.

**You** are my God and I will thank You; You are my God, I will exalt You.

You are my God and I will thank You; You are my God, I will exalt You.

**Thank** the Lord for He is good, His loving-kindness is for ever.

Thank the Lord for He is good, His loving-kindness is for ever.

**All Your works** will praise You, Lord our God, and Your devoted ones – the righteous who do Your will, together with all Your people the house of Israel – will joyously thank, bless, praise, glorify, exalt, revere, sanctify, and proclaim the sovereignty of Your name, our King. For it is good to thank You and fitting to sing psalms to Your name, for from eternity to eternity You are God.

# THANK THE LORD

אָנָּא יהוה הוֹשִׁיעָה נָּא:

אָנָּא יהוה הוֹשִׁיעָה נָּא:

אָנָּא יהוה הַצְלִיחָה נָּא:

אָנָּא יהוה הַצְלִיחָה נָּא:

בָּרוּךְ הַבָּא בְּשֵׁם יהוה, בֵּרַכְנוּכֶם מִבֵּית יהוה:
בָּרוּךְ הַבָּא בְּשֵׁם יהוה, בֵּרַכְנוּכֶם מִבֵּית יהוה:

אֵל יהוה וַיָּאֶר לָנוּ, אִסְרוּ־חַג בַּעֲבֹתִים עַד־קַרְנוֹת
הַמִּזְבֵּחַ:
אֵל יהוה וַיָּאֶר לָנוּ, אִסְרוּ־חַג בַּעֲבֹתִים עַד־
קַרְנוֹת הַמִּזְבֵּחַ:

אֵלִי אַתָּה וְאוֹדֶךָּ, אֱלֹהַי אֲרוֹמְמֶךָּ:
אֵלִי אַתָּה וְאוֹדֶךָּ, אֱלֹהַי אֲרוֹמְמֶךָּ:

הוֹדוּ לַיהוה כִּי־טוֹב, כִּי לְעוֹלָם חַסְדּוֹ:
הוֹדוּ לַיהוה כִּי־טוֹב, כִּי לְעוֹלָם חַסְדּוֹ:

יְהַלְלוּךָ יהוה אֱלֹהֵינוּ כָּל מַעֲשֶׂיךָ וַחֲסִידֶיךָ
צַדִּיקִים עוֹשֵׂי רְצוֹנֶךָ וְכָל עַמְּךָ בֵּית יִשְׂרָאֵל בְּרִנָּה
יוֹדוּ וִיבָרְכוּ וִישַׁבְּחוּ וִיפָאֲרוּ וִירוֹמְמוּ וְיַעֲרִיצוּ
וְיַקְדִּישׁוּ וְיַמְלִיכוּ אֶת שִׁמְךָ מַלְכֵּנוּ כִּי לְךָ טוֹב
לְהוֹדוֹת וּלְשִׁמְךָ נָאֶה לְזַמֵּר כִּי מֵעוֹלָם וְעַד עוֹלָם
אַתָּה אֵל.

Thank the Lord, for He is good,
>His loving-kindness is for ever.
Thank the God of gods,
>His loving-kindness is for ever.
Thank the Lᴏʀᴅ of lords,
>His loving-kindness is for ever.
To the One who alone works great wonders,
>His loving-kindness is for ever.
Who made the heavens with wisdom,
>His loving-kindness is for ever.
Who spread the earth upon the waters,
>His loving-kindness is for ever.
Who made the great lights,
>His loving-kindness is for ever.
The sun to rule by day,
>His loving-kindness is for ever.
The moon and the stars to rule by night;
>His loving-kindness is for ever.
Who struck Egypt through their firstborn,
>His loving-kindness is for ever.
And brought out Israel from their midst,
>His loving-kindness is for ever.
With a strong hand and outstretched arm,
>His loving-kindness is for ever.
Who split the Reed Sea into parts,
>His loving-kindness is for ever.
And made Israel pass through it,
>His loving-kindness is for ever.
Casting Pharaoh and his army into the Red Sea;
>His loving-kindness is for ever.
Who led His people through the wilderness;
>His loving-kindness is for ever.
Who struck down great kings,
>His loving-kindness is for ever.
And slew mighty kings,
>His loving-kindness is for ever.
Siḥon, king of the Amorites,
>His loving-kindness is for ever.

| | |
|---|---|
| כִּי לְעוֹלָם חַסְדּוֹ: | הוֹדוּ לַיהוה כִּי־טוֹב |
| כִּי לְעוֹלָם חַסְדּוֹ: | הוֹדוּ לֵאלֹהֵי הָאֱלֹהִים |
| כִּי לְעוֹלָם חַסְדּוֹ: | הוֹדוּ לַאֲדֹנֵי הָאֲדֹנִים |
| כִּי לְעוֹלָם חַסְדּוֹ: | לְעֹשֵׂה נִפְלָאוֹת גְּדֹלוֹת לְבַדּוֹ |
| כִּי לְעוֹלָם חַסְדּוֹ: | לְעֹשֵׂה הַשָּׁמַיִם בִּתְבוּנָה |
| כִּי לְעוֹלָם חַסְדּוֹ: | לְרֹקַע הָאָרֶץ עַל־הַמָּיִם |
| כִּי לְעוֹלָם חַסְדּוֹ: | לְעֹשֵׂה אוֹרִים גְּדֹלִים |
| כִּי לְעוֹלָם חַסְדּוֹ: | אֶת־הַשֶּׁמֶשׁ לְמֶמְשֶׁלֶת בַּיּוֹם |
| אֶת־הַיָּרֵחַ וְכוֹכָבִים לְמֶמְשְׁלוֹת בַּלָּיְלָה כִּי לְעוֹלָם חַסְדּוֹ: | |
| כִּי לְעוֹלָם חַסְדּוֹ: | לְמַכֵּה מִצְרַיִם בִּבְכוֹרֵיהֶם |
| כִּי לְעוֹלָם חַסְדּוֹ: | וַיּוֹצֵא יִשְׂרָאֵל מִתּוֹכָם |
| כִּי לְעוֹלָם חַסְדּוֹ: | בְּיָד חֲזָקָה וּבִזְרוֹעַ נְטוּיָה |
| כִּי לְעוֹלָם חַסְדּוֹ: | לְגֹזֵר יַם־סוּף לִגְזָרִים |
| כִּי לְעוֹלָם חַסְדּוֹ: | וְהֶעֱבִיר יִשְׂרָאֵל בְּתוֹכוֹ |
| כִּי לְעוֹלָם חַסְדּוֹ: | וְנִעֵר פַּרְעֹה וְחֵילוֹ בְיַם־סוּף |
| כִּי לְעוֹלָם חַסְדּוֹ: | לְמוֹלִיךְ עַמּוֹ בַּמִּדְבָּר |
| כִּי לְעוֹלָם חַסְדּוֹ: | לְמַכֵּה מְלָכִים גְּדֹלִים |
| כִּי לְעוֹלָם חַסְדּוֹ: | וַיַּהֲרֹג מְלָכִים אַדִּירִים |
| כִּי לְעוֹלָם חַסְדּוֹ: | לְסִיחוֹן מֶלֶךְ הָאֱמֹרִי |

# HE WORKS WONDERS

And Og, king of Bashan,
> His loving-kindness is for ever.

And gave their land as a heritage,
> His loving-kindness is for ever.

A heritage for His servant Israel;
> His loving-kindness is for ever.

Who remembered us in our lowly state,
> His loving-kindness is for ever.

And rescued us from our tormentors,
> His loving-kindness is for ever.

Who gives food to all flesh,
> His loving-kindness is for ever.

Give thanks to the God of heaven.
> His loving-kindness is for ever.

**The soul** of all that lives shall bless Your name, LORD our God, and the spirit of all flesh shall always glorify and exalt Your remembrance, our King. From eternity to eternity You are God. Without You, we have no King, Redeemer or Savior, who liberates, rescues, sustains and shows compassion in every time of trouble and distress. We have no King but You, God of the first and last, God of all creatures, Master of all ages, extolled by a multitude of praises, who guides His world with loving-kindness and His creatures with compassion. The LORD neither slumbers nor sleeps. He rouses the sleepers and wakens the slumberers. He makes the dumb speak, sets the bound free, supports the fallen, and raises those bowed down. To You alone we give thanks: If our mouths were as full of song as the sea, and our tongue with jubilation as its myriad waves, if our lips were full of praise like the spacious heavens, and our eyes shone like the sun and moon, if our hands were outstretched like eagles of the sky, and our feet as swift as hinds – still we could not thank You enough, LORD our God and God of our ancestors, or bless Your name for even one of the thousand thousands and myriad myriads of favors

FULL
OF
SONG

FULL
OF
PRAISE

כִּי לְעוֹלָם חַסְדּוֹ: וּלְעוֹג מֶלֶךְ הַבָּשָׁן

כִּי לְעוֹלָם חַסְדּוֹ: וְנָתַן אַרְצָם לְנַחֲלָה

כִּי לְעוֹלָם חַסְדּוֹ: נַחֲלָה לְיִשְׂרָאֵל עַבְדּוֹ

כִּי לְעוֹלָם חַסְדּוֹ: שֶׁבְּשִׁפְלֵנוּ זָכַר לָנוּ

כִּי לְעוֹלָם חַסְדּוֹ: וַיִּפְרְקֵנוּ מִצָּרֵינוּ

כִּי לְעוֹלָם חַסְדּוֹ: נֹתֵן לֶחֶם לְכָל־בָּשָׂר

כִּי לְעוֹלָם חַסְדּוֹ: הוֹדוּ לְאֵל הַשָּׁמָיִם

נִשְׁמַת כָּל חַי תְּבָרֵךְ אֶת שִׁמְךָ, יהוה אֱלֹהֵינוּ, וְרוּחַ כָּל בָּשָׂר תְּפָאֵר וּתְרוֹמֵם זִכְרְךָ מַלְכֵּנוּ תָּמִיד. מִן הָעוֹלָם וְעַד הָעוֹלָם אַתָּה אֵל, וּמִבַּלְעָדֶיךָ אֵין לָנוּ מֶלֶךְ גּוֹאֵל וּמוֹשִׁיעַ, פּוֹדֶה וּמַצִּיל וּמְפַרְנֵס וּמְרַחֵם בְּכָל עֵת צָרָה וְצוּקָה, אֵין לָנוּ מֶלֶךְ אֶלָּא אָתָּה. אֱלֹהֵי הָרִאשׁוֹנִים וְהָאַחֲרוֹנִים, אֱלוֹהַּ כָּל בְּרִיּוֹת אֲדוֹן כָּל תּוֹלָדוֹת, הַמְהֻלָּל בְּרֹב הַתִּשְׁבָּחוֹת, הַמְנַהֵג עוֹלָמוֹ בְּחֶסֶד וּבְרִיּוֹתָיו בְּרַחֲמִים. וַיהוה לֹא יָנוּם וְלֹא יִישָׁן, הַמְעוֹרֵר יְשֵׁנִים וְהַמֵּקִיץ נִרְדָּמִים וְהַמֵּשִׂיחַ אִלְּמִים וְהַמַּתִּיר אֲסוּרִים וְהַסּוֹמֵךְ נוֹפְלִים וְהַזּוֹקֵף כְּפוּפִים. לְךָ לְבַדְּךָ אֲנַחְנוּ מוֹדִים. אִלּוּ פִינוּ מָלֵא שִׁירָה כַּיָּם וּלְשׁוֹנֵנוּ רִנָּה כַּהֲמוֹן גַּלָּיו וְשִׂפְתוֹתֵינוּ שֶׁבַח כְּמֶרְחֲבֵי רָקִיעַ וְעֵינֵינוּ מְאִירוֹת כַּשֶּׁמֶשׁ וְכַיָּרֵחַ וְיָדֵינוּ פְרוּשׂוֹת כְּנִשְׁרֵי שָׁמָיִם וְרַגְלֵינוּ קַלּוֹת כָּאַיָּלוֹת, אֵין אֲנַחְנוּ מַסְפִּיקִים לְהוֹדוֹת לְךָ, יהוה אֱלֹהֵינוּ וֵאלֹהֵי אֲבוֹתֵינוּ, וּלְבָרֵךְ אֶת שִׁמְךָ עַל אַחַת מֵאָלֶף אֶלֶף אַלְפֵי אֲלָפִים וְרִבֵּי רְבָבוֹת פְּעָמִים

You did for our ancestors and for us. You redeemed us from Egypt, LORD our God, and freed us from the house of bondage. In famine You nourished us; in times of plenty You sustained us. You delivered us from the sword, saved us from the plague, and spared us from serious and lasting illness. Until now Your mercies have helped us. Your love has not forsaken us. May You, LORD our God, never abandon us. There-fore the limbs You formed within us, the spirit and soul You breathed into our nostrils, and the tongue You placed in our mouth – they will thank and bless, praise and glorify, exalt and esteem, hallow and do homage to Your name, O our King. For every mouth shall give thanks to You, every tongue vow allegiance to You, every knee shall bend to You, every upright body shall bow to You, all hearts shall fear You, and our innermost being sing praises to Your name, as is written: "All my bones shall say: LORD, who is like You? You save the poor from one stronger than him, the poor and needy from one who would rob him." Who is like You? Who is equal to You? Who can be compared to You? O great, mighty and awesome God, God Most High, Maker of heaven and earth. We will laud, praise and glorify You and bless Your holy name, as it is said: "Of David. Bless the LORD, O my soul, and all that is within me bless His holy name."

**God** – in Your absolute power, Great – in the glory of Your name, Mighty – for ever, Awesome – in Your awe-inspiring deeds, the King – who sits on a throne. High and lofty He inhabits eternity; exalted and holy is His name. And it is written: Sing joyfully to the LORD, you righteous, for praise from the upright is seemly. By the mouth of the upright You shall be praised. By the words of the righteous You shall be blessed. By the tongue of the devout You shall be extolled, and in the midst of the holy You shall be sanctified.

HANDS LIKE EAGLES' WINGS

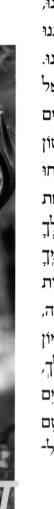

FEET
SWIFT
AS
HINDS

הַטּוֹבוֹת שֶׁעָשִׂיתָ עִם אֲבוֹתֵינוּ וְעִמָּנוּ. מִמִּצְרַיִם
גְּאַלְתָּנוּ, יהוה אֱלֹהֵינוּ, וּמִבֵּית עֲבָדִים פְּדִיתָנוּ,
בְּרָעָב זַנְתָּנוּ וּבְשָׂבָע כִּלְכַּלְתָּנוּ, מֵחֶרֶב הִצַּלְתָּנוּ
וּמִדֶּבֶר מִלַּטְתָּנוּ, וּמֵחֳלָיִים רָעִים וְנֶאֱמָנִים דִּלִּיתָנוּ.
עַד הֵנָּה עֲזָרוּנוּ רַחֲמֶיךָ, וְלֹא עֲזָבוּנוּ חֲסָדֶיךָ, וְאַל
תִּטְּשֵׁנוּ, יהוה אֱלֹהֵינוּ, לָנֶצַח. עַל כֵּן אֵבָרִים
שֶׁפִּלַּגְתָּ בָּנוּ, וְרוּחַ וּנְשָׁמָה שֶׁנָּפַחְתָּ בְּאַפֵּנוּ, וְלָשׁוֹן
אֲשֶׁר שַׂמְתָּ בְּפִינוּ הֵן הֵם יוֹדוּ וִיבָרְכוּ וִישַׁבְּחוּ
וִיפָאֲרוּ וִירוֹמְמוּ וְיַעֲרִיצוּ וְיַקְדִּישׁוּ וְיַמְלִיכוּ אֶת
שִׁמְךָ מַלְכֵּנוּ, כִּי כָל פֶּה לְךָ יוֹדֶה, וְכָל לָשׁוֹן לְךָ
תִשָּׁבַע, וְכָל בֶּרֶךְ לְךָ תִכְרַע, וְכָל קוֹמָה לְפָנֶיךָ
תִשְׁתַּחֲוֶה, וְכָל לְבָבוֹת יִירָאוּךָ, וְכָל קֶרֶב וּכְלָיוֹת
יְזַמְּרוּ לִשְׁמֶךָ, כַּדָּבָר שֶׁכָּתוּב, כָּל עַצְמֹתַי תֹּאמַרְנָה,
יהוה מִי כָמוֹךָ, מַצִּיל עָנִי מֵחָזָק מִמֶּנּוּ, וְעָנִי וְאֶבְיוֹן
מִגֹּזְלוֹ: מִי יִדְמֶה לָּךְ וּמִי יִשְׁוֶה לָּךְ וּמִי יַעֲרָךְ לָךְ,
הָאֵל הַגָּדוֹל, הַגִּבּוֹר וְהַנּוֹרָא אֵל עֶלְיוֹן, קוֹנֵה שָׁמַיִם
וָאָרֶץ. נְהַלֶּלְךָ וּנְשַׁבֵּחֲךָ וּנְפָאֶרְךָ וּנְבָרֵךְ אֶת שֵׁם
קָדְשֶׁךָ, כָּאָמוּר, לְדָוִד, בָּרְכִי נַפְשִׁי אֶת־יהוה, וְכָל־
קְרָבַי אֶת־שֵׁם קָדְשׁוֹ:

הָאֵל בְּתַעֲצֻמוֹת עֻזֶּךָ, הַגָּדוֹל בִּכְבוֹד שְׁמֶךָ, הַגִּבּוֹר
לָנֶצַח וְהַנּוֹרָא בְּנוֹרְאוֹתֶיךָ, הַמֶּלֶךְ הַיּוֹשֵׁב עַל כִּסֵּא.
רָם וְנִשָּׂא. שׁוֹכֵן עַד מָרוֹם וְקָדוֹשׁ שְׁמוֹ, וְכָתוּב:
רַנְּנוּ צַדִּיקִים בַּיהוה, לַיְשָׁרִים נָאוָה תְהִלָּה: בְּפִי
יְשָׁרִים תִּתְהַלָּל, וּבְדִבְרֵי צַדִּיקִים תִּתְבָּרַךְ, וּבִלְשׁוֹן
חֲסִידִים תִּתְרוֹמָם, וּבְקֶרֶב קְדוֹשִׁים תִּתְקַדָּשׁ.

## PRAYING LEGS

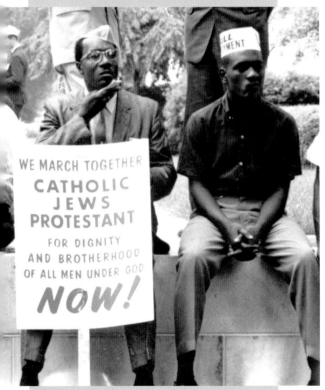

*Selma to Montgomery civil rights marchers rest at a roadside stop, 1965*

will never be past to me – that day will continue to be this day. A great Hasidic sage compares the service of God to a battle being waged in war. An army consists of infantry, artillery, and cavalry. In critical moments cavalry and artillery may step aside from the battle-front. Infantry, however, carries the brunt. I am glad to belong to infantry! May I add that I have rarely in my life been privileged to hear a sermon as glorious as the one you delivered at the service in Selma prior to the march."

Believing that King's use of the Exodus would be strengthened if he were to participate in a Passover celebration, Heschel invited King and his wife to his family's Seder, to take place on April 16, 1968: "The ritual and the celebration of that evening seek to make present to us the spirit and the wonder of the Exodus from Egypt. It is my feeling that your participation at a Seder celebration would be of very great significance." King was assassinated just days before Passover.

וְכָל בֶּרֶךְ לְךָ תִכְרַע, וְכָל קוֹמָה לְפָנֶיךָ תִשְׁתַּחֲוֶה, וְכָל לְבָבוֹת
יִירָאוּךָ, וְכָל קֶרֶב וּכְלָיוֹת יְזַמְּרוּ לִשְׁמֶךָ.

*"Every knee shall bend to You, every upright body shall bow to You, all hearts shall fear You, and our innermost being sing praises to Your name."*

Rabbi Abraham Joshua Heschel with Martin Luther King Jr.

To the utter shock of the citizens of Alabama, hundreds of Black marchers who made the journey on foot from Selma to Montgomery in March 1965 wore kippot to show solidarity with Rabbi Abraham Joshua Heschel who marched with them. Susannah Heschel recalled how her father was so deeply moved by the event that he felt his legs "were praying." Heschel was a dear friend of Reverend Dr. Martin Luther King Jr., and was deeply impressed by the latter's use of Exodus imagery in furthering the cause of civil rights.

A comparison of King and Heschel reveals theological affinities in addition to shared political sympathies…. For Heschel, the primacy of the Exodus in the Civil Rights movement was a major step in the history of Christian-Jewish relations. Heschel's concept of divine pathos, a category central to his theology, is mirrored in King's understanding of the nature of God's involvement with humanity. For both, the theological was intimately intertwined with the political and that conviction provided the basis of the spiritual affinity they felt for each other.…

Heschel, for example, was particularly touched during the march from Selma to Montgomery by King's references to the Exodus in his sermon, describing three types among the Israelites who left Egypt…. Shortly after returning from the march, he wrote to King: "The day we marched together out of Selma was a day of sanctification. That day I hope

Marching in the civil rights march from Selma to Montgomery, 1965

**And in the assemblies** of tens of thousands of Your people, the house of Israel, with joyous song shall Your name, our King, be glorified in every generation. For this is the duty of all creatures before You, Lord our God and God of our ancestors: to thank, praise, laud, glorify, exalt, honor, bless, raise high and acclaim – even beyond all the words of song and praise of David, son of Jesse, Your servant, Your anointed.

THE
HOUSE
OF
ISRAEL

וּבְמַקְהֲלוֹת רִבְבוֹת עַמְּךָ בֵּית יִשְׂרָאֵל,
בְּרִנָּה יִתְפָּאַר שִׁמְךָ מַלְכֵּנוּ בְּכָל דּוֹר וָדוֹר,
שֶׁכֵּן חוֹבַת כָּל הַיְצוּרִים לְפָנֶיךָ, יהוה אֱלֹהֵינוּ
וֵאלֹהֵי אֲבוֹתֵינוּ, לְהוֹדוֹת, לְהַלֵּל, לְשַׁבֵּחַ,
לְפָאֵר, לְרוֹמֵם לְהַדֵּר, לְבָרֵךְ, לְעַלֵּה וּלְקַלֵּס
עַל כָּל דִּבְרֵי שִׁירוֹת וְתִשְׁבְּחוֹת דָּוִד בֶּן יִשַׁי,
עַבְדְּךָ מְשִׁיחֶךָ.

**May Your name** be praised for ever, our King, the great and holy God, King in heaven and on earth. For to You, LORD our God and God of our ancestors, it is right to offer song and praise, hymn and psalm, strength and dominion, eternity, greatness and power, song of praise and glory, holiness and kingship, blessings and thanks, from now and for ever. Blessed are You, LORD, God and King, exalted in praises, God of thanksgivings, Master of wonders, who delights in hymns of song, King, God, Giver of life to the worlds.

### Blessed are You, LORD our God, King of the Universe, who creates the fruit of the vine.

Drink the fourth cup while reclining to the left.

# THE FOURTH CUP

**Blessed** are You, LORD our God, King of the Universe, for the vine and the fruit of the vine, and for the produce of the field; for the desirable, good and spacious land that You willingly gave as heritage to our ancestors, that they might eat of its fruit and be satisfied with its goodness. Have compassion, LORD our God, on Israel Your people, on Jerusalem, Your city, on Zion the home of Your glory, on Your altar and Your Temple. May You rebuild Jerusalem, the holy city swiftly in our time, and may You bring us back there, rejoicing in its rebuilding, eating from its fruit, satisfied by its goodness, and blessing You for it in holiness and purity. (On Shabbat: Be pleased to refresh us on this Sabbath Day.) Grant us joy on this festival of matzot. For You, God, are good and do good to all and we thank You for the land and for the fruit of the vine / wine from Israel: her vine /. Blessed are You, LORD, for the land and for the fruit of the vine / wine from Israel: her vine /.

יִשְׁתַּבַּח שִׁמְךָ לָעַד מַלְכֵּנוּ, הָאֵל הַמֶּלֶךְ הַגָּדוֹל
וְהַקָּדוֹשׁ בַּשָּׁמַיִם וּבָאָרֶץ, כִּי לְךָ נָאֶה, יהוה אֱלֹהֵינוּ
וֵאלֹהֵי אֲבוֹתֵינוּ, שִׁיר וּשְׁבָחָה, הַלֵּל וְזִמְרָה עֹז
וּמֶמְשָׁלָה, נֶצַח, גְּדֻלָּה וּגְבוּרָה, תְּהִלָּה וְתִפְאֶרֶת,
קְדֻשָּׁה וּמַלְכוּת, בְּרָכוֹת וְהוֹדָאוֹת, מֵעַתָּה וְעַד
עוֹלָם. בָּרוּךְ אַתָּה יהוה, אֵל מֶלֶךְ גָּדוֹל בַּתִּשְׁבָּחוֹת,
אֵל הַהוֹדָאוֹת, אֲדוֹן הַנִּפְלָאוֹת, הַבּוֹחֵר בְּשִׁירֵי
זִמְרָה, מֶלֶךְ, אֵל, חֵי הָעוֹלָמִים.

בָּרוּךְ אַתָּה יהוה אֱלֹהֵינוּ מֶלֶךְ הָעוֹלָם
בּוֹרֵא פְּרִי הַגָּפֶן.

Drink the fourth cup while reclining to the left.

The fruit of the vine

בָּרוּךְ אַתָּה יהוה אֱלֹהֵינוּ מֶלֶךְ הָעוֹלָם, עַל הַגֶּפֶן
וְעַל פְּרִי הַגֶּפֶן, וְעַל תְּנוּבַת הַשָּׂדֶה, וְעַל אֶרֶץ חֶמְדָּה
טוֹבָה וּרְחָבָה שֶׁרָצִיתָ וְהִנְחַלְתָּ לַאֲבוֹתֵינוּ, לֶאֱכֹל
מִפִּרְיָהּ וְלִשְׁבֹּעַ מִטּוּבָהּ. רַחֶם נָא יהוה אֱלֹהֵינוּ עַל
יִשְׂרָאֵל עַמֶּךָ וְעַל יְרוּשָׁלַיִם עִירֶךָ וְעַל צִיּוֹן מִשְׁכַּן
כְּבוֹדֶךָ וְעַל מִזְבְּחַךָ וְעַל הֵיכָלֶךָ. וּבְנֵה יְרוּשָׁלַיִם עִיר
הַקֹּדֶשׁ בִּמְהֵרָה בְיָמֵינוּ, וְהַעֲלֵנוּ לְתוֹכָהּ וְשַׂמְּחֵנוּ
בְּבִנְיָנָהּ וְנֹאכַל מִפִּרְיָהּ וְנִשְׂבַּע מִטּוּבָהּ וּנְבָרֶכְךָ עָלֶיהָ
בִּקְדֻשָּׁה וּבְטָהֳרָה. (בשבת: וּרְצֵה וְהַחֲלִיצֵנוּ בְּיוֹם הַשַּׁבָּת
הַזֶּה) וְשַׂמְּחֵנוּ בְּיוֹם חַג הַמַּצּוֹת הַזֶּה, כִּי אַתָּה יהוה
טוֹב וּמֵטִיב לַכֹּל, וְנוֹדֶה לְךָ עַל הָאָרֶץ וְעַל פְּרִי הַגֶּפֶן
/ מארץ ישראל: גַּפְנָהּ / בָּרוּךְ אַתָּה יהוה עַל הָאָרֶץ
וְעַל פְּרִי הַגֶּפֶן/ מארץ ישראל: גַּפְנָהּ /.

שִׁיר וּשְׁבָחָה, הַלֵּל וְזִמְרָה, עֹז וּמֶמְשָׁלָה.

*"To offer song and praise, hymn and psalm, strength and dominion."*

On January 1, 1863, in celebration of the Emancipation Proclamation, a choir of freed slaves gathered in Boston's Tremont Temple to sing Irish poet Thomas Moore's jubilant poem about the deliverance of Israel from bondage, "Sound the Loud Timbrel." Echoing the verses of the Song of the Sea, the freed slaves saw themselves as having newly emerged from the cloven waters to freedom.

*And Miriam, the Prophetess, the sister of Aaron, took a timbrel in her hand; and all the women went out after her with timbrels and with dances.*

— Ex. 15:20

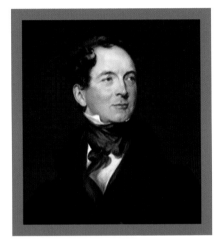

Thomas Moore

*SOUND the loud timbrel o'er Egypt's dark sea:*

*Jehovah has triumphed – his people are free!*

*Sing – for the pride of the tyrant is broken:*

*His chariots, his horsemen, all splendid and brave –*

*How vain was their boast; for the Lord hath but spoken,*

*And chariots and horsemen are sunk in the wave.*

*Sound the loud timbrel o'er Egypt's dark sea:*

*Jehovah has triumphed – his people are free!*

*Praise to the Conqueror, praise to the Lord!*

*His word was our arrow, his breath was our sword.*

*Who shall return to tell Egypt the story*

*Of those she sent forth in the hour of her pride?*

*For the Lord hath looked out from his pillar of glory,*

*And all her brave thousands are dashed in the tide.*

*Sound the loud timbrel o'er Egypt's dark sea:*

*Jehovah has triumphed – his people are free!*

הַלֵּל
זִמְרָה

*"The Songs of Joy," by James
Jacques Joseph Tissot*

SOUND
THE
LOUD
TIMBREL

**The Pesaḥ service** is finished, as it was meant to be performed, in accordance with all its rules and laws. Just as we have been privileged to lay out its order, so may we be privileged to perform it [in the Temple]. Pure One, dwelling in Your heaven, raise up this people, too abundant to be counted. Soon, lead the shoots of [Israel's] stock, redeemed, into Zion with great joy.

### Next year in Jerusalem rebuilt!

Outside Israel, the Omer is counted on the second night of the festival.

**Blessed** are You, LORD our God, King of the Universe, who has made us holy through His commandments, and has commanded us about counting the Omer.

### Today is the first day of the Omer.

*Jerusalem at sunset*

172

נִרְצָה

חֲסַל סִדּוּר פֶּסַח כְּהִלְכָתוֹ, כְּכָל מִשְׁפָּטוֹ וְחֻקָּתוֹ, כַּאֲשֶׁר זָכִינוּ לְסַדֵּר אוֹתוֹ, כֵּן נִזְכֶּה לַעֲשׂוֹתוֹ. זָךְ שׁוֹכֵן מְעוֹנָה, קוֹמֵם קְהַל עֲדַת מִי מָנָה, קָרֵב נַהֵל נִטְעֵי כַנָּה, פְּדוּיִים לְצִיּוֹן בְּרִנָּה.

לְשָׁנָה הַבָּאָה בִּירוּשָׁלַיִם הַבְּנוּיָה.

Outside ארץ ישראל, the עומר is counted
on the second night of the festival.

בָּרוּךְ אַתָּה יהוה אֱלֹהֵינוּ מֶלֶךְ הָעוֹלָם, אֲשֶׁר קִדְּשָׁנוּ בְּמִצְוֹתָיו, וְצִוָּנוּ עַל סְפִירַת הָעֹמֶר.

הַיּוֹם יוֹם אֶחָד בָּעֹמֶר.

NEXT
YEAR
IN JERUSALEM

## "Next year in Jerusalem rebuilt!"

President Abraham Lincoln often made reference to the Exodus in his campaign to preserve the Union and abolish slavery. In his 1852 "Eulogy on Henry Clay," Lincoln reminded his audience that:

> Pharaoh's country was cursed with plagues, and his hosts were drowned in the Red Sea for striving to retain a captive people who had already served them more than four hundred years. May like disasters never befall us!

In 1862, when then-Governor of Illinois Richard Yates berated Lincoln for delaying the Emancipation Proclamation, the President paraphrased words first spoken by Moses at the Red Sea: "Dick, hold still and see the salvation of God."

According to his widow, Abraham Lincoln's last words were, "How I should like to visit Jerusalem sometime." One scholar found that out of 372 eulogies of the President, nearly half compared Lincoln to Moses. The most memorable was delivered in Lincoln's hometown of Springfield, IL by Methodist Bishop Matthew Simpson, who saw in Lincoln a redeemer who crossed religious boundaries:

> Among the events of history there have been great processions of mourners.... There was mourning when Moses fell upon the heights of Pisgah and was hid from human view…but never was

*Abraham Lincoln's Emancipation Proclamation*

there in the history of man such mourning as that which has accompanied this funeral procession, and has gathered around the mortal remains of he who was our loved one, and who now sleeps among us.... We have all been taught to revere the sacred characters. Among them Moses stands preeminently high. He received the Law from God, and his name is honored among the hosts of heaven. Was not his greatest act the delivering of three millions of his kindred out of bondage? Yet we may assert that Abraham Lincoln, by his proclamation, liberated more enslaved people than ever Moses set free, and those not of his kindred or his race.

לְשָׁנָה
הַבָּאָה

*View of the Promised Land
from Mount Nebo, Jordan,
Moses's presumed burial place*

## LINCOLN'S
## LAST
## WISH

Outside Israel, this poem is recited on the first night of the festival only.

## It Happened at Midnight

Many were the miracles You performed long ago, at
   night.
At the beginning of the watch, on this night,
You won [Abraham]'s battle, when [his men were]
   split, and the night.
                              **It happened at midnight.**

You judged the king of Gerar in his dream at night.
You put dread into [Laban] the Aramean's heart that
   night.
And Israel struggled with an angel and overcame him
   at night.
                              **It happened at midnight.**

You crushed the firstborns of Patros [Egypt] in the
   middle of the night.
They could not find their strength, when they rose up
   [against Israel] at night.
You flung [Sisera] the commander of Haroshet off
   course with the stars of night.
                              **It happened at midnight.**

[Sennacherib] the blasphemer thought to raise his
   hand against the beloved [city]; but You dried up
   the bodies of his fallen in the night.
You overthrew Bel, idol and pedestal together, in the
   dead of night.
To [Daniel] the beloved man were revealed the se-
   crets of that vision of the night.
                              **It happened at midnight.**

[Belshazzar], who drank himself merry from the holy
   vessels, was killed on that same night.
[Daniel] was brought out unharmed from the lions'
   den; he who had explained those terrors of the night.
[Haman] the Agagite bore his hatred and wrote his
   orders at night.
                              **It happened at midnight.**

*The smiting of Sisera*

ON
THIS
NIGHT

Outside ישראל ארץ, this poem is recited
on the first night of the festival only.

*Sennacherib, king of Assyria
from 705–681 BCE*

וּבְכֵן וַיְהִי בַּחֲצִי הַלַּיְלָה

אָז רֹב נִסִּים הִפְלֵאתָ בַּלַּיְלָה
בְּרֹאשׁ אַשְׁמוּרוֹת זֶה הַלַּיְלָה
גֵּר צֶדֶק נִצַּחְתּוֹ, כְּנֶחֱלַק לוֹ לַיְלָה
וַיְהִי בַּחֲצִי הַלַּיְלָה

דַּנְתָּ מֶלֶךְ גְּרָר בַּחֲלוֹם הַלַּיְלָה
הִפְחַדְתָּ אֲרַמִּי בְּאֶמֶשׁ לַיְלָה
וְיִשְׂרָאֵל יָשַׂר לָאֵל, וַיּוּכַל לוֹ לַיְלָה
וַיְהִי בַּחֲצִי הַלַּיְלָה

זֶרַע בְּכוֹרֵי פַתְרוֹס מָחַצְתָּ בַּחֲצִי הַלַּיְלָה
חֵילָם לֹא מָצְאוּ בְּקוּמָם בַּלַּיְלָה
טִיסַת נְגִיד חֲרֹשֶׁת סִלִּיתָ בְּכוֹכְבֵי לַיְלָה
וַיְהִי בַּחֲצִי הַלַּיְלָה

יָעַץ מְחָרֵף לְנוֹפֵף אִוּוּי, הוֹבַשְׁתָּ פְגָרָיו בַּלַּיְלָה
כָּרַע בֵּל וּמַצָּבוֹ בְּאִישׁוֹן לַיְלָה
לְאִישׁ חֲמוּדוֹת נִגְלָה רָז חֲזוֹת לַיְלָה
וַיְהִי בַּחֲצִי הַלַּיְלָה

מִשְׁתַּכֵּר בִּכְלֵי קֹדֶשׁ נֶהֱרַג בּוֹ בַּלַּיְלָה
נוֹשַׁע מִבּוֹר אֲרָיוֹת, פּוֹתֵר בְּעִתּוּתֵי לַיְלָה
שִׂנְאָה נָטַר אֲגָגִי, וְכָתַב סְפָרִים בַּלַּיְלָה
וַיְהִי בַּחֲצִי הַלַּיְלָה

# AMERICA
# VERSUS
# THE
# AGAGITE

*Ahasuerus and Haman*
*at the Feast of Esther*

שִׂנְאָה נָטַר אֲגָגִי, וְכָתַב סְפָרִים בַּלַּיְלָה, וַיְהִי בַּחֲצִי הַלַּיְלָה.

*"[Haman] the Agagite bore his hatred and wrote his orders at night. It happened at midnight."*

*John Witherspoon*

While the nascent United States saw the promise of redemption in the Exodus narrative, the story of Esther was also often cited to inspire hope for salvation from wicked plots. On May 17, 1776, the Continental Congress, like the biblical Esther, declared a public fast day in order to "humbly implor[e] His assistance to frustrate the cruel purposes of our unnatural enemies; and by inclining their hearts to justice and benevolence."

John Witherspoon, then president of what would later become Princeton University, delivered a sermon on that fast day, enlisting Esther into the American cause:

> We have also an instance in Esther in which the most mischievous designs of Haman, the son of Hammedatha the Agagite against Mordecai the Jew, and the nation from which he sprung, turned out at last to his own destruction, the honor of Mordecai, and the salvation and peace of his people.

# "The nation from which he sprung, turned out at last to his own destruction."

You awakened Your might against him, disturbing [King Ahasuerus's] sleep at night.

You shall tread the winepress of [Se'ir], who asks anxiously, "What of the night?"

You will cry out like the watchman, calling, "Morning is come, and also night."

**It happened at midnight.**

Draw near the day that will be neither day nor night.

Highest One, make known that day is Yours and also night.

Appoint watchmen [to guard] Your city all day long and all night.

Light up like daylight the darkness of night.

**It happened at midnight.**

Outside Israel, this poem is recited on the second night of the festival only.

## Tell [Your Children]: "This Is the Pesaḥ"

You showed Your immense power in wonders on Pesaḥ;

to the head of all seasons You have raised up Pesaḥ.

You revealed to [Abraham] the Ezraḥi what would come at midnight on Pesaḥ.

**Tell [your children]: "This is the Pesaḥ."**

You knocked at his doors in the heat of the day on Pesaḥ;

he gave Your shining [messengers] unleavened cakes to eat on Pesaḥ;

and he ran to the herd, hinting at the ox in the Torah reading of Pesaḥ.

**Tell [your children]: "This is the Pesaḥ."**

*Abraham greeting
God's messengers*

עוֹרַרְתָּ נִצְחֲךָ עָלָיו בְּנֶדֶד שְׁנַת לַיְלָה
פּוּרָה תִדְרֹךְ לְשׁוֹמֵר מַה מִלַּיְלָה
צָרַח כַּשּׁוֹמֵר, וְשָׂח אָתָא בֹקֶר וְגַם לַיְלָה
וַיְהִי בַּחֲצִי הַלַּיְלָה

קָרֵב יוֹם אֲשֶׁר הוּא לֹא יוֹם וְלֹא לַיְלָה
רָם הוֹדַע כִּי לְךָ הַיּוֹם אַף לְךָ הַלַּיְלָה
שׁוֹמְרִים הַפְקֵד לְעִירְךָ כָּל הַיּוֹם וְכָל הַלַּיְלָה
תָּאִיר כְּאוֹר יוֹם חֶשְׁכַת לַיְלָה
וַיְהִי בַּחֲצִי הַלַּיְלָה

"Appoint watchmen [to guard] Your city...."

Outside ארץ ישראל, this poem is recited on the second night of the festival only.

**וּבְכֵן וַאֲמַרְתֶּם זֶבַח פֶּסַח**

אֹמֶץ גְּבוּרוֹתֶיךָ הִפְלֵאתָ בַּפֶּסַח
בְּרֹאשׁ כָּל מוֹעֲדוֹת נִשֵּׂאתָ פֶּסַח
גִּלִּיתָ לְאֶזְרָחִי חֲצוֹת לֵיל פֶּסַח
וַאֲמַרְתֶּם זֶבַח פֶּסַח

דְּלָתָיו דָּפַקְתָּ כְּחֹם הַיּוֹם בַּפֶּסַח
הִסְעִיד נוֹצְצִים עֻגוֹת מַצּוֹת בַּפֶּסַח
וְאֶל הַבָּקָר, רָץ זֵכֶר לְשׁוֹר עֵרֶךְ פֶּסַח
וַאֲמַרְתֶּם זֶבַח פֶּסַח

The men of Sodom raged and burned in fire on Pesaḥ.

Lot was saved; he baked matzot at the end of Pesaḥ.

You swept bare the land of Mof and Nof [Egypt] in Your great rage on Pesaḥ.

**Tell [your children]: "This is the Pesaḥ."**

The firstborns of [Egypt's] vigor You crushed, Lord, on the night of guarding, on Pesaḥ.

[But,] Mighty One, You passed over Your firstborn son when You saw the blood of the Pesaḥ,

allowing no destruction through my doors on Pesaḥ.

**Tell [your children]: "This is the Pesaḥ."**

The walled city [of Jericho] was closed [for fear] when it was Pesaḥ.

Midian was destroyed in the din, [after a dream of] Omer barley on Pesaḥ.

The fat ones of [Assyria; of] Pul and Lud were burned away in fires on Pesaḥ.

**Tell [your children]: "This is the Pesaḥ."**

This day [Sennacherib] halted at Nob [and laid siege] until the time of Pesaḥ.

A hand wrote Babylonia's doom on the wall at Pesaḥ: the lamp was lit, the table was laid on Pesaḥ.

**Tell [your children]: "This is the Pesaḥ."**

Hadassa gathered the people to fast three days at Pesaḥ;

You crushed [Haman,] the head of that evil family, on a gallows fifty cubits high on Pesaḥ.

[Loss and widowhood –] You will bring these two in a moment to [Edom, which rules us now,] on Pesaḥ.

Strengthen Your hand, raise Your right hand, as on the night first sanctified as Pesaḥ.

**Tell [your children]: "This is the Pesaḥ."**

*TELL YOUR CHILD*

*Belshazzar and the writing on the wall*

זֹעֲמוּ סְדוֹמִים, וְלֹהֲטוּ בָּאֵשׁ בְּפֶסַח

חֻלַּץ לוֹט מֵהֶם, וּמַצּוֹת אָפָה בְּקֵץ פֶּסַח

טֵאטֵאתָ אַדְמַת מֹף וְנֹף בְּעָבְרְךָ בְּפֶסַח

וַאֲמַרְתֶּם זֶבַח פֶּסַח

יָהּ, רֹאשׁ כָּל אוֹן מָחַצְתָּ בְּלֵיל שִׁמּוּר פֶּסַח

כַּבִּיר, עַל בֵּן בְּכוֹר פָּסַחְתָּ בְּדָם פֶּסַח

לְבִלְתִּי תֵּת מַשְׁחִית לָבֹא בִּפְתָחַי בְּפֶסַח

וַאֲמַרְתֶּם זֶבַח פֶּסַח

The walls of Jericho

מְסֻגֶּרֶת סֻגְּרָה בְּעִתּוֹתֵי פֶּסַח

נִשְׁמְדָה מִדְיָן בִּצְלִיל שְׂעוֹרֵי עֹמֶר פֶּסַח

שֹׂרְפוּ מִשְׁמַנֵּי פּוּל וְלוּד, בִּיקַד יְקוֹד פֶּסַח

וַאֲמַרְתֶּם זֶבַח פֶּסַח

עוֹד הַיּוֹם בְּנֹב לַעֲמֹד, עַד גָּעָה עוֹנַת פֶּסַח

פַּס יָד כָּתְבָה לְקַעֲקֵעַ צוּל בַּפֶּסַח

צָפֹה הַצָּפִית עָרוֹךְ הַשֻּׁלְחָן בְּפֶסַח

וַאֲמַרְתֶּם זֶבַח פֶּסַח

קָהָל כִּנְּסָה הֲדַסָּה, צוֹם לְשַׁלֵּשׁ בְּפֶסַח

רֹאשׁ מִבֵּית רָשָׁע מָחַצְתָּ בְּעֵץ חֲמִשִּׁים בְּפֶסַח

שְׁתֵּי אֵלֶּה, רֶגַע תָּבִיא לְעוּצִית בְּפֶסַח

תָּעֹז יָדְךָ, תָּרוּם יְמִינֶךָ, כְּלֵיל הִתְקַדֵּשׁ חַג פֶּסַח

וַאֲמַרְתֶּם זֶבַח פֶּסַח

## For Him It Is Fitting

Majestic in Kingship, truly chosen: His legions say to Him: "Yours and Yours; Yours, for it is Yours; Yours, only Yours; Yours, Lord, is the Kingdom."
**For Him it is fitting, for Him it is right.**

Unmistakable in His Kingship, truly glorious: His venerable ones say to Him: "Yours and Yours; Yours, for it is Yours; Yours, only Yours; Yours, Lord, is the kingdom."
**For Him it is fitting, for Him it is right.**

Worthy of Kingship, truly mighty: His officers say to Him: "Yours and Yours; Yours, for it is Yours; Yours, only Yours; Yours, Lord, is the kingdom."
**For Him it is fitting, for Him it is right.**

One in Kingship, truly omnipotent: His learned ones say to Him: "Yours and Yours; Yours, for it is Yours; Yours, only Yours; Yours, Lord, is the kingdom."
**For Him it is fitting, for Him it is right.**

King in His Kingship, truly awesome: those surrounding Him say to Him: "Yours and Yours; Yours, for it is Yours; Yours, only Yours; Yours, Lord, is the kingdom."
**For Him it is fitting, for Him it is right.**

Humble in Kingship, truly the Redeemer, His righteous ones say to Him: "Yours and Yours; Yours, for it is Yours; Yours, only Yours; Yours, Lord, is the kingdom."
**For Him it is fitting, for Him it is right.**

Holy in Kingship, truly compassionate, His angels say to Him: "Yours and Yours; Yours, for it is Yours; Yours, only Yours; Yours, Lord, is the kingdom."
**For Him it is fitting, for Him it is right.**

Powerful in Kingship, truly our Support, His perfect ones say to Him: "Yours and Yours; Yours, for it is Yours; Yours, only Yours; Yours, Lord, is the kingdom."
**For Him it is fitting, for Him it is right.**

# כִּי לוֹ נָאֶה, כִּי לוֹ יָאֶה

אַדִּיר בִּמְלוּכָה בָּחוּר כַּהֲלָכָה גְּדוּדָיו יֹאמְרוּ לוֹ
לְךָ וּלְךָ, לְךָ כִּי לְךָ, לְךָ אַף לְךָ, לְךָ יהוה הַמַּמְלָכָה
כִּי לוֹ נָאֶה, כִּי לוֹ יָאֶה

דָּגוּל בִּמְלוּכָה הָדוּר כַּהֲלָכָה וָתִיקָיו יֹאמְרוּ לוֹ
לְךָ וּלְךָ, לְךָ כִּי לְךָ, לְךָ אַף לְךָ, לְךָ יהוה הַמַּמְלָכָה
כִּי לוֹ נָאֶה, כִּי לוֹ יָאֶה

זַכַּאי בִּמְלוּכָה חָסִין כַּהֲלָכָה טַפְסְרָיו יֹאמְרוּ לוֹ
לְךָ וּלְךָ, לְךָ כִּי לְךָ, לְךָ אַף לְךָ, לְךָ יהוה הַמַּמְלָכָה
כִּי לוֹ נָאֶה, כִּי לוֹ יָאֶה

יָחִיד בִּמְלוּכָה כַּבִּיר כַּהֲלָכָה לִמּוּדָיו יֹאמְרוּ לוֹ
לְךָ וּלְךָ, לְךָ כִּי לְךָ, לְךָ אַף לְךָ, לְךָ יהוה הַמַּמְלָכָה
כִּי לוֹ נָאֶה, כִּי לוֹ יָאֶה

מֶלֶךְ בִּמְלוּכָה נוֹרָא כַּהֲלָכָה סְבִיבָיו יֹאמְרוּ לוֹ
לְךָ וּלְךָ, לְךָ כִּי לְךָ, לְךָ אַף לְךָ, לְךָ יהוה הַמַּמְלָכָה
כִּי לוֹ נָאֶה, כִּי לוֹ יָאֶה

עָנָו בִּמְלוּכָה פּוֹדֶה כַּהֲלָכָה צַדִּיקָיו יֹאמְרוּ לוֹ
לְךָ וּלְךָ, לְךָ כִּי לְךָ, לְךָ אַף לְךָ, לְךָ יהוה הַמַּמְלָכָה
כִּי לוֹ נָאֶה, כִּי לוֹ יָאֶה

קָדוֹשׁ בִּמְלוּכָה רַחוּם כַּהֲלָכָה שִׁנְאַנָּיו יֹאמְרוּ לוֹ
לְךָ וּלְךָ, לְךָ כִּי לְךָ, לְךָ אַף לְךָ, לְךָ יהוה הַמַּמְלָכָה
כִּי לוֹ נָאֶה, כִּי לוֹ יָאֶה

תַּקִּיף בִּמְלוּכָה תּוֹמֵךְ כַּהֲלָכָה תְּמִימָיו יֹאמְרוּ לוֹ
לְךָ וּלְךָ, לְךָ כִּי לְךָ, לְךָ אַף לְךָ, לְךָ יהוה הַמַּמְלָכָה
כִּי לוֹ נָאֶה, כִּי לוֹ יָאֶה

**He is Majestic** may He build His House soon, soon, speedily in our days. Build, O God, build, O God, build Your House soon.

| | | |
|---|---|---|
| He is chosen, | He is great, | He is unmistakable |
| He is glorious, | He is venerable, | He is worthy |
| He is kind, | He is pure, | He is One |
| He is mighty, | He is learned, | He is King |
| He is awesome, | He is elevated, | He is strong |
| He is Savior, | He is righteous, | He is holy |
| He is compassionate, | | He is Almighty, |
| | He is powerful | |

may He build His House soon, soon, speedily in our days. Build, O God, build, O God, build Your House soon.

MAY
HE
BUILD
HIS
HOUSE
SOON

אַדִּיר הוּא יִבְנֶה בֵּיתוֹ בְּקָרוֹב, בִּמְהֵרָה
בִּמְהֵרָה, בְּיָמֵינוּ בְּקָרוֹב, אֵל בְּנֵה, אֵל בְּנֵה,
בְּנֵה בֵיתְךָ בְּקָרוֹב

| | | |
|---|---|---|
| בָּחוּר הוּא | גָּדוֹל הוּא | דָּגוּל הוּא |
| הָדוּר הוּא | וָתִיק הוּא | זַכַּאי הוּא |
| חָסִיד הוּא | טָהוֹר הוּא | יָחִיד הוּא |
| כַּבִּיר הוּא | לָמוּד הוּא | מֶלֶךְ הוּא |
| נוֹרָא הוּא | סַגִּיב הוּא | עִזּוּז הוּא |
| פּוֹדֶה הוּא | צַדִּיק הוּא | קָדוֹשׁ הוּא |
| רַחוּם הוּא | שַׁדַּי הוּא | תַּקִּיף הוּא |

יִבְנֶה בֵּיתוֹ בְּקָרוֹב בִּמְהֵרָה בִּמְהֵרָה, בְּיָמֵינוּ
בְּקָרוֹב אֵל בְּנֵה אֵל בְּנֵה בְּנֵה בֵּיתְךָ בְּקָרוֹב

# SACRED
# WALLS

The Assembly Room inside
Independence Hall, Philadelphia

אַדִּיר הוּא יִבְנֶה בֵּיתוֹ בְּקָרוֹב.

*"He is Majestic may He build His House soon."*

*Abraham Lincoln raising the flag at Independence Hall*

Lincoln often invoked imagery of the Jerusalem Temple in order to inspire reverence for the Founding Documents and establish America's role in disseminating the principles embodied by these documents. In the Lyceum Address (January 27, 1838), Lincoln paralleled civil obedience to the Temple service, referring to the American ideal allegorically as the "Temple of Liberty" and exhorting Americans to "sacrifice unceasingly upon [the] altars" of the Law.

Lincoln also used the metaphor in his "Reply to Mayor Alexander Henry of Philadelphia" (February 21, 1861), in which he likened Philadelphia to Jerusalem and Independence Hall to the Temple by citing Psalm 137, "On the Waters of Babylon," and Isaiah 2:3, "For Out of Zion Shall Go Forth the Law."

Mr. Mayor and Fellow Citizens of Philadelphia, I appear before you to make no lengthy speech…. The reception you have given me to-night is not to me, the man, the individual, but to the man who temporarily represents, or should represent, the majesty of the nation…

Your worthy Mayor has expressed the wish, in which I join with him, that if it were convenient for me to remain with you in your city long enough to consult, [your merchants and manufacturers;] or, as it were, to listen to those breathings rising within the consecrated walls where the Constitution of the United States, and, I will add, the Declaration of American Independence was originally framed, I would do so.

I assure you and your Mayor that I had hoped on this occasion, and upon all occasions during my life, that I shall do nothing inconsistent with the teachings of those holy and most sacred walls….

All my political warfare has been in favor of the teachings coming forth from that sacred hall. May my right hand forget its cunning and my tongue cleave to the roof of my mouth, if ever I prove false to those teachings.

## Who Knows One?

**Who knows one?** I know one: our God is One, in heaven and on earth.

**Who knows two?** I know two: two Tablets of the Covenant; but our God is One, in heaven and on earth.

**Who knows three?** I know three: three fathers, two Tablets of the Covenant; but our God is One, in heaven and on earth.

**Who knows four?** I know four: four mothers, three fathers, two Tablets of the Covenant; but our God is One, in heaven and on earth.

**Who knows five?** I know five: five books of the Torah, four mothers, three fathers, two Tablets of the Covenant; but our God is One, in heaven and on earth.

**Who knows six?** I know six: six divisions of the Mishna, five books of the Torah, four mothers, three fathers, two Tablets of the Covenant; but our God is One, in heaven and on earth.

**Who knows seven?** I know seven: seven days from Sabbath to Sabbath, six divisions of the Mishna, five books of the Torah, four mothers, three fathers, two Tablets of the Covenant; but our God is One, in heaven and on earth.

**Who knows eight?** I know eight: eight days to a brit, seven days from Sabbath to Sabbath, six divisions of the Mishna, five books of the Torah, four mothers, three fathers, two Tablets of the Covenant; but our God is One, in heaven and on earth.

BUT OUR GOD IS ONE

# אֶחָד מִי יוֹדֵעַ

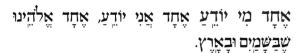

אֶחָד מִי יוֹדֵעַ אֶחָד אֲנִי יוֹדֵעַ, אֶחָד אֱלֹהֵינוּ שֶׁבַּשָׁמַיִם וּבָאָרֶץ.

שְׁנַיִם מִי יוֹדֵעַ, שְׁנַיִם אֲנִי יוֹדֵעַ, שְׁנֵי לוּחוֹת הַבְּרִית, אֶחָד אֱלֹהֵינוּ שֶׁבַּשָׁמַיִם וּבָאָרֶץ.

שְׁלוֹשָׁה מִי יוֹדֵעַ, שְׁלוֹשָׁה אֲנִי יוֹדֵעַ, שְׁלוֹשָׁה אָבוֹת, שְׁנֵי לוּחוֹת הַבְּרִית, אֶחָד אֱלֹהֵינוּ שֶׁבַּשָׁמַיִם וּבָאָרֶץ.

אַרְבַּע מִי יוֹדֵעַ, אַרְבַּע אֲנִי יוֹדֵעַ, אַרְבַּע אִמָּהוֹת, שְׁלוֹשָׁה אָבוֹת, שְׁנֵי לוּחוֹת הַבְּרִית, אֶחָד אֱלֹהֵינוּ שֶׁבַּשָׁמַיִם וּבָאָרֶץ.

חֲמִשָׁה מִי יוֹדֵעַ, חֲמִשָׁה אֲנִי יוֹדֵעַ, חֲמִשָׁה חֻמְשֵׁי תוֹרָה, אַרְבַּע אִמָּהוֹת, שְׁלוֹשָׁה אָבוֹת, שְׁנֵי לוּחוֹת הַבְּרִית, אֶחָד אֱלֹהֵינוּ שֶׁבַּשָׁמַיִם וּבָאָרֶץ.

שִׁשָׁה מִי יוֹדֵעַ, שִׁשָׁה אֲנִי יוֹדֵעַ, שִׁשָׁה סִדְרֵי מִשְׁנָה, חֲמִשָׁה חֻמְשֵׁי תוֹרָה, אַרְבַּע אִמָּהוֹת, שְׁלוֹשָׁה אָבוֹת, שְׁנֵי לוּחוֹת הַבְּרִית, אֶחָד אֱלֹהֵינוּ שֶׁבַּשָׁמַיִם וּבָאָרֶץ.

שִׁבְעָה מִי יוֹדֵעַ, שִׁבְעָה אֲנִי יוֹדֵעַ, שִׁבְעָה יְמֵי שַׁבַּתָּא, שִׁשָׁה סִדְרֵי מִשְׁנָה, חֲמִשָׁה חֻמְשֵׁי תוֹרָה, אַרְבַּע אִמָּהוֹת, שְׁלוֹשָׁה אָבוֹת, שְׁנֵי לוּחוֹת הַבְּרִית, אֶחָד אֱלֹהֵינוּ שֶׁבַּשָׁמַיִם וּבָאָרֶץ.

שְׁמוֹנָה מִי יוֹדֵעַ, שְׁמוֹנָה אֲנִי יוֹדֵעַ, שְׁמוֹנָה יְמֵי מִילָה, שִׁבְעָה יְמֵי שַׁבַּתָּא, שִׁשָׁה סִדְרֵי מִשְׁנָה, חֲמִשָׁה חֻמְשֵׁי תוֹרָה, אַרְבַּע אִמָּהוֹת, שְׁלוֹשָׁה אָבוֹת, שְׁנֵי לוּחוֹת הַבְּרִית, אֶחָד אֱלֹהֵינוּ שֶׁבַּשָׁמַיִם וּבָאָרֶץ.

**Who knows nine?** I know nine: nine months until birth, eight days to a brit, seven days from Sabbath to Sabbath, six divisions of the Mishna, five books of the Torah, four mothers, three fathers, two Tablets of the Covenant; but our God is One, in heaven and on earth.

**Who knows ten?** I know ten: Ten Commandments, nine months until birth, eight days to a brit, seven days from Sabbath to Sabbath, six divisions of the Mishna, five books of the Torah, four mothers, three fathers, two Tablets of the Covenant; but our God is One, in heaven and on earth.

**Who knows eleven?** I know eleven: eleven stars [in Joseph's dream], Ten Commandments, nine months until birth, eight days to a brit, seven days from Sabbath to Sabbath, six divisions of the Mishna, five books of the Torah, four mothers, three fathers, two Tablets of the Covenant; but our God is One, in heaven and on earth.

**Who knows twelve?** I know twelve: twelve tribes, eleven stars, Ten Commandments, nine months until birth, eight days to a brit, seven days from Sabbath to Sabbath, six divisions of the Mishna, five books of the Torah, four mothers, three fathers, two Tablets of the Covenant; but our God is One, in heaven and on earth.

**Who knows thirteen?** I know thirteen: thirteen attributes [of God's compassion], twelve tribes, eleven stars, Ten Commandments, nine months until birth, eight days to a brit, seven days from Sabbath to Sabbath, six divisions of the Mishna, five books of the Torah, four mothers, three fathers, two Tablets of the Covenant; but our God is One, in heaven and on earth.

IN HEAVEN AND ON EARTH

תִּשְׁעָה מִי יוֹדֵעַ, תִּשְׁעָה אֲנִי יוֹדֵעַ, תִּשְׁעָה יַרְחֵי לֵדָה, שְׁמוֹנָה יְמֵי מִילָה, שִׁבְעָה יְמֵי שַׁבַּתָּא, שִׁשָּׁה סִדְרֵי מִשְׁנָה, חֲמִשָּׁה חֻמְשֵׁי תוֹרָה, אַרְבַּע אִמָּהוֹת, שְׁלוֹשָׁה אָבוֹת, שְׁנֵי לוּחוֹת הַבְּרִית, אֶחָד אֱלֹהֵינוּ שֶׁבַּשָּׁמַיִם וּבָאָרֶץ.

עֲשָׂרָה מִי יוֹדֵעַ, עֲשָׂרָה אֲנִי יוֹדֵעַ, עֲשָׂרָה דִבְּרַיָּא, תִּשְׁעָה יַרְחֵי לֵדָה, שְׁמוֹנָה יְמֵי מִילָה, שִׁבְעָה יְמֵי שַׁבַּתָּא, שִׁשָּׁה סִדְרֵי מִשְׁנָה, חֲמִשָּׁה חֻמְשֵׁי תוֹרָה, אַרְבַּע אִמָּהוֹת, שְׁלוֹשָׁה אָבוֹת, שְׁנֵי לוּחוֹת הַבְּרִית, אֶחָד אֱלֹהֵינוּ שֶׁבַּשָּׁמַיִם וּבָאָרֶץ.

אַחַד עָשָׂר מִי יוֹדֵעַ, אַחַד עָשָׂר אֲנִי יוֹדֵעַ, אַחַד עָשָׂר כּוֹכְבַיָּא, עֲשָׂרָה דִבְּרַיָּא, תִּשְׁעָה יַרְחֵי לֵדָה, שְׁמוֹנָה יְמֵי מִילָה, שִׁבְעָה יְמֵי שַׁבַּתָּא, שִׁשָּׁה סִדְרֵי מִשְׁנָה, חֲמִשָּׁה חֻמְשֵׁי תוֹרָה, אַרְבַּע אִמָּהוֹת, שְׁלוֹשָׁה אָבוֹת, שְׁנֵי לוּחוֹת הַבְּרִית, אֶחָד אֱלֹהֵינוּ שֶׁבַּשָּׁמַיִם וּבָאָרֶץ.

שְׁנֵים עָשָׂר מִי יוֹדֵעַ, שְׁנֵים עָשָׂר אֲנִי יוֹדֵעַ, שְׁנֵים עָשָׂר שִׁבְטַיָּא, אַחַד עָשָׂר כּוֹכְבַיָּא, עֲשָׂרָה דִבְּרַיָּא, תִּשְׁעָה יַרְחֵי לֵדָה, שְׁמוֹנָה יְמֵי מִילָה, שִׁבְעָה יְמֵי שַׁבַּתָּא, שִׁשָּׁה סִדְרֵי מִשְׁנָה, חֲמִשָּׁה חֻמְשֵׁי תוֹרָה, אַרְבַּע אִמָּהוֹת, שְׁלוֹשָׁה אָבוֹת, שְׁנֵי לוּחוֹת הַבְּרִית, אֶחָד אֱלֹהֵינוּ שֶׁבַּשָּׁמַיִם וּבָאָרֶץ.

שְׁלוֹשָׁה עָשָׂר מִי יוֹדֵעַ, שְׁלוֹשָׁה עָשָׂר אֲנִי יוֹדֵעַ, שְׁלוֹשָׁה עָשָׂר מִדַּיָּא, שְׁנֵים עָשָׂר שִׁבְטַיָּא, אַחַד עָשָׂר כּוֹכְבַיָּא, עֲשָׂרָה דִבְּרַיָּא, תִּשְׁעָה יַרְחֵי לֵדָה, שְׁמוֹנָה יְמֵי מִילָה, שִׁבְעָה יְמֵי שַׁבַּתָּא, שִׁשָּׁה סִדְרֵי מִשְׁנָה, חֲמִשָּׁה חֻמְשֵׁי תוֹרָה, אַרְבַּע אִמָּהוֹת, שְׁלוֹשָׁה אָבוֹת, שְׁנֵי לוּחוֹת הַבְּרִית, אֶחָד אֱלֹהֵינוּ שֶׁבַּשָּׁמַיִם וּבָאָרֶץ.

*Stained glass depictions representing the twelve tribes*

# One Little Goat, One Little Goat

my father bought for two zuzim; one little goat, one little goat.

**Along came a cat** and ate the goat my father bought for two zuzim; one little goat, one little goat.

**Then came a dog** and bit the cat that ate the goat my father bought for two zuzim; one little goat, one little goat.

**Then came a stick** and hit the dog that bit the cat that ate the goat my father bought for two zuzim; one little goat, one little goat.

**Then came a fire** and burned the stick that hit the dog that bit the cat that ate the goat my father bought for two zuzim; one little goat, one little goat.

**Then came water** and put out the fire that burned the stick that hit the dog that bit the cat that ate the goat my father bought for two zuzim; one little goat, one little goat.

**Then came an ox** and drank the water that put out the fire that burned the stick that hit the dog that bit the cat that ate the goat my father bought for two zuzim; one little goat, one little goat.

**Then came a slaughterer** and slew the ox that drank the water that put out the fire that burned the stick that hit the dog that bit the cat that ate the goat my father bought for two zuzim; one little goat, one little goat.

**Then came the angel of death** and slew the slaughterer who slew the ox that drank the water that put out the fire that burned the stick that hit the dog that bit the cat that ate the goat my father bought for two zuzim; one little goat, one little goat.

**Then came the Holy One** and slew the angel of death, who slew the slaughterer who slew the ox that drank the water that put out the fire that burned the stick that hit the dog that bit the cat that ate the goat my father bought for two zuzim; one little goat, one little goat.

# חַד גַּדְיָא  חַד גַּדְיָא

דְּזַבֵּן אַבָּא בִּתְרֵי זוּזֵי חַד גַּדְיָא חַד גַּדְיָא.

וְאָתָא שׁוּנְרָא וְאָכְלָה לְגַדְיָא דְּזַבֵּן אַבָּא בִּתְרֵי זוּזֵי חַד גַּדְיָא חַד גַּדְיָא.

וְאָתָא כַלְבָּא וְנָשַׁךְ לְשׁוּנְרָא דְּאָכְלָה לְגַדְיָא דְּזַבֵּן אַבָּא בִּתְרֵי זוּזֵי חַד גַּדְיָא חַד גַּדְיָא.

וְאָתָא חֻטְרָא וְהִכָּה לְכַלְבָּא דְּנָשַׁךְ לְשׁוּנְרָא דְּאָכְלָה לְגַדְיָא דְּזַבֵּן אַבָּא בִּתְרֵי זוּזֵי חַד גַּדְיָא חַד גַּדְיָא.

וְאָתָא נוּרָא וְשָׂרַף לְחֻטְרָא דְּהִכָּה לְכַלְבָּא דְּנָשַׁךְ לְשׁוּנְרָא דְּאָכְלָה לְגַדְיָא דְּזַבֵּן אַבָּא בִּתְרֵי זוּזֵי חַד גַּדְיָא חַד גַּדְיָא.

וְאָתָא מַיָּא וְכָבָה לְנוּרָא דְּשָׂרַף לְחֻטְרָא דְּהִכָּה לְכַלְבָּא דְּנָשַׁךְ לְשׁוּנְרָא דְּאָכְלָה לְגַדְיָא דְּזַבֵּן אַבָּא בִּתְרֵי זוּזֵי חַד גַּדְיָא חַד גַּדְיָא.

וְאָתָא תוֹרָא וְשָׁתָה לְמַיָּא דְּכָבָה לְנוּרָא דְּשָׂרַף לְחֻטְרָא דְּהִכָּה לְכַלְבָּא דְּנָשַׁךְ לְשׁוּנְרָא דְּאָכְלָה לְגַדְיָא דְּזַבֵּן אַבָּא בִּתְרֵי זוּזֵי חַד גַּדְיָא חַד גַּדְיָא.

וְאָתָא הַשּׁוֹחֵט וְשָׁחַט לְתוֹרָא דְּשָׁתָה לְמַיָּא דְּכָבָה לְנוּרָא דְּשָׂרַף לְחֻטְרָא דְּהִכָּה לְכַלְבָּא דְּנָשַׁךְ לְשׁוּנְרָא דְּאָכְלָה לְגַדְיָא דְּזַבֵּן אַבָּא בִּתְרֵי זוּזֵי חַד גַּדְיָא חַד גַּדְיָא.

וְאָתָא מַלְאַךְ הַמָּוֶת וְשָׁחַט לְשׁוֹחֵט דְּשָׁחַט לְתוֹרָא דְּשָׁתָה לְמַיָּא דְּכָבָה לְנוּרָא דְּשָׂרַף לְחֻטְרָא דְּהִכָּה לְכַלְבָּא דְּנָשַׁךְ לְשׁוּנְרָא דְּאָכְלָה לְגַדְיָא דְּזַבֵּן אַבָּא בִּתְרֵי זוּזֵי חַד גַּדְיָא חַד גַּדְיָא.

וְאָתָא הַקָּדוֹשׁ בָּרוּךְ הוּא וְשָׁחַט לְמַלְאַךְ הַמָּוֶת דְּשָׁחַט לְשׁוֹחֵט דְּשָׁחַט לְתוֹרָא דְּשָׁתָה לְמַיָּא דְּכָבָה לְנוּרָא דְּשָׂרַף לְחֻטְרָא דְּהִכָּה לְכַלְבָּא דְּנָשַׁךְ לְשׁוּנְרָא דְּאָכְלָה לְגַדְיָא דְּזַבֵּן אַבָּא בִּתְרֵי זוּזֵי חַד גַּדְיָא חַד גַּדְיָא.

חַד גַּדְיָא חַד גַּדְיָא.

*"One little goat, one little goat."*

Mark Twain (whose given name was Samuel Clemens) was notorious for his irreverent satires of biblical themes. In his travelogue of his journeys through Europe and Palestine, Twain described the Holy Land as a "hopeless, dreary, heart-broken land" and was thoroughly unimpressed by its biblical sites.

However, while Twain saw the Land of Israel as a dead country, he saw in the Israelite people a vigorous immortality in spite of perpetual persecution which he describes in his essay, "Concerning the Jews" (1899). Like the "one little kid," the Jewish people have endured one cruel regime after another for centuries, and yet thrive.

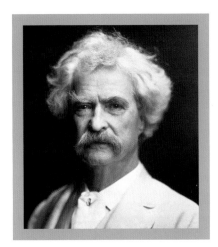

*Mark Twain*

He has made a marvellous fight in this world, in all the ages; and has done it with his hands tied behind him. He could be vain of himself, and be excused for it. The Egyptian, the Babylonian, and the Persian rose, filled the planet with sound and splendor, then faded to dream-stuff and passed away; the Greek and the Roman followed, and made a vast noise, and they are gone; other peoples have sprung up and held their torch high for a time, but it burned out, and they sit in twilight now, or have vanished. The Jew saw them all, beat them all, and is now what he always was, exhibiting no decadence, no infirmities of age, no weakening of his parts, no slowing of his energies, no dulling of his alert and aggressive mind. All things are mortal but the Jew; all other forces pass, but he remains. What is the secret of his immortality?

## "All things are mortal but the Jew."

חַד
גַּדְיָא

*Sunrise over planet Earth from space (elements of this photo provided by NASA)*

## THE SECRET OF JEWISH IMMORTALITY

# ESSAYS

should be pleased that political leaders make such efforts to reach out to the Jewish community. These activities are a refreshing improvement over much of Jewish history, in which Jews hoped that their host governments would not kick them out, or worse, kill them.

Even as we celebrate this new development, we should also recognize that there are, and should be, limits to how far we take this. It is best that future administrations not go too far in their efforts to court the Jewish community. White House Yom Kippur, with mandatory fasting and the strictures against leather shoes could cause rampant violations of the buttoned-down White House dress code. A White House sukka, with the traditional hut built on the South Lawn where Marine One is supposed to touch down, could also be problematic. These examples are obviously absurd (I hope), but a continued search by politicians for Jewish communal events to latch on to runs the risk of mixing that which is holy with that which is common. Sticking with Hanukka parties and virtual Seders seems like a good place to settle, and a worthy development to celebrate.

Of course, switching to a virtual Seder will not avoid controversy. For example, a conservative blogger did not like the fact that a Jewish critic of Israel was invited to the 2021 Seder. Yet wise and careful guest selection can alleviate some of the potential pitfalls. In the 2022 Biden online Seder, guests like Mayim Bialik, Deborah Lipstadt, and Yeshiva

University President Rabbi Dr. Ari Berman participated and brought meaningful religious content to the discussion. In addition, the White House was careful to make sure that the Orthodox, Conservative, and Reform movements all were represented. Vice President Kamala Harris even displayed a bottle of wine from a vineyard in Judea and Samaria. (She also said, "Next Year in Jerusalem," which was a pleasant surprise.) And Biden released a Passover statement that said, in part, "The enduring spirit of this holiday continues to teach us that with faith, the driest desert can be crossed, the mightiest sea can be split, and hope never stops marching towards the Promised Land."

As a Modern Orthodox Jew and a former White House Jewish liaison, I find White House Seder tradition meaningful and powerful because it shows that we are welcome and accepted in this great country. Long may the virtual Seder continue as an American Jewish political tradition. ■

# WHITE HOUSE SEDERS SHOW THAT AMERICAN JEWS BELONG

## Dr. Tevi Troy

*Dr. Tevi Troy is a Senior Fellow and Director of the Presidential Leadership Initiative at the Bipartisan Policy Center, and a former White House aide, White House Jewish Liaison, and Deputy Secretary of the U.S. Department of Health and Human Services.*

While America has never had a Jewish president, it has begun a relatively new tradition that demonstrates the deep impact Passover has had on the collective American consciousness. Beginning in 2009, President Barack Obama began hosting Seders in the White House, becoming the first president to attend a Seder there. This White House Seder is the latest in a series of escalating steps taken by presidents of both parties to appeal to Jewish voters. President George W. Bush, for example, initiated the tradition of hosting Hanukka parties in the White House, while Jimmy Carter was the first president to allow a menora lighting on the Ellipse, behind the White House.

Donald Trump followed Obama and hosted a Seder run by some of his Jewish staffers. But then Covid interceded, and for once, the Covid intercession was a good one. When Joe Biden became president, his Covid-careful administration chose to have an online "People's Seder." Because it was online, the People's Seder took place before Passover, so that it would not interfere with the actual Seder ritual.

The Seder is one of the most recognized Jewish rituals, and one can hardly fault the Obama and Trump administrations for trying to promote better relations with the Jewish community by hosting one. Yet there are multiple reasons why hosting a Seder is far more challenging than throwing a Hanukka party, which is basically just a holiday party with an all-Jewish guest list and candle-lighting ceremony. (That being said, the White House Hanukka parties have met with multiple logistical challenges regarding the provision of kosher food and intense lobbying regarding the number of attendees.) A Seder, in contrast, is an explicitly religious event and therefore fraught with pitfalls which can diminish the goodwill these types of events are supposed to engender. For this reason, the streaming "Seder" is actually a helpful improvement that can potentially bring different streams of Jews together (from both political parties) without emphasizing their denominational differences.

Navigation of religious and political differences aside, Passover is an important Jewish holiday, and politicians seeking to reach out to the Jewish community are wise to acknowledge the festival. And we as Jews

should be ▶

How many of us are walking around with deep pain that we keep locked away, feeling as if no one else can understand it, not bothering to try? While most of us have never seen combat, or had a friend die in our arms, pain is a part of life, and even seemingly insignificant experiences shape us against our will. And we all carry unresolved intergenerational trauma, a burdensome and sacred inheritance of its own.

The Jewish experience has been defined both by inexplicable miracles and unimaginable tragedies, from the bloody wars documented in the Tanakh to the modern expulsion of Jews from the Middle East and North Africa and the calculated decimation of Europe's Jews during the Holocaust. Our current period of safety and affluence in America is an aberration, not the historic norm.

This has all taken a toll. If you are focused on merely getting through the day, as earlier generations often were, it is only natural to keep your pain locked away, out of reach, where you think it cannot hurt you.

Why, then, does the Haggada implore us each year to look back and experience the profoundly painful Passover story, as if it had happened to each of us personally?

Imagine, after generations of enslavement in Egypt, running for your life and leaving behind everything you've ever known. Imagine giving up a culture and a land you know only to be thrust into an even more vulnerable existence. Imagine doing all that and never leaving exile. Is it any wonder that the Talmud tells us most Jews refused to leave Egypt? Most of us simply cannot fathom the depths of our ancient ancestors' pain.

Perhaps this is precisely why the Haggada demands that we try. "Now that you're comfortable," it reminds us, "it's time to open that box." It's time to imagine, just once a year, the unimaginable. As our Sages in "Ethics of our Fathers" say of the Torah more broadly, so too with this ancestral pain: "Turn it, and turn it, for everything is in it."

Recalling the story of our enslavement and the Exodus in vivid detail, discussing the ways our ancestors reacted to it, as we do during the Seder, is certainly not the same as truly healing. It is a start. The effort is necessary. Unaddressed trauma tends to reverberate through subsequent generations. It is not quiet suffering that our tradition demands – to be whole, we must sit with and process this avalanche

> "Our current period of safety and affluence in America is an aberration, not the historic norm."

of Jewish ▶

# LEARNING FROM OUR PAIN ON PASSOVER
## Laura E. Adkins

*Iron Dome launching an intercept missile*

*Laura E. Adkins is the Opinion Editor of The Forward.*

On the Fourth of July, a friend texted me with a "random question."

She was at a party in the suburbs, and the hosts were shooting off fireworks in their backyard. As the sky lit up above her, my friend had a panic attack.

"Probably because of that summer we spent in Israel," she texted. "I am shocked because nothing has happened in the intervening 8 years.... I've seen fireworks so many times, but I guess they've never been directly above my head like that."

And then came the question I had no idea how to answer: "Has anything like that happened to you?"

My friend and I lived in a beautiful South Tel Aviv apartment in the summer of 2014. During that period, militant groups in Gaza fired over 4,500 rockets and projectiles into Israel. The first time the warning sirens blared, my friend and I had been on a bus home from work. The second time, later that night, we were walking in the street; I grasped my friend's hand as we ran to crouch against the steep shoulder of the road, poignantly aware of our vulnerability. We felt the air shake as we heard a barrage of Iron Dome missiles intercept a nearby rocket overhead.

Recalling my own sense of helplessness during that time, I empathize with my friend's response years later. But even when we share an experience with another person, we can never fully understand the depths of how it felt for them. It was easy for me to recall the shared experience. It was impossible for me to truly feel her pain.

An acquaintance who served in the Israeli army during a much earlier war and watched much of his unit die in combat recently told me that he'd built a wall around his trauma so high that he couldn't touch it for twenty years. Sometimes, he said, the impenetrable wall still comes in handy.

How many ▶

# "NEXT YEAR WE WILL BE FREE": WE HAVE A DREAM

## Joseph I. Lieberman
## with Rabbi Menachem Genack

*Now Senior Counsel at the law firm of Kasowitz, Benson, Torres LLP in New York, Joseph I. Lieberman was for 24 years a member of the US Senate from Connecticut.*

*Rabbi Menachem Genack is the Rabbinic Administrator and CEO of OU Kosher and General Editor of OU Press.*

Through the millennia, the Jewish people have recited the Haggada, our national paean to freedom, even while living under conditions closer to slavery than to freedom and, indeed, under conditions far worse than slavery. Facing the persecutions of ancient Romans, medieval Inquisitors, and the uniquely modern menace of the Third Reich, Jews continued to sing God's praises for their deliverance from slavery to freedom. How can we understand this phenomenon? Although these Jews were no longer slaves to the Egyptian Pharaohs, in what sense were they free?

In its introductory paragraph, the Haggada addresses this fundamental question in one line: "This year we are here, next year we will be in the Land of Israel; this year we are slaves, next year we will be free." Who is freer, the man who is currently unconfined but is about to be sentenced to life in prison, or a prisoner who is imminently

*March on Washington, August 1963*

reaching the end of his prison sentence and eagerly anticipating living out the rest of his life as a free man? The Haggada is telling us that though externally we may be in chains, internally and existentially we are free because of our confident belief in redemption. We acknowledge that the present is not perfect, but we recognize that it is not permanent. We know that the future redemption is at hand and that the era of our final freedom is about to be realized. As the saying goes, the present is but a blink of an eye. In our collective mind's eye, we already see the future actualization and culmination of God's plan.

During the ▶

of Jewish pain, in our own homes, as if it had happened to us that very night.

Of course, the Haggada itself is a roadmap for doing so.

We begin our retelling of the Passover story each year with a physical reminder of acute suffering: "*ha laḥma anya*," "this [matza] is the bread of oppression." And then comes a strange refrain: "All those who are hungry, let them enter and eat."

Why should the hungry take part in this sad affair? Because the Seder asks us to *lesader*, to get ourselves in order. As the late Rabbi Sacks wrote in his Haggada commentary, "What transforms the bread of oppression into the bread of freedom is the willingness to share it with others."

We are not being asked to wallow in our pain. But we are being asked to let it deeply move us, and to learn from it.

It is not enough, our tradition teaches us, to simply gain freedom and forget who we are. It is not acceptable to bury our past and block out what we have endured. We must heal ourselves and articulate what we stand for before we can ever hope to heal the world. To heal your deepest pain, the Haggada whispers, you must find a reason to live for more than just yourself.

As the inheritors of Jewish tradition churning in the American melting pot, this task is an enormously sacred one. Our forefathers and foremothers, scrambling to make it out of persecution alive, did not always have the luxury of such rumination. Picking up where they left off is our sacred task to fulfill.

The radical premise of Judaism is that we are God's partners in creation. And the radical promise of America, to generations of immigrants, has been that effort, coupled with liberty, brings reward, making a better life possible for future generations.

Forging a better future, of course, is more easily said than done. How can we stay grounded by what our tradition demands without being felled by it? How can we learn and benefit from the American spirit of independence without making an idol of it?

The Israelites in the wilderness had the clouds of glory to protect them when they were afraid. Today, we have smartphones to distract us from our pain instead.

At the Seder, we are commanded to remind ourselves that we are the recipients of the miracle of redemption. The freedoms that liberty grants us in our generation create immense individual and collective responsibilities.

It is up to each of us to be strong enough to sit with whatever our pain – individual and collective, personal and historical – demands. And it is also our sacred responsibility to invite others in, reminding them of our shared purpose and sharing with them the taste of redemptive possibility. ∎

be, and by envisioning, by dreaming, we can bring about a new reality.

Inspired by Dr. King, I traveled with other college students to Mississippi during the fall that year to participate in a Freedom Vote campaign. After I returned to Yale, I heard that Dr. King was coming to Bridgeport, Connecticut, to speak at a rally. Of course, I went.

Dr. King was running a little late, so someone asked me to tell the crowd about what I had seen and done in Mississippi. When I concluded my remarks and began to walk off the stage, Dr. King walked on. He shook my hand and said in his extraordinary, resonant voice, "Very good, young man." My first thought was that the voice I had just heard was like the voice of Moses – strong, calm, and encouraging.

During my time in the Civil Rights Movement, I was struck that so many of the African American leaders I met were clergymen and women. I was moved by the way they told and retold the biblical story of the Exodus to inspire and give hope to African Americans fighting for their freedom. Dr. King continued his speech with one final dream: "I have a dream that one day every valley shall be exalted, every hill and mountain shall be made low, the rough places will be made plain, and the crooked places will be made straight, and the glory of the Lord shall be revealed, and all flesh shall see it together." This dream first envisioned by the prophet Isaiah has always been our dream as a nation, and through the dream we will achieve the reality. "This year we are here, next year we will be in the Land of Israel; this year we are slaves, next year we will be free." ∎

During the summer of 1963, I was one of hundreds of thousands who attended the March on Washington for Jobs and Freedom, which ended at the Lincoln Memorial with Dr. Martin Luther King's "I Have a Dream" speech, one of the greatest orations of my time, or any other. The participants in that march were diverse – racially and religiously – in good part, I believe, because Dr. King placed the struggle for civil rights in the context of broadly shared religious values and religious narratives, including, of course, God's liberation of the Israelites from slavery in Egypt. Dr. King's message to his audience that day was:

> Let us not wallow in the valley of despair, I say to you today, my friends.

> So even though we face the difficulties of today and tomorrow, I still have a dream. It is a dream deeply rooted in the American dream. I have a dream that one day this nation will rise up and live out the true meaning of its creed: We hold these truths to be self-evident, that all men are created equal.

> I have a dream that one day on the red hills of Georgia, the sons of former slaves and the sons of former slave owners will be able to sit down together at the table of brotherhood.

> I have a dream that one day even the state of Mississippi, a state sweltering with the heat of injustice, sweltering with the heat of oppression will be transformed into an oasis of freedom and justice.

> I have a dream that my four little children will one day live in a nation where they will not be judged by the color of their skin but by the content of their character. I have a dream today.

"I have a dream today." Dr. King knew that while the struggle for civil rights could not be won simply by dreaming, dreams do possess a transformative power. The great nineteenth century biblical commentator known as the Malbim explains the opening verse of Psalm 26, "When God brought back those who returned to Zion we were like dreamers," to mean: "We were like dreamers who saw God bringing back Zion's exiles" – even though the event had not yet taken place. We were able to visualize it, Malbim writes, "like a prophet, who sees the future as if it is happening right now." When reality is not what it should be, our dreams can envision things as they should be, and ▶

## "The era of our final freedom is about to be realized."

sermon but he was so overcome that he could not continue. Alfred T. Jones, Parnas of Beth El-emeth Congregation of Philadelphia, asked [the well-known Jewish scholar and writer] Isaac Leeser to say something to comfort the worshippers; he did, but it was so disconnected that he had to apologize: "the dreadful news and its suddenness have in a great measure overcome my usual composure, and my thoughts refuse to arrange themselves in their wonted order."

Because the president died on Saturday, the Jewish Sabbath, the first utterances from the pulpit in response to the assassination were heard in synagogues, as Isaac Marken explains in *Abraham Lincoln and the Jews*. One of the most striking – and indeed, controversial – moments took place in Congre-

gation Shearith Israel, in New York, the oldest Jewish congregation in America. There, Marken recounts, "the rabbi recited the Hashkaba (prayer for the dead) for Lincoln. This, according to the *Jewish Messenger*, was the first time that this prayer had been said in a Jewish house of worship for any other than those professing the Jewish religion." This seeming deviation from tradition in Shearith Israel – known to this day for its fierce devotion to preserving religious and liturgical tradition – was noted by many, and defended by the aforementioned Isaac Leeser, who also edited American Jewry's most prominent newspaper:

It is, indeed, somewhat unusual to pray for one not of our faith, but by no means in opposition to its spirit, and therefore not inadmissible. We pray for the dead,

*General Lee surrenders at Appomattox Court House*

because we ▶

# WHEN LINCOLN DIED ON PASSOVER
## Rabbi Dr. Meir Y. Soloveichik

*Rabbi Dr. Meir Y. Soloveichik is the Rabbi of Congregation Shearith Israel in New York and Director of the Straus Center for Torah and Western Thought at Yeshiva University. This essay is adapted with permission from The Weekly Standard.*

On Sunday, April 9, 1865, Generals Grant and Lee met in Appomattox Court House, Virginia. Lee surrendered, and the Civil War came to an end, with 360,000 Union and 260,000 Confederate soldiers dead. The news broke all over the United States on April 10, which, in the Hebrew calendar, was the morning before the eight-day holiday of Passover was to begin. We can imagine the elegant symmetry that those Jews sympathetic to the Union cause saw in the advent of their Festival of Freedom, commemorating the Israelite Exodus from slavery, coinciding with the Confederacy's defeat. Thinking of their own relatives, who like other Americans had fought, bled, and died for several terrible years, we can imagine their finding a double meaning at their Seder tables that Monday evening, as they uttered the immortal words of the Haggada: "Why is this night different from all other nights?"

It was four days later, on Friday evening, that the president ventured out into a joyful, festive Washington for an evening at Ford's Theatre and was shot. Carried to a boarding house across the street, Lincoln died at 7:22 a.m. on Saturday. It is often told that all those crowded around his deathbed turned to Secretary of War Edwin Stanton, who said simply, "Now he belongs to the ages." As the writer Adam Gopnik has noted, these words are the best-known epitaph in American history, and probably the finest: "They seem perfectly chosen, in their bare and stoical evocation of a Lincoln who belongs to history alone, their invocation not of an assumption to an afterlife but of a long reign in the corridors of time, a man now part of eternity."

Conveyed by telegraph, the news soon reached the rest of the country. Jews heard it from their fellow Americans on the day of the celebratory service held on the Sabbath during Passover. Bertram Korn, in his *American Jewry and the Civil War*, describes the scene:

> Jews were on their way to synagogue or already worshipping when tidings of the assassination reached them…. Jews who had not planned on attending services hastened to join their brethren in the sanctuaries where they could find comfort in the hour of grief. The Rabbis put their sermon notes aside and spoke extemporaneously, haltingly, reaching out for the words to express their deep sorrow…. Samuel Adler of Temple Emmanuel in New York began to deliver a

sermon but ▶

Stanton's original reference, then, may have been to Lincoln's place amongst the angels, not the ages. The question of what Stanton actually said, Gopnik notes, "leads to the most vexed question in all the Lincoln literature, that of his faith. How religious – how willing to credit more than metaphoric angels – did the men in the room think that Lincoln was?" After all, as anticlerical as Lincoln may have been in his youth, there is no question that his most famous speeches are laced with biblical references, and he began to see the work of Divine Providence in the history of the United States and the elimination of slavery from a nation conceived in liberty. "The Second Inaugural," Gopnik notes, "is the most famous instance, with its insistence that 'if God wills that [the war] continue until all the wealth piled by the bondsman's two hundred and fifty years of unrequited toil shall be sunk, and until every drop of blood drawn with the lash shall be paid by another drawn with the sword, as was said three thousand years ago, so still it must be said "the judgments of the Lord are true and righteous altogether."'" It was this Lincoln about whom Stanton likely said, "Now he belongs to the angels"; and if he did not say it, then perhaps the first ones to say it were the members of Congregation Shearith Israel.

As terrible as it was, Lincoln's death on Passover, and the Jews' joining their observance of this holiday with their mourning of his death, is curiously fitting. For as Britain's former chief rabbi, Lord Jonathan Sacks z"l, notes in his commentary on the Haggada,

In a strange way civil religion has the same relationship to the United States as Pesaḥ [Passover] does to the Jewish people. It is first and foremost not a philosophy but a story. It tells of how a persecuted group escaped from the old world and made a hazardous journey to an unknown land, there to construct a new society, in Abraham Lincoln's famous words, "conceived in liberty, and dedicated to the proposition that all men are created equal." Like the Pesaḥ story, it must be told repeatedly, as it is in every inaugural address. It defines the nation, not merely in terms of its past but also as a moral, spiritual commitment to the future. It is no accident that the founders of America turned to the Hebrew Bible, or that successive presidents have done likewise, because there is no other text in Western literature that draws [on] these themes. . . . Israel, ancient and modern, and the United States are the two supreme examples of societies constructed in conscious pursuit of an idea.

The Passover story, in other words, has always been linked to that of America. Indeed, Benjamin Franklin first suggested that the seal of the United States depict Pharaoh drowning at the Red Sea, with the motto "Rebellion to Tyrants Is Obedience to God." Matthew Holbreich, a scholar at Yeshiva University's Straus Center, and Yale's Danilo Petranovich, note in a coauthored article that even before the Civil War, Lincoln drew on the same biblical imagery to predict the possibility of Divine punishment for slavery;

in his ▶

*Edwin Stanton, Abraham Lincoln's
secretary of war*

because we believe that the souls of the departed as well as of the living are in the keeping of God…. The prayers, therefore, offered up this day for the deceased President are in accordance with the spirit of the faith which we have inherited as children of Israel, who recognize in all men those created like them in the image of God, and all entitled to His mercy, grace and pardon, though they have not yet learned to worship and adore Him as we do who have been especially selected as the bearers of His law.

The prayer for Lincoln, in other words – one of the first religious reactions to Lincoln's death – embodied the belief in human equality that lay at the heart of Lincoln's worldview: that this was a nation conceived in liberty and dedicated to the idea that all men are created equal. At the same time, the reciting of the prayer – which asks on behalf of the deceased for a "goodly portion in the life of the World to Come" – also embodied the belief the members of Congregation Shearith Israel had in Lincoln's spiritual immortality. A focus on spiritual immortality may have been Stanton's original intent as well; because, as Gopnik himself has noted, as perfect as our version of Stanton's epitaph may seem to us today, it very possibly is not quite accurate. The closest source we have to an eyewitness is a Corporal Tanner, a soldier, who took dictation from Stanton. Tanner described the final moments of Lincoln's life in his own words:

> The Reverend Dr. Gurley stepped forward and lifting his hands began "Our Father and our God" and I snatched pencil and notebook from my pocket, but my haste defeated my purpose. My pencil point (I had but one) caught in my coat and broke, and the world lost the prayer, a prayer that was only interrupted by the sobs of Stanton as he buried his face in the bedclothes. As "Thy will be done, Amen" in subdued and tremulous tones floated through the little chamber, Mr. Stanton raised his head, the tears streaming down his face. A more agonized expression I never saw on a human countenance as he sobbed out the words: "He belongs to the angels now."

Stanton's original ▶

In invoking this image, Holbreich and Petranovich write, "Lincoln envisioned the eradication of slavery in terms of a moral resurrection."

Here, however, is what no scholar has noted before: the story of the Valley of the Dry Bones from the Book of Ezekiel is read in synagogues all over the world when the Sabbath takes place in the middle of Passover, as it did the year Lincoln died. The tale in Ezekiel is read on Passover because the holiday itself commemorates, for Jews, our moment of national resurrection, our new birth of freedom. The prophetic portion is read immediately after the reading from the Torah and the recitation of memorial prayers, so at Congregation Shearith Israel in 1865, it would have almost immediately followed the memorial prayer for Lincoln.

We are now able to reconstruct what happened in Shearith Israel that day. The news of the assassination broke as services were beginning. The rejoicing over the Passover holiday and the Northern victory were all of a sudden turned to mourning. A traditional Jewish prayer was recited for the soul of a Gentile, the Gentile who embodied for these Jews the best of humanity. By saying the prayer on his behalf, Jews expressed their faith both in his spiritual immortality and in the posterity of his principles; they were, one might say, stressing that he belonged both to the ages and to the angels. These Jews then read the first half of Ezekiel's thirty-seventh chapter, the story of the Valley of the Dry Bones, a tale embodying a new birth of

*The assassination of Abraham Lincoln*

freedom, at the moment that the Civil War came to an end. Holbreich and Petranovich reflect that Lincoln, in referencing Ezekiel's Valley of the Dry Bones in his "House Divided" speech, surely knew that chapter's final verses. The prophet concludes by referencing ancient Israel, which had been split into a northern and southern kingdom; and one can conceive of no more fitting verse with which to capture Lincoln's legacy:

> And I will make them into one nation in the land upon the mountains of Israel, and one king shall be to them all as a king; and they shall no longer be two nations, neither shall they be divided into two kingdoms anymore.

For American Jews, the story of Lincoln's death on Passover, and of the Jewish memorial prayer in response, inspires us to dedicate ourselves with renewed vigor to the principles for which Lincoln stood, and for which he died, that they shall not soon perish from the earth. ∎

in his eulogy for Henry Clay in 1852, Lincoln reflected that "Pharaoh's country was cursed with plagues, and his hosts were drowned in the Red Sea for striving to retain a captive people, who already served them more than four hundred years. May like disasters never befall us!" The eternal link between Lincoln's life and Passover – the fact that Lincoln's death, marked in the Hebrew calendar, coincides with Passover every year – is certainly fitting, and perhaps even part of the providence that Lincoln began to see in his own life, and the life of his nation.

With this in mind, we are now able to glean one more fascinating link between Lincoln's life and death and the Passover holiday. In his famous "House Divided" speech, delivered on June 16, 1858, when he accepted the nomination of the Republican Party for a seat in the U.S. Senate, Lincoln reflected on the new political party that had been born to fight slavery:

Two years ago the Republicans of the nation mustered over thirteen hundred thousand strong. We did this under the single impulse of resistance to a common danger, with every external circumstance against us. Of strange, discordant, and even hostile elements, we gathered from the four winds, and formed and fought the battle through, under the constant hot fire of a disciplined, proud, and pampered enemy. Did we brave all then to falter now? – now – when that same enemy is wavering, dissevered, and belligerent? The result is not doubtful. We shall not fail – if we stand firm, we shall not fail.

As Holbreich and Petranovich have noted, Lincoln's phrase, "gathered from the four winds," is biblical, a reference to the story in Ezekiel where the prophet sees a field full of dry bones, a symbol of Israel's loss of hope following exile. As the bones come together to form bodies, Ezekiel is told:

"Prophesy to the spirit, prophesy, O son of man, and say to the spirit, 'So says the Lord God: From four winds come, O spirit, and breathe into these slain ones that they may live.'" And I prophesied as He had commanded me, and the spirit came into them, and they lived and stood on their feet, a very great army, exceedingly so.

"The holiday itself commemorates, for Jews, our moment of national resurrection, our new birth of freedom."

In invoking ▶

from that place with a mighty hand and an outstretched arm," I envision my African American ancestors who saw the sea had split with the Emancipation Proclamation, only for new overwhelming oceans of Jim Crow to be created and barriers upheld by the echoes and afterlife of American slavery.

"We" are commanded to ensure that every free person – from the poor to cushioned royalty, adult and child alike – asks why. Why engage with the symbols and stories, performative theatrics, and songs of yesteryear? Why do we, as twenty-first-century Jews, need to read the histories of our ancestors we never knew?

Because we must never take our freedom for granted. We must always remember that Pharaoh never died. So many have been and are still caught in his shackles. What makes the Seder night different from all other nights for Black American Jews is different. Our origin stories from slavery to freedom are complex and ongoing.

For my enslaved ancestors, America was a lighthouse and beacon, a Zion, amidst a long and tired exile. As a Jew of Color today, I am an America scarred by social hierarchies and bruised by bigotry that has yet to fully heal.

I have come to know that people who are color-blind deny that there is a difference in how a person of color is treated. America still holds onto its Pharaohs.

An evening to be safeguarded, and night to be remembered, the Passover Seder resets the table of our lives with a call to stand for freedom in every generation and a call to stand against tyranny in every generation. As *Avadim Hayinu* echoes throughout the centuries, its reverberations whisper, "You are able to speak, and to be carried away on the wings of words from millennia ago, bound to no Pharaoh's story, but liberated by your own."

By calling to the table not just the free of today but also those who yearn to be free tomorrow – not just our ancient ancestors, but my own parents and grandparents – we recenter the Jewish people's greatest teaching: that the Lord liberates the enslaved. ∎

> ## "The Passover Seder resets the table of our lives with a call to stand for freedom."

# FROM SLAVERY TO FREEDOM: AN AMERICAN PASSOVER STORY

## Rabbi Isaiah Rothstein

*Freed African American women*

*Rabbi Isaiah Rothstein is the Rabbinic Scholar and Public Affairs Advisor at Jewish Federations of North America*

As a youth from Monsey, NY, I learned about the Passover story through Torah coloring books that depicted the epic and dramatic narratives of the Exodus. One particular comic depicted Moshe as an eighteenth-century hasidic Jew with a *shtreimel* (fur hat), long *kapota* (robe), and side-locks down to his shoulders. I remember bringing home my masterpiece fully crayoned in purple and my mother saying, "You know Moshe didn't look like this, right?! He had brown skin like me."

The Mishna teaches that the central mitzva of telling the Jewish people's liberation story must begin by sharing our ancestors'

hard beginnings and difficult moments and only then the joyous ending, so one can fully embrace God's miracles and convey gratitude for being liberated. As a mixed-race Jew from the ultra-Orthodox community of Monsey, NY, my own freedom story for which I am grateful is that I am a seventh-generation survivor of America's slave trade.

With a mother who converted to Judaism after being raised Methodist and a Chabad father living in Monsey, I had a lot to think about while growing up.

Both sides of my family have been victimized because of who they were and what they believe in, and so, both sides have made it their life's purpose to stand for the other, and to advocate for civil liberties and justice for all. Beyond the threading of colors and convergence of different faiths, both sides of my family know all too well that there is still a Pharaoh lurking in unfriendly places with every evil intention to harm, cast away, and degrade others based on their color or religion. Indeed, you only truly know racism exists if you experience it.

So when the story of the Haggada begins with the declaration: "We were enslaved to Pharaoh in Egypt and God liberated us

from that ▶

makes simple, straightforward sense, since freedom can only be fully appreciated in contrast with its opposite, enslavement: no one can truly understand the import of freedom and truly savor it as vividly as a former slave.

But Rav's opinion, that we need to remember our inglorious roots in idolatry, is less easily understood.

It would seem that while Shmuel focuses on the liberation of the Jewish people from physical enslavement, Rav chooses to highlight the process of the people's *spiritual* liberation. It began with the idol worship of their distant ancestors, continued through

radation to truly appreciating subsequent spiritual growth.

Someone who has gone from spiritual degradation to refinement, the Talmud is teaching us, should not try to erase the darkness of his past from his consciousness. On the contrary, recalling it is part and parcel of truly understanding the import, and the blessing, of his present.

That truth is pertinent not only to our perception of ancient Jewish history, and not only to an individual's appreciation of his personal spiritual growth, but to our, and all American citizens', perception of our country's history.

> ## "Freedom can only be fully appreciated in contrast with its opposite, enslavement."

the dark days of Egyptian slavery, when, the mystical text Zohar Ḥadash (*Parashat Yitro*) tells us, the Jews fell to a low level of spiritual contamination, and then attained the lofty spiritual heights reached at the Exodus – when, the Midrash tells us, even a "lowly maidservant" perceived what later prophets could not – and culminated with the revelation at Sinai.

And so, it seems, as essential as experiencing slavery is to truly appreciating physical freedom, so is recalling one's moral deg-

That the United States is a beacon of freedom and democracy today is no reason to obscure or ignore elements of our country's past that leave us far from proud. It is reason to remember them.

It can't be denied that, before the republic was founded, the English colonists who landed on our shores in 1607 and laid the groundwork for what would later become a country, committed terrible crimes against the human beings they found here. Over

the course ▶

# THE BAD OLD TIMES
## Rabbi Avi Shafran

*The Pilgrims meet Samoset, the first Native American to make contact with the European settlers*

*Rabbi Avi Shafran taught Talmud, Humash and Jewish history at the secondary level for many years and is the author of several books and writes widely in Jewish and general media. He also serves as Director of Public Affairs for Agudath Israel of America.*

A disagreement in the Talmud between two famous rabbis about how to tell the story of the Exodus from Egypt was resolved by the Haggada's author in the spirit of… "you're both right."

Babylonian scholar Rav maintained that the Exodus account should begin with how "our forefathers were idolaters," a reference to the Jewish ancestor Abraham's idol-wor-

shipping father, Terah. Shmuel, a contemporary of Rav, held otherwise, that the story should start with how "We were slaves to Pharaoh in the land of Egypt."

Both Rav's and Shmuel's opinions are born of a strange Mishnaic directive about how one should fulfill the Torah commandment (Exodus 13:8) to "tell" (Hebrew, *vihigadta* – the source of the word "Haggada") the next generation about the Exodus.

The Talmud's odd stipulation (Pesaḥim 116a) is that the recounting needs to "begin with degradation" before proceeding to "praise" – the description of how God took our ancestors out of Egypt and into service to Him.

Truth be told, Rav's and Shmuel's opinions, different though they may be, are not exclusive of one another, and so, that's likely why both are layered into our Haggada's text.

What is interesting, though, is what elicited those different opinions – the Talmud's requirement to retell the history of the Jews' escape from Egypt by beginning "with degradation."

It seems clear that, when it comes to celebrating freedom, there is something essential in first stressing the "bad old times" of the past.

Shmuel's understanding of that need – to begin with the degradation of slavery –

makes simple ▶

# THE AMERICAN SEDER AND ITS ENEMIES
## Adam Kirsch

*Adam Kirsch is a poet and critic whose books include* The People and the Books: 18 Classics of Jewish Literature. *He is an editor at* The Wall Street Journal.

Part of the power of the Haggada is that the things it tells us can change even as it stays exactly the same. Growing up, I listened every year to the words recited with the matza uncovered and the cup of wine held up: "And it is this that has stood for our ancestors and for us; since it is not one that has stood against us to destroy us, but rather in each generation, they stand against us to destroy us. But the Holy One, blessed be He, rescues us from their hand."

Yet until I was in my mid-20s, I was never stopped by the gravity of what these words meant. Maybe that was because the basic idea can be found everywhere in Jewish life. The rescue of the Jews by the parting of the Red Sea is a prototype for so many later skin-of-our-teeth escapes: the Jews of Persia on Purim, the Jews of Greek Judea on Hanukka, even the Jews of Israel in the Six Day War. American Jews of my generation grew up with these stories, but they remained stories – things we knew from books or testimonies, not first-hand.

The purpose of the Seder, however, is to convert history to memory, the third person to the first person. What does the father tell the son who doesn't know how to

*Remembering 9/11*

ask about the meaning of the Seder? He quotes Exodus 13: "And you shall explain to your child on that day, 'It is because of what the Lord did for me when I went free from Egypt.'" Only for the generation of the Exodus could this answer be literally true. For every Jew born since, it is a statement of identification and continuity, and the Haggada itself is one of Judaism's best technologies of continuity.

It was in 2002 that I went beyond understanding what the Haggada means by "those who stand against us" to feeling it as a personal reality. On the first night of Passover that year, Hamas carried out a suicide

bombing at ▶

the course of the next two centuries, millions – quite literally – of Native Americans were killed by the European settlers of the land, not only while repelling attacks but also, and overwhelmingly, for no morally defensible reason.

But knowing, and dwelling, on that fact doesn't mar in any way the wonderful democracy that we live in today. Quite the opposite. The "degradation" we note by acknowledging the flaw of some of the Europeans who settled the land, just like the idolatry at the beginning of the Jewish people, deserves our focus not only because it is true but because it can help us better appreciate how far our country has traveled.

And the same is true of other, more recent, "degradation" truths in the American national past, be they slavery and its defense over so many decades, the erstwhile popularity of the Ku Klux Klan, Jim Crow laws, the internment of tens of thousands of Japanese-Americans during World War II, or Vietnam-era atrocities like the My Lai massacre.

Sadly, these days, many in our country have become infected with a partisan "us vs. them" mentality and view the incorporation into educational curricula of regrettable facts of our nation's history as some sort of a betrayal of America.

But it is nothing of the sort. Truth cannot betray history. And the past's uncomfortable truths not only don't contradict an evolved, better present. They are precisely what allow us to most appreciate just where and what we are. ∎

the Newport synagogue in 1790 is a direct refutation of Haman's way of thinking: "The Government of the United States, which gives to bigotry no sanction, to persecution no assistance, requires only that they who live under its protection should demean themselves as good citizens, in giving it on all occasions their effectual support."

This pluralism has made America a good home not just for individual Jews, but for Judaism. For the late Rabbi Lord Jonathan Sacks, one of the important roles Judaism plays in the world is to demonstrate "the dignity of difference." In his book of that name, produced as a response to the 9/11 attacks, he wrote that "Judaism was born as a protest against…attempts to impose a single truth on a plural world."

Yet the freedom Jews have found in America also challenges one of the key assumptions of the Haggada. The recitation of the Exodus story begins by stating that all Jews are in the same situation as the Israelites in Egypt and need the same kind of redemption: "Now we are here, next year we will be in the Land of Israel; this year we are slaves, next year we will be free people." At most Seders over the last two thousand years, this would have been a statement of messianic hope: maybe this will finally be the year when the Temple is rebuilt and we are restored to the Promised Land.

But if American Jews are already free people, how can we feel like slaves? And if we aren't slaves, what kind of redemption is it that we look forward to on Passover? What does it mean to say, "Next year we will be in the Land of Israel," when nothing is stopping us from booking a flight there tomorrow? Today, the opportunity to ask and answer these questions is one of the most important gifts the Haggada can give us. ∎

*The Touro Synagogue in Newport*

bombing at a Seder in a Netanya hotel, killing 30 people and wounding 140 more. The attack seemed designed to show that "in each generation they stand against us to destroy us." What brought it especially close to me in and American values. In European countries where belonging depends on ethnicity or religion, Jews could only be outsiders, whether tolerated or despised. But the United States was founded on the idea that

> ## "The way Jews have thrived in America reveals a deep consonance between Jewish and American values."

New York was that this was the first Seder after the attacks of September 11, 2001, in which a different group of terrorists had killed a hundred times as many people. I was not directly endangered by either attack, but reading the passage suddenly felt suffocating.

That night, the Haggada helped me think in new ways about the blessing and challenge of being an American Jew. What makes this country different from all other Diaspora countries? For one thing, in no other time or place in Jewish history could it have taken me until adulthood to feel the shadow of "those who stood against us to destroy us." Think of all the Seders over the centuries that have taken place in watchful secrecy, in fear of blood libels or police spies. Only in America could Passover be publicly celebrated in the seat of government, as it was at the White House Seders held every year during Barack Obama's presidency.

The way Jews have thrived in America reveals a deep consonance between Jewish

as citizens we are individuals, not representatives of groups. All Americans are free to pursue happiness as they see fit, not as the majority or the State demands.

The common embrace of individual liberty by Americans and Jews also explains why the enemies of one are so often enemies of the other, as that Passover in 2002 showed so bloodily. Whatever their declared politics or goals, those who "stand against us to destroy us" have always seen difference as a danger and the toleration of difference as weakness. That was the logic Haman used to persuade Ahasuerus that the Jews were a threat to Persia: "There is a certain people, scattered and dispersed among the other peoples in all the provinces of your realm, whose laws are different from those of any other people and who do not obey the king's laws; and it is not in Your Majesty's interest to tolerate them."

In America, by contrast, difference is a blessing. George Washington's famous letter to

the Newport ▶

appealed particularly to Eastern European Jews who faced economic hardship and persistent antisemitism. And in the post-World War II period, Israel served as a haven for Holocaust refugees and then for Jews fleeing Arab countries. But American Jews have never emigrated en masse to the State of Israel, and their loyalty to the United States has shaped their relationship to Zionism from the beginning.

During the last century and a half, American Jews have navigated their American patriotism and their Zionism, articulating at least three distinct approaches to the relationship between the two: incompatibility, fundamental compatibility, and conditional compatibility.

Those who felt the relationship with America and modern Israel as incompatible saw the particularism of Jewish peoplehood as driving a wedge between Jews and other nationalities and cultures. Thus, the Reform Movement's Pittsburgh Platform of 1885 stated: "We consider ourselves no longer a nation, but a religious community, and therefore expect neither a return to Palestine, nor a sacrificial worship under the sons of Aaron, nor the restoration of any of the laws concerning the Jewish state."

Others argued both that America and Israel shared common values, and moreover, that particularistic loyalties make one a better American. Rather than worrying about dual loyalties, this position articulates a value in having compatible multiple loyalties. As Judge Louis Brandeis wrote in 1915: "A man

*Jacob's funeral, by James Jacques Tissot*

is a better citizen of the United States for being also a loyal citizen of his state, and of his city; for being loyal to his family, and to his profession or trade; for being loyal to his college or his lodge…"

Still other Jews emphasized the difference between the type of loyalty they have to America and the type of loyalty they have to Israel: Jews are politically loyal to the United States while they only pledge resources – economic, social and otherwise – to the (then emerging) State of Israel. Proponents of this approach often pointed out how important Israel could be as a safe haven for Jews from *other* countries rather than the United States, where Jews were fundamentally safe. AJC President Jacob Blaustein repeated this basic argument to Israeli Prime Minister David Ben Gurion in 1950.

By the end of the twentieth century, the compatibility model basically became the norm for American Jews. But what of the twenty-first?

Today there ▶

# "AND THEY VILIFIED US": NEGOTIATING MULTIPLE LOYALTIES
## Dr. Elana Stein Hain

*Dr. Elana Stein Hain is the Rosh Beit Midrash and a Senior Fellow at the Shalom Hartman Institute of North America.*

A well-worn antisemitic charge paints Jews as disloyal to their host countries in exile, stressing that they belong to a global people that longs for a return to the Land of Israel.

In fact, in the Torah itself, Pharaoh enslaves his Israelite subjects "lest they multiply and in the event of war, they may join our enemies and fight against us and leave the land (Ex. 1:10)." Some say this accusation is implied by Deuteronomy 26:6, read each year at the Seder, "*vayarei'u otanu haMitzrim vaya'annunu, vayittnu aleinu avoda kasha.*" Most translate this phrase as: "the Egyptians dealt harshly with us and oppressed us; they imposed heavy labor upon us."

*Pharaoh vilifies the Israelites.*

But the Netziv, Rabbi Naftali Zvi Yehuda Berlin (1816–1893), objected to this translation because the Hebrew does not say "they dealt harshly to, or, with us." Rather, the Netziv suggested the Hebrew means "the Egyptians vilified us." The Egyptians, he explained, painted the Israelites as a fifth column, accusing them of planning to ally with Egypt's enemies. Vilifying the Israelites was Egypt's foundational crime.

What was Pharaoh's justification for the accusation of the Israelites' disloyalty? Some posit that the charge emerged from the Israelites' well-known relationship to the land of Canaan. Contemporary scholar Dr. Brachi Elitzur points out that when Joseph asked permission from Pharaoh to bury Jacob in Canaan, Pharaoh sent along an Egyptian entourage (Gen. 50:4-9). Rather than reading this accompaniment as a sign of respect, Dr. Elitzur understands it as a means of guaranteeing that Joseph and his brothers would not betray Egypt by remaining in Canaan. The Torah also relates that the mourners left their cattle and their children back in Egypt, perhaps another assurance, required by the Egyptians, that they would return (Gen. 50: 7).

In modernity, Zionism continues to raise questions of loyalty for American Jews. Initially, the modern Zionist movement

appealed particularly ▶

# AN AMERICAN MOSES...AND JOSHUA
## Kylie Unell

*Kylie Unell is a podcaster, content creator and a Dean's Doctoral Fellow at NYU concentrating in Jewish philosophy. In 2021, she was named an "aspiring Jewish philosopher" by The New York Jewish Week in their annual 36 Under 36.*

History has come to know many different Moseses. Some only incidentally have the name Moses, while possessing both the name and, like the original, the ability to articulate a different future for a newly emancipated people. Moses Maimonides, the medieval Sephardic philosopher and rabbi, and Moses Mendelssohn, the eighteenth century German theologian who paved the way for Jewish integration into Western culture, were both credited by contemporaries as being the "Moses of their time."

Non-Jewish historical figures like Christopher Columbus, George Washington, and Harriet Tubman too were deemed the Moses of their eras.

But in a 1907 address delivered in Edinburgh, the industrialist Andrew Carnegie told his Scottish audience about the American Moses who had no parallel in any time. "Booker T. Washington," he lauded, "is the combined Moses and Joshua of his people. Not only has he led them to the Promised Land, but still lives to teach them by example and precept how properly to enjoy it.

*A statue of Maimonides in Córdoba, Spain*

He is one of these extraordinary men who rise at rare intervals and work miracles."

Born a slave in Virginia in 1856, Booker T. Washington was freed at the age of nine, two years after the Emancipation. At sixteen, Washington heard about a vocational school for Black students in West Virginia and made his way by foot to the Hampton Institute where he received an education that emphasized moral training alongside a practical, industrial education. Only a few years later, Washington was selected to head the Tuskegee Normal School, a newly-established vocational school established to educate Black students in Tuskegee, Alabama.

Washington literally ▶

Today there are new tensions around the compatibility between Americanness and Zionism: many American Jews wish to see Israel and America mirror each other politically. Those on the right in American politics see an Israel which reflects conservative politics and policies. Those on the left have split: some wish to see an Israel which reflects liberal politics and policies. Others have started to argue that Zionism is fundamentally incompatible with American progressive values. This leaves liberal Zionists feeling less confident about their own home within American politics, and it leaves Zionists on the right concerned for the future of the America-Israel relationship.

These trends demand serious reckoning and conversation. Some of the questions we need to ask ourselves include:

1. In what ways does trying to align American politics with Israeli politics help the State of Israel and in what ways does it harm the State of Israel?

2. How should communities navigate differences of opinion regarding Israel – its policies and its vision? What are the boundaries of acceptable disagreement within our own communities?

As the Israelites of old, we would be wise to consider how best to navigate our multiple commitments as Jews who do not live in Israel in ways that can continue to strengthen Jewish life – rather than divide us. ∎

> **"In modernity, Zionism continues to raise questions of loyalty for American Jews."**

upon visiting Washington's school that it was an anomaly in all of America. As he remarked to reporters after his visit: "I was astonished at the progressiveness in the schools. I don't believe there is a White industrial school in America or anywhere that compares to Mr. Washington's at Tuskegee." German American Jews felt a certain kinship for the man who was helping to uplift members of his community, much like the they were doing for the newly arriving Eastern European Jews.

Synagogues around America, particularly Reform temples, wanted to book the man dubbed the most influential Black leader and educator of his time for speaking engagements. Rosenwald's daughters, Gussie and Ethel Rosenwald, recalled one such occasion when Washington's presence at their temple, Chicago's Sinai Congregation, was so sought after that people were turned away: "The Temple this morning could not take care of the crowd that poured in, and as

thropists and businessmen Jacob Schiff, Paul Sachs (son of Samuel Sachs of Goldman Sachs), the Lehman brothers, Joseph Pulitzer, and Julius Rosenwald. Each joined the Board of Trustees (at different times) at Tuskegee after reading *Up From Slavery*.

Among Washington's connections with American Jews, his relationship with Julius Rosenwald stands out above the rest. Long before Rabbi Abraham Joshua Heschel and Dr. Martin Luther King Jr.'s friendship, Washington and Rosenwald forged one of the most important relationships in Black history. Rosenwald served on Tuskegee's Board of Trustees for twenty-one years, staying involved with the school well after Washington's death. But his commitment to Black education expanded beyond Tuskegee. Rosenwald and Washington carried out the most important initiative to advance Black education in the twentieth century. Together they built over 5,300 schoolhouses

> ## "Of all the minority groups in America, it was the Jews alone who Washington believed could sympathize with the Black experience."

many were turned away as were in the Temple and people had to sit on the platform."

The timing of his popularity was not coincidental. *Up From Slavery*, Washington's autobiography and the book for which he is best known, captivated the minds of many leaders of the community, including philan-

in the South that carried Washington's philosophy of pairing a vocational education with moral and intellectual development.

Washington may very well have been a Moses and a Joshua of his time. And American Jews played a crucial role in helping make manifest his vision of a Promised Land. ∎

*Booker T. Washington*

Washington literally and metaphorically built the school up from nothing. He came to a school that had no buildings or land and barely any funds. At the young age of twenty-five, with no leadership experience to speak of, he became responsible for building a school, raising the funds to sustain it, and creating the curriculum that would improve the lives of Blacks living in the South after the Civil War. He followed the example of his alma mater and developed a curriculum at Tuskegee built on pairing vocational education with moral and intellectual development to help Black southerners cultivate the character traits and skills he believed were necessary for achieving success in the racist and segregated South. His efforts at Tuskegee and unique approach caught the attention of America's wealthiest, including Carnegie. It also led to the development of a groundbreaking relationship between Washington and American Jews.

Of all the minority groups in America, it was the Jews alone who Washington believed could sympathize with the Black experience. "With the possible exception of the Jews," he once wrote, "no race has ever been subjected to criticisms so searching and candid, to state it mildly, as the Negroes." Washington deeply respected the resourcefulness he saw in the Jews. To him, the Jewish people were willing to work hard to become successful and committed to the process no matter how long it took. Through focusing on their skills and labor, Washington saw a people that ignored race-based contempt and focused on improving their lives and the lives of future generations. Many Jews felt the same way about Washington.

In the early twentieth century, Washington became immensely popular among Jewish Americans who had emigrated from Germany. His model for leadership and education was widely admired. American Jewish philanthropist Julius Rosenwald observed

*A history class conducted at Tuskegee Institute in 1902*

upon visiting ▶

something similar has happened in our lives, and we did not think to feel about it as our compatriot has. Public thanks attunes us to God's goodness.

A later commentator, the Gerrer Rebbe (R. Avraham Alter, d. 1948) has still another answer that touches on gratitude contagion. He teaches that to eat the entire sacrifice in one day suggests full confidence that there will be more the next day. And this is what one should feel about miracles in general.

Let us apply both of these teachings to *Dayeinu*. The first has Israel saying, in essence: "Had you created a public miracle, one the whole world would witness, it would have been enough." Such inspiration would have moved others to be grateful as well. The miracle, once public, would not have ended with the miracle. We acknowledge our gratitude thousands of years later because word of You back then endures today.

More powerfully, utilizing the Gerrer Rebbe's insight, *Dayeinu* reminds us of the proliferation of miracles, not all of them supernatural. "It would have been enough" because we are daily showered with other miracles. Given God's initial push, we would have made it through. As we say in the *Amida* of our daily prayers, "…for Your miracles which are daily with us."

This approach found its way into the very origins of our American nation. The Pilgrims, despite enormous hardships, instituted a holiday of thanksgiving. "That which was most sad and lamentable," Governor William Bradford later recalled, "was

*The first Thanksgiving*

that in ▶

# IS IT REALLY ENOUGH?
## Rabbi David Wolpe

*Rabbi David Wolpe is the Emeritus Rabbi of Sinai Temple in Los Angeles. His most recent book is David: The Divided Heart.*

"The food is terrible."

"Yes – and such small portions!"

The old Jewish joke reminds us of the paradox of desire – we want an ample supply even of things we aren't that fond of. The idea of *Dayeinu* – enough! – goes against the very grain of human nature. There is never enough. And the song itself amplifies the problem.

Children notice the difficulty with *Dayeinu* right away. "Had God divided the sea for us and not led us to dry land – it would have been enough." Wait – the fate of the Israelites standing on the seabed for eternity does not seem like a cause for thanksgiving. Would it really have been enough if God had stranded us? But the song is not done. "Had God led us across to dry land and not taken care of us for forty years in the desert, it would have been enough." Had God taken us out of Egypt, it would have been enough? Most assuredly not! Israel would have perished in the wilderness, without food, without water, without guidance. And we would never have received the Torah. How can we sing that it would have been sufficient had God chosen to withhold the Torah from Israel?

The parade of imponderables does not stop there. Had God done this, and not done that – brought us to Sinai and not given us the Torah…given us the Torah and not led us to enter Israel.… In other words, had God truncated the story, created Israel and then abandoned Israel, it would have been enough. The literal meaning of the song is clearly not what the song is teaching.

Let us look anew.

In Leviticus 7:15 there is a strange regulation. It says the thanksgiving offering "shall be eaten on the day that it is offered; none of it shall be set aside until morning."

Of all the sacrifices, why must the one that offers thanks be eaten that day? Why no leftovers?

The great Spanish biblical commentator Abravanel (1437-1508) has a beautiful answer, one amplified by the Netziv. Since the sacrifice entails a lot of food – not only an animal but four types of bread, and 10 breads of each type, 40 loaves in all, one person could not possibly consume it. Therefore, others will join. Thus an individual's expression of gratitude becomes a public celebration – and the miracle that occasioned the sacrifice is publicized.

This is the lesson of "gratitude contagion." When we hear about someone's good fortune and see that they are genuinely grateful, it helps us be grateful as well. Perhaps

something similar ▸

# LETTING THE DESTROYER LOOSE: A POLITICAL LESSON FROM THE FIRST PASSOVER

## Rabbi Mark Gottlieb

*Rabbi Mark Gottlieb is Senior Director of the Tikvah Fund.*

Take a bunch of hyssop, dip it in the blood that is in the basin, and apply some of the blood that is in the basin to the lintel [*mashkof*] and to the two doorposts [*mezuzot*]. None of you shall go outside the door of his house until morning. For when the Lord goes through to smite the Egyptians, He will see the blood on the lintel [*mashkof*] and the two doorposts [*mezuzot*], and the Lord will pass over the door and not let the Destroyer [*HaMashkhit*] enter and smite your home. (Ex. 12:22–23)

Among the more familiar details of this first Passover is the requirement of all Israelites to paint the lintels and doorways of their homes with the blood of the *korban Pesaḥ*, the Paschal offering. In the midst of the destruction waged upon Egypt with the death of their firstborn sons, God will see the blood on the Israelite homes and bypass their dwelling places, leaving them unharmed for the long-awaited Exodus on the dawn of the very next day. Additionally, the Israelites are not to leave their homes the night of the plague of the firstborn sons, perhaps out of concern that the *Mashkhit*, the Destroyer, will not discern innocent Israelite from guilty Egyptian.

*The drafting committee of the Declaration of Independence*

While the symbolic resonances of these requirements of the first Passover are powerful and well-known, upon closer examination they appear to the modern reader somewhat strange. Why does an omniscient God need a distinguishing mark of blood on the Israelite doorposts and lintels to direct Him to the proper destination to unleash His destructive forces? Similarly, what is the nature of the quarantine required of all Israelite homes? Would the Israelites somehow be in mortal danger by venturing out on that fateful night of wanton destruction? As if to address this concern, the Rabbis teach that once the powers of destruction are let loose, there is no real discernment between wicked and pure, guilty or innocent. In a more

naturalistic spirit ▸

that in two or three months' time, half of their company died, especially in January and February, being the depth of winter, and wanting houses and other comforts; being infected with the scurvy and other diseases.... There died sometimes two or three of a day." Yet Bradford also expressed a sense of thanksgiving, saying: "Thus out of small beginnings greater things have been produced by His hand that made all things of nothing, and gives being to all things that are; and, as one small candle may light a thousand, so the light here kindled hath shone unto many…"

Gratitude is the fundamental religious emotion, and it shaped the American consciousness. Entitlement and expectation are the opposite of gratitude. We do not ask for more, we say "*Dayeinu*," because we are so grateful for what we have been given. The first words a worshipper says upon waking in the morning are "*modeh ani*" –

we are grateful to You. When the *shaliaḥ tzibur*, the cantor, repeats the *Amida*, the one prayer the congregation must say on its own is *Modim*, the prayer for thanks. Each person must be thankful – no one else can express your gratitude for you.

*Dayeinu* is deeper than the literal meaning. It reminds us of the wonder of God's gifts, every single day. It insists that the world is showered with blessing, that we receive more than we merit, and even if we did not get this or that – *Dayeinu* – we are grateful and satisfied with the beneficence that is our life.

As we sit around the table on Passover, with food and family and history, we are grateful for the abundant blessings of our lives and our history. And we know we could have been grateful even with less. So we say to the One responsible for our blessings, *Dayeinu*. ∎

> ## "Gratitude is the fundamental religious emotion, and it shaped the American consciousness."

practically none of the off-battlefield savagery which we now assume to be inevitable in revolutions. There were no revolutionary tribunals dispensing "revolutionary justice;" there was no reign of terror; there were no bloodthirsty procla-

My heart is with you. My eye cannot have its fill of your flaming flag…And yet… And yet I have my fear for you. I fear the oppressed who are victorious lest they turn into oppressors…Is there not already talk among you that humanity must

> ## "The Jew must always remain above the revengeful rage that comes so naturally to humanity."

mations by the Continental Congress.… As Tocqueville later remarked, with only a little exaggeration, the [American] Revolution "contracted no alliance with the turbulent passions of anarchy, but its course was marked, on the contrary, by a love of order and law."

The Haggada is teaching us this "love of order and law," a way at odds with the conventional psychology of the newly-freed slave. God Himself will mete out the long-awaited justice to the Israelites' oppressors; the Jew must always remain above the revengeful rage and violent resentment that comes so naturally to humanity.

In 1914, in the midst of the bloody battles between Red and White Russian factions, the revered Yiddish writer and lifelong socialist Y.L. Peretz sent greetings on the occasion of an important workers' victory:

march like an army?… And yet humanity is not an army. With real joy I see you tear down the walls of Sodom. But my heart trembles lest you build on its ruins a new, worse Sodom – more cold, more gloomy!

Peretz's prescience was uncanny, as history would prove just a few years later. Perhaps in addition to whatever metaphysical force, whatever avenging angel, present on that first Passover, the Haggada is reminding us of another force of fury and rage, and a deep political truth – not in the sense of partisan politics like left and right, but in the perennial sense of what constitutes a life of human and societal flourishing. More damaging than anything occult or demonic is the force of destruction which lies within the heart of every human being wronged, persecuted, or oppressed. And once that destructive force is let loose, it can no longer discern between righteous and wicked, innocent and guilty. ∎

naturalistic spirit, it could be suggested that if the blood-stained lintel and door-posts are surely not necessary for God to distinguish between Egyptian and Israelite, perhaps they are intended not to keep the Destroyer out, but to keep the Israelites in, to prod them to some deeper realization as to why they should not venture out of doors that devastating night. More generally, what is the deeper meaning of the Destroyer and why should the Israelites remain indoors that night?

The late Rabbi Joseph B. Soloveitchik offered an original insight, as recounted in Rabbi Hershel Schachter's *Nefesh HaRav*. God, Rabbi Soloveitchik suggested, did not want the Israelites to leave their homes that night not because of any danger directed to them from a mysteriously indiscriminate and inhuman destructive force, but because, under these unique circumstances, the Israelites would be tempted to unleash their own destructive fury on the already besieged and debilitated Egyptians. In this historically-prescient reading, a reading Rabbi Soloveitchik calls *peshat*, contextually-driven or the simple meaning of the text, the Destroyer is not some supernatural force, an occult power designated by God to mete out unholy punishment to the Egyptians for their sins of oppression and genocide. Rather, it is the all-too-natural, all-too-human rage that the oppressed classes are likely to visit upon their oppressors when the tables are finally turned in their favor. The Torah is telling us not to indulge in that deadly comeuppance so

common in human history, the leveling of the field when rulers are toppled and former victims are given free rein to mete out their sense of justice. The Israelites must remain indoors, lest they indulge their (understandable from a human perspective) blood lust, visiting the pent-up furies of righteous indignation upon their hapless former rulers.

History has seen this form of mob justice and revolutionary rage play out in numerous settings, from the French and Haitian Revolutions of the eighteenth and nineteenth centuries to the Russian, Chinese, and Cambodian Revolutions of the twentieth century. Interestingly, this form of bloody revolution, of unbridled rage meted out on the once mighty but now vanquished, was largely absent from the American context. There are many reasons why this is so, but one might wonder whether the Israelite precedent of freedom without wanton revenge on one's previous rulers served as a model for the American Revolution. As the institution-building political thinker Irving Kristol observed in an essay in honor of America's Bicentennial, "The American Revolution as a Successful Revolution":

> The American Revolution was also successful in another important aspect: it was a mild and relatively bloodless revolution…there was none of the butchery which we have come to accept as a natural concomitant of revolutionary warfare. More important, there was

practically none ▶

233    ESSAYS

The ability to imagine is an essential part of our religious experience. We are called upon to use our personal experiences to access emotional relevance to ritual; without stories, stories that feel intimate, the ritual risks feeling irrelevant, distant, academic even. It is our secret hardships which help us understand what Egypt is, and it is jubilant victories which help us understand the crossing of the Sea.

But note what exactly we are being asked to imagine here, at this point of the Seder. Note that the text does not specify that we must empathize with either the oppression of slavery or the miracles of the Exodus.

Rather, what does the text ask us to imagine in our individual memories?

*Ke'ilu hu yatza miMitzrayim*. The leaving of Egypt. It is the process of leaving that we are commanded to tap into.

It is perhaps the journey, the exit, that matters most of all. Whether exile from the comforts of Egypt (and the Midrash tells us that it was, indeed, an exile from a plush existence), or the wandering in the desert, or our current Diaspora – all of this can be defined as exile.

And it is these experiences, of walking through a desert, barefoot, humbled, and uncertain, which can expand us as human beings. As the Russian-American poet Joseph Brodsky once wrote: "If there is anything good about exile, it is that it teaches one humility. It accelerates one's drift into isolation, an absolute perspective into the condition

*The Kremlin*

at which all one is left with is oneself and one's language, with nobody or nothing in between. Exile brings you overnight where it would normally take a lifetime to go."

Perhaps we are called upon to insert ourselves into the ancient Exodus narrative not only to marvel at God's greatness but also to examine, deeply, how the experience of exile changes us.

Perhaps then, and only then, once we recognize the good that difficult journeys offer us – only then can we go on to, in the words of Rabban Gamliel in the Haggada, to "thank, praise, laud, glorify, exalt, honor, bless, extol, and adore" our Redeemer. Only when we imagine that journey and recognize the good that even the painful experience offers us, only when we can see how exile improves us as individuals and as collectives – then, and only then, can we truly see the goodness of God, the ultimate Writer, and the Divine plot that is ever unfolding. ∎

# ON THE POWER OF IMAGINATION
## Avital Chizhik-Goldschmidt

*Avital Chizhik-Goldschmidt is a journalist living in New York City; her work has appeared in publications including The Atlantic, The New York Times, The New Republic, and Foreign Policy. She and her husband lead the Altneu Synagogue in Manhattan's Upper East Side.*

As schoolchildren, we used to paste a small circular mirror into our Haggada, smack in the middle of a childish illustration of the Exodus, right next to the words: *"Bekhol dor vador ḥayav adam lirot et atzmo ke'ilu hu yatza miMitzrayim,"* "In every generation a person must see themselves as if they left Egypt themselves."

The intention was that we should look into the mirror and see ourselves as if we, too, left Egypt. It was hard, perhaps, for the typical American Jewish kid growing up on the rolling green lawns of suburban New Jersey, that *goldene medina*, to imagine the life of a refugee, at least two degrees of separation away.

Yet that craft project always felt like a bit of a joke for me. I didn't need kitsch to remember exoduses. As a child of Soviet refugees who had left their Egypt in 1979, I found the refugee experience inescapable. Seders growing up were always, to my mind, an awkward collision of Sovietisms and my own burgeoning (and irritatingly self-righteous) American Orthodox Jewish

identity. At our table, the Haggada text was, in the first years, read in Russian, and then eventually in heavily accented English. My grandfathers would stand up and offer long toasts in Russian, addresses that seemed to belong more at a New Year's party and less at a *frum* ritual. No one knew how to sing the traditional songs – my parents would turn to me, the eldest child, the first American in the family, the first in yeshiva, to perform and to explain.

For years, I longed for the "right" kind of Seder – a litany of *divrei Torah* and of songs sung by the whole table. I dreamt of a Seder where the intergenerational transmission of tradition went from old to young, rather than from young to old, which was how I (rather arrogantly) saw our Seder. And the transposing of Soviet memory onto the text felt, at first, inauthentic. It was as if the towers of the Kremlin were blocking my view of the pyramids of Pithom and Raamses.

Little did I realize that this was, in fact, the embodiment of "In every generation a person must see themselves as if they left Egypt themselves." Little did I understand that those memories, those stories of oppression, antisemitism, hunger, taking place across the landscape of Kiev, Kharkov, and the steppes of northern Siberia – they were the ultimate fulfillment of the *ḥiyuv*, the obligation, to imagine.

The ability ▶

thirteenth-century Persian poet Rumi, in "Humble Living," writes, "When a man makes up a story for his child/he becomes a father and a child/ together, listening."

A powerful family story inspires, protects, shapes, and provides hope through life's troughs and challenges. Modern research has demonstrated that this kind of storytelling correlates with resilience in children. Contemporary master storyteller Bruce Feiler popularized these findings, articulating them through the presentation of three typical family narratives. The first, the ascending family narrative, boils down to "with every generation, we become more successful." The second, the descending family narrative, amounts to, "we had everything, but now we have nothing." The third is the oscillating narrative – "Good things happened to our family, then bad things, and then good things."

It is this last narrative of the ups and downs of a family history which is deemed the most healthy in building a resilient muscle in children. As Feiler writes in his essay, "The Stories that Bind Us," "The bottom line: if you want a happier family, create, refine and retell the story of your family's positive moments and your ability to bounce back from the difficult ones."

America has long embraced a historical narrative of ascent. We are the rags to riches country. This dream of streets paved with gold has inspired millions of immigrants to come here in search of better lives. Emma Lazarus's sonnet, "The New Colossus," greeted so many of our own ancestors by sea with this very sentiment: "Give me your tired, your poor/Your huddled masses yearning to breathe free/The wretched refuse of your teeming shore." And life was, indeed, better for so many in the United States. But this is not the full story. There is also loneliness and heartache in the immigrant story. There is anger and false hope. There are ups and downs.

What the Haggada offers us with its insertion of these three difficult verses is the emotional counterbalance to a happy ending; it's a not-so-gentle reminder that good times will end. Bad times are on the horizon, but we have the mettle and adaptability to manage them as well. The matza itself is an oscillating symbol, reflecting both slavery and freedom. Our oscillating narrative of transition is redemptive, to be sure, and also complicated because life is complicated. *Shefokh Hamatkha* reminds us that in the ever-developing story of our people – and of our own lives – we have the resilience to manage the bad times and will always cycle out of them towards better days. ∎

## "A powerful family story inspires, protects, shapes, and provides hope."

# "POUR OUT YOUR WRATH" AND THE POWER OF STORYTELLING

## Dr. Erica Brown

*Dr. Erica Brown is the Vice Provost for Values and Leadership at Yeshiva University and the founding Director of its Rabbi Lord Jonathan Sacks-Herenstein Center for Values and Leadership.*

After the first half of Hallel and the meal, when we are about to sing songs of victory and joy, we open the door for Elijah and suddenly read *Shefokh Ḥamatkha*, three biblical verses that are strung together in an attempt to invoke God's revenge against our enemies. Each year the recitation blindsides us emotionally. Everything was moving upwards in a positive direction in the Exodus narration, and now we are reminded once again that evil and hatred persist.

Some contemporary Haggadot have actually scrubbed these three verses or changed them to avoid their "negative" messaging. However, this reflects a failure to understand the intentional and important placement, which takes us to the beginning of the Haggada. Once the Passover table is laden with all of the story-provoking foods, we are given the imperative "to tell" that emerges from four separate verses:

> When in time your children ask you… (Deut. 6:20)

> And when your children ask you, 'What do you mean by this rite?' you shall say… (Ex. 12:26)

> And you shall explain to your son on that day… (Ex. 13:8)

> And when, in time to come, your son asks you… (Ex. 13:14)

Storytelling is subjective. The Haggada offers one script. Yet we are advised to go off-script and elaborate. "*Vekhol hamarbeh meshubakh*," "Everyone who discusses the Exodus from Egypt at length is praiseworthy." The very telling of an oscillating narrative also shapes the storyteller. The

thirteenth-century ▶

meanwhile, an exalted portion of his spirit, and his mantle, to an Adams."

A fellow Philadelphian preacher, William Rogers, offered a similar message on February 22, 1800, referring to Adams as being "Like Elisha of Old…may he possess a double portion of the Spirit and virtues of his once intimate – affectionate – but now entombed friend!"

To these preachers, Washington, like Elijah, was a wonderworking figure beyond time. His legacy unperishable, he left behind a national moral compass to be followed by future generations.

Despite preachers' politics, Thomas Jefferson defeated Adams in the election of 1800.

Yet Elijah would remain. In an 1817 letter from Adams to Jefferson regarding the recently defeated Napoleon, Adams evoked the prophet in a critique of the French emperor. "A Whirlwind raised him and a Whirlwind blowed him a Way to St Helena," Adams wrote. "He is very confident that the Age of Reason is not past; and So am I; but I hope that Reason will never again rashly and hastily create Such Creatures as him." In 1865, the Italian artist Constantino Brumidi rendered a fresco that adorns the United States Capitol building. In it, Washington is sitting amid the clouds of heaven. Titled "The Apotheosis of Washington," it depicts America's first president being carried by a whirlwind.

*Washington being carried away on a whirlwind in a scene from Constantino Brumidi's "The Apotheosis of Washingon"*

Every Elijah ▶

# AMERICA'S FAVORITE PROPHET
## Rabbi Dr. Stuart Halpern

*Rabbi Dr. Stuart Halpern is Senior Advisor to the Provost and Deputy Director of the Zahava and Moshael Straus Program for Torah and Western Thought at Yeshiva University. This essay originally appeared in Tablet and is adapted with permission.*

Everyone's favorite Passover guest is a ghost.

In one of the Seder's most mystical moments, we pour a glass for Elijah – that mysterious ancient prophet whose arrival will signify the messianic redemption. And we open the door for his anticipated entrance.

For those who might need a refresher on Elijah's biblical backstory, the book of Kings describes how this native of Gilead, circa 900 BCE, had the ability to declare famine, resuscitate dead children, outshine and then slaughter 450 prophets of Ba'al in a game of "who worships the real true God?," rebuke the wicked King Ahab, hear God's "still small voice" (per the King James Version rendering of I Kings 19:12) on a mountain after despairing of his ability to inspire his fellow Israelites to repent, and mentor his successor Elisha before ascending to heaven in a chariot amid a whirlwind. His eventual return, the tradition goes, will come when the world is to be redeemed.

While Jews think about Elijah primarily

at Passover, he's actually been a fixture of American political culture from the very beginning – not only at Passover, and not even only for Jews.

Upon George Washington's death on December 14, 1799, the Pennsylvanian priest Samuel Magaw offered a sermon titled, "An Oration Commemorative of the Virtues and Greatness of General Washington." In it, Magaw invoked Elijah both to praise the president's virtues as everlasting – and to signal the preacher's own political support for John Adams as the bearer of Washington's mantle in the election of 1800. He sermonized:

> Consolation is that your venerable Chief is not to be considered as moldering in dust, and gone forever – but, gone a little before, assuredly invested with a life unperishable…as the sage Franklin expressed, on a valuable friend's decease…. "His carriage was first ready, and he is gone before us. We could not all conveniently start together; and why should you and I be grieved at this, since we are soon to follow, and we know where to find him." – He hath gone before you! He hath ascended like Elijah, in his triumphal car, and bids us follow.

Reassuring his flock that their leader had appointed a worthy successor as Elijah had appointed Elisha before ascending to heaven, Magaw continued: "He hath left,

meanwhile, an ►

*If you get there before I do*
*Comin' for to carry me home*
*Tell all my friends that I'm a-comin' too.*

During and after Reconstruction, Elijah kept coming, sipping from the cup of liberation. Francis James Grimke, one of the leading African American clergy until his death in 1937, in a sermon in 1900, compared Elijah's efforts to steer Israel back toward its God to America's need to morally repent. "For years he had labored hard for the reformation of his countrymen," Grimke preached. "He saw the people rushing headlong into idolatry and every form of wickedness and under the direction and inspiration of the Almighty, he threw himself with all the energy and impetuosity of his nature into the work of reforming them."

In 1909, William Jennings Bryan, later to become secretary of state, also evoked Elijah as a symbol of American courage. Addressing the Northwestern Law School banquet, he told the assembled: "We need more Elijahs in the pulpit today – more men who will dare to upbraid an Ahab and defy a Jezebel."

American politicians continue to evoke Elijah today. In 2019, Hillary Clinton eulogized Congressman and civil rights advocate Elijah Cummings as having, like his biblical namesake, "weathered storms and earthquakes but never lost his faith" as he "raised the next generation of leaders" and "even worked a few miracles." With the road towards social equality taking longer than

*Elijah Cummings*

hoped, it was the harshness of Elijah's moral rebuke that was hearkened to.

The 21st century's self-help ethos has also enlisted Elijah. In her 2013 commencement address at Harvard, Oprah Winfrey told the graduates, "If you're willing to listen to, be guided by, that still small voice that is the GPS within yourself – to find out what makes you come alive – you will be more than OK. You will be happy."

Jews aren't the only ones, American history has shown, who have been looking for Elijah with expectant eyes. A harbinger of hope, a rebuker of the unrighteous, a hearer of stillness amid fractured times, the Seder night's specter continues to visit, stirring Americans to perceive in his cup their own redemptive possibilities. ∎

Every Elijah needs his King Ahab – his nemesis – and Washington's was England's King George III. Thus Charleston's John Lewis delivered a sermon titled "Naboth's Vineyard" in 1777. Just as Ahab had unlawfully seized the vineyard of and killed an innocent man in I Kings 21 at the urging of his wife Jezebel, Lewis argued, the British crown was unjustly stealing colonists' property for personal gain. It was up to General Washington to offer George III's army an Elijah-style rebuke in the manner of 21:19's "hast thou killed and also taken possession?"

In America's earliest decades then, it was Elijah to whom Americans turned in referencing a peerless figure of political ambition, fortitude, and lasting civic influence.

Fernando Wood. Urging him to make peace with the South, Wood referenced I Kings 19:12 when he wrote: "your Inaugural address… pointed out with prophetic vision…that after a bloody and terrible struggle 'the still small voice of reason' would intervene and settle the controversy." Frederick Douglass had earlier praised the British emancipation of West Indies as having come "not by the sword, but by the word; not by the brute force of numbers, but by the still small voice of truth." The former slave, Wallace Willis, also saw in Elijah the hope for a more tranquil and unified polity, as Daniel Matt notes in his recent biography of the biblical figure. Willis's spiritual "Swing Low, Sweet Chariot" is a lyrical interpretation of the prophet's ascension.

> # "In America's earliest decades then, it was Elijah to whom Americans turned."

Antebellum America was also visited by Elijah. In 1854, Congress passed the Kansas-Nebraska Act, repealing the Missouri Compromise. As historian Mark Noll notes in *America's Book: The Rise and Decline of a Bible Civilization*, President Franklin Pierce, who supported the South on this issue, was criticized as a "latter day Ahab, deaf to the warnings of his Elijahs, the anti-Nebraska clergy." Abraham Lincoln, too, encountered Elijah – in the form of a letter from the former mayor of New York,

To these advocates for national unity, it wasn't Elijah's fiery wonder-working whirlwind riding that resonated. It was his having heard God's quietly rendered call. Perhaps, they hoped, this tranquil Divine uttering might usher in a more united United States.

*I'm sometimes up, and I'm sometimes down*
*Comin' for to carry me home*
*But I know my soul is heavenly bound*
*Comin' for to carry me home…*

If you ▶

the Maxwell House Haggada of 1932, by far the most widely-distributed Haggada in history, likewise looked to God to "grant us to be in Jerusalem." By then, the Zionist Organization of America, Hadassah, and many other Jewish organizations were laboring mightily to rebuild a Jewish homeland in the Land of Israel. Still, the idea that Jews might someday return to Jerusalem of their own free will found no support in any American translation of the Haggada.

Theodor Herzl had long before insisted that Jews *should* voluntarily return to the Land of Israel. His *Der Judenstaat*, published in English translation in 1904, specifically linked the idea of a Jewish state to the "kingly dream" embodied in the "old phrase, 'Next year in Jerusalem.'" He challenged readers to seize the opportunity, "to prove that the dream may be converted into a living reality." When he famously declared, "if you will it, it is no dream," the "it" referred to "next year in Jerusalem." Herzl thus transformed "next year in Jerusalem" from a dream into a manifesto. Rather than concealing the hope that long underlay the exclamation, "*leshana haba'a biYerushalayim*," he and his followers transvalued the "old phrase" into a catch phrase, a pithy statement of Zionism's goals.

In 1934, a young Zionist historian in England, Cecil Roth, finally broke the taboo against "next year in Jerusalem" and embraced the "living reality" that Herzl had anticipated. He daringly published the four forbidden words "NEXT YEAR IN JERUSALEM" in capital letters, accompanied by an illustration of ḥalutzim, Zionist pioneers, in his popular Haggada issued by London's Soncino Press. The Zionist writer, translator and intellectual, Maurice Samuel, followed suit in 1942 in his popular Haggada, the first time an American publisher broke the longstanding taboo. By then, the battle against Nazism and the plight of hundreds of thousands of Jewish refugees whom no country in the world would consent to rescue, persuaded Jews and non-Jews alike in the United States that the Jewish people needed a homeland of their own. Where "next year in Jerusalem" had once reflected age-old hopes for the rebuilding of the Temple, now it became an urgent necessity, a matter of life and death.

Against this background, David and Tamar de Sola Pools' Haggada "for Members of the Armed Forces" takes on heightened significance. It made clear that praying for a return to Zion was in no way inconsistent with American patriotism; even soldiers could safely embrace Zionism's goals. The Pools' opening message echoed the paeans to liberty and freedom that were commonplace

"So long as Israel cherishes the Haggada, freedom will not die."

during World ▶

# NEXT YEAR IN JERUSALEM
## Dr. Jonathan D. Sarna

*President Barack Obama holds a Passover Seder using the Maxwell House Haggada*

*Dr. Jonathan D. Sarna is University Professor and the Joseph H. & Belle R. Braun Professor of American Jewish History at Brandeis University, as well as Chief Historian of the Weitzman National Museum of American Jewish History in Philadelphia.*

During World War II, hundreds of thousands of Jewish soldiers received a small paper-covered Haggada funded by the United States government, printed on the press of the Jewish Publication Society and distributed by the National Jewish Welfare Board. Edited by Rabbi David de Sola Pool, esteemed rabbi of America's oldest congregation, the Spanish and Portuguese Synagogue in New York (Shearith Israel), along with his learned wife, Tamar, a leader of Hadassah, the Haggada "for Members of the Armed Forces" linked the Passover story to the battle against the Nazis. "The Passover Festival of Freedom," it declared, "has never been observed more poignantly than today, when we are struggling to preserve freedom." The Haggada included the Hebrew words for the Zionist anthem, "*Hatikva*," along with the words of "The Star-Spangled Banner" and "America." In addition, the narrative portion of the Haggada concluded with the traditional exclamation "*leshana haba'a biYerushalayim*," translated, in most printings, as "Next year in Jerusalem!"

Prior to the 1940s, Hebrew-English Haggadot published in the United States, even if they included in Hebrew the three words "*leshana haba'a biYerushalayim*," carefully eschewed this familiar English equivalent. A strict taboo surrounded "Next Year in Jerusalem," for nobody wanted to provide fodder for antisemites or arouse suspicions of Jewish disloyalty. Instead, Jews generally employed clumsy translations that underscored the Divine role in returning Jews to Jerusalem. The widely emulated first American Haggada of 1837 employed the translation, "The year that approaches, O bring us to Jerusalem." Placing the onus upon God ("O bring us") calmed fears that Jews might prefer Jerusalem to wherever they lived in the United States. Almost a century later,

the Maxwell ▶

# FOR FURTHER READING

For more on the Passover story's impact on America, we recommend the following works that inspired this Haggada:

Michael Walzer, *Exodus and Revolution*

Eric Nelson, *The Hebrew Republic: Jewish Sources and the Transe formation of European Political Thought*

Eran Shalev, *American Zion: The Old Testament as a Political Text from the Revolution to the Civil War*

John Coffey, *Exodus and Liberation: Deliverance Politics from John Calvin to Martin Luther King Jr.*

James P. Byrd, *Sacred Scripture, Sacred War: The Bible and the American Revolution*

James P. Byrd, *A Holy Baptism of Fire and Blood: The Bible and the American Civil War*

Meir Y. Soloveichik, Matthew Holbreich, Jonathan Silver and Stuart W. Halpern (eds.), *Proclaim Liberty Throughout the Land: The Hebrew Bible in the United States – A Source Reader*

during World War II: "Though dictatorships may rise up intent on burying human liberty, so long as Israel cherishes the Haggada of Passover, freedom will not die from the world." At the same time, their translation exuded an unapologetic yearning for Zion, literally from the beginning of the Maggid narration ("next year may we be in the Land of Israel") to the closing lines of *ḥasal siddur Pesaḥ* ("Oh, be thy people redeemed in our time/In freedom to sing and Zion to build").

Earlier American Jewish translations, like the Maxwell House Haggada, obscured most Zionistic references; the Pools gloried in them. In the hymn, "And It Came to Pass at Midnight," for example, the Maxwell House translated the concluding lines enigmatically: "Appoint watchmen to thy city (Jerusalem) all day and all night. Illuminate, as with the light of day, the darkness of our night." The forthright Pool translation, by contrast, read: "In Zion rebuilt and secure set watch. May darkness of exile now yield to light."

The Pools' decision to include *Hatikva* in their Haggada, as well as their use of the translation "Next Year in Jerusalem" and other Zionist renderings, conveyed an important lesson to Jewish members of the armed forces – one that bore the imprimatur of the National Jewish Welfare Board and, implicitly, of the United States military. It provided reassurance that fighting for liberty and freedom as soldiers of the United States of America and rebuilding a secure Jewish state in the Land of Israel were thoroughly compatible goals. Whenever I see *"leshana haba'a biYerushalayim"* translated in a contemporary Haggada as "Next year in Jerusalem," I recall that lesson. ∎

Wikimedia Commons; page 62, Joseph and brothers, the Providence Lithograph Company, public domain, via Wikimedia Commons; page 63, Albert Murray, © Photo by Chris Felver / Getty Images; page 64, Reagan, public domain, via Wikimedia Commons; page 65, Concord Bridge, The National Guard, public domain, via Wikimedia Commons; page 68, Ship, Fred Pansing (1844–1912), public domain, via Wikimedia Commons; page 69, Melville, Joseph Oriel Eaton, public domain, via Wikimedia Commons; page 70, Martin Luther King Jr., Library of Congress NKR; page 71, Entering Israel, the Providence Lithograph Company, public domain, via Wikimedia Commons; pages 72-73, Building in Egypt, public domain; page 74, Ten Commandments, Aron de Chaves \ de Chavez (painter at Amsterdam in 1700), public domain, via Wikimedia Commons; page 75, Einhorn, unknown, this upload by Concord, public domain, via Wikimedia Commons; page 76, Pharaoh, James Tissot, public domain, via Wikimedia Commons; page 77, Joseph in Egypt, Jewish Museum, public domain, via Wikimedia Commons; page 78, Slaves, William Clark, CC0, via Wikimedia Commons; page 79, Jubilee singers, public domain, via Wikimedia Commons; page 79, Slave ship, P. Oursel, public domain, via Wikimedia Commons; page 80, Grimke, public domain, via Wikimedia Commons; page 81, Pharaoh and midwives, James Tissot, public domain, via Wikimedia Commons; page 82, Pharaoh, James Tissot, public domain, via Wikimedia Commons; page 83, Firstborn sign, James Tissot, public domain, via Wikimedia Commons; page 84, Leaving Egypt, David Roberts, public domain, via Wikimedia Commons; page 85, Higginson, public domain, via Wikimedia Commons; page 85, Prosser,

Schomburg Center for Research in Black Culture, Photographs and Prints Division, The New York Public Library; page 86, Locusts, James Tissot, public domain, via Wikimedia Commons; page 87, Blood, James Tissot, public domain, via Wikimedia Commons; page 89, Washington, Gilbert Stuart, public domain, via Wikimedia Commons; page 95, Chandler, Unknown author, perhaps commissioned by Benjamin Lundy, public domain, via Wikimedia Commons; page 96, Washington, Junius Brutus Stearns, public domain, via Wikimedia Commons; page 100, Solomon, Salomon de Bray, public domain, via Wikimedia Commons; page 100, Torah, HOWI – Horsch, Willy, CC BY-SA 4.0, via Wikimedia Commons; page 101, Manna, James Tissot, public domain, via Wikimedia Commons; page 101, Kiddush cup, Flickr / CC BY-SA 2.0, Shalom Gurewicz; page 102, Pharaoh's army, Frederick Arthur Bridgman, public domain, via Wikimedia Commons; page 103, Declaration of Independence, Jean Leon Gerome Ferris, public domain, via Wikimedia Commons; page 103, Seal, Benson John Lossing, public domain, via Wikimedia Commons; page 104, Jefferson, Rembrandt Peale, public domain, via Wikimedia Commons; page 107, Bush, White House photo by Eric Draper, public domain, via Wikimedia Commons; page 108, Burgoyne, John Trumbull, public domain, via Wikimedia Commons; page 108, Rush, Charles Willson Peale, public domain, via Wikimedia Commons; page 113, Clark, United States Army Signal Corps, public domain, via Wikimedia Commons; page 113, Army Seder, public domain / Flickr NKR; page 117, Douglass, Courtesy of The Miriam and Ira D. Wallach Division of Art, Prints and Photographs: Print Collection, The New York Public Library. Frederick Douglass;

# IMAGE CREDITS

Page 6, Moon, Bill Anders, public domain, via Wikimedia Commons; page 7, Apollo 8, NASA, public domain, via Wikimedia Commons; page 7, Liftoff, NASA, public domain, via Wikimedia Commons; page 9, Washing cup, CC BY-SA 2.5 http://hadadbros.com/; page 10, Civil War, © ClassicStock / Alamy Stock Photo; page 11, Forest, © Metropolitan Museum of Art / Gilman Collection, Purchase, The Horace W. Goldsmith Foundation Gift, through Joyce and Robert Menschel, 2005; page 12, Mordecai Manuel Noah, Library of Congress, public domain, via Wikimedia Commons; page 18, Boston Tea Party, Nathaniel Currier, public domain, via Wikimedia Commons; page 19, Adams, © National Gallery of Art / Gift of Mrs. Robert Homans; page 20, White House Seder, © GM/Current Affairs / Alamy Stock Photo; page 20, Abolition, Library of Congress NKR; page 21, Portrayal Black slavery, Library of Congress NKR; pages 22-23, Rabbis, Created by AI; page 24, Wildnerness, CC BY-SA 1.0 / Wellcome Collection 37108ip; page 25, Congress voting, public domain / Historical Society of Pennsylvania, via Explore PA History; page 26, Higginson, Library of Congress NKR; page 26, Soldiers, Library of Congress NKR; page 27, Moon, Freepik; pages 28-29, Four sons, Created by AI; page 30, Torah, Lawrie Cate, CC BY 2.0, via Wikimedia Commons; page 31, Mendes Seixas, CC BY-SA 4.0, via Wikimedia Commons; page 34, Battle Lexington, © National Army Museum; page 35, Paine, Courtesy of The Miriam and Ira D. Wallach Division of Art, Prints and Photographs: Print Collection, The New York Public Library; page 35, King George III, Allan Ramsay, public domain, via Wikimedia Commons; page 36, Carigal, © Yale University Art Gallery / Gift of Ann Jenkins Prouty; page 36, Stiles, © Yale University Art Gallery / Bequest of Dr. Charles Jenkins Foote, B.A. 1883, M.D. 1890; page 38, Euphrates, © A.D. Riddle / BiblePlaces.com; page 41, Underground Railroad, Photographer: Horatio Seymour Squyer, 1848–18, Dec. 1905, public domain, via Wikimedia Commons; page 44, Battle of Antietam, Library of Congress NKR; page 45, Lincoln, Library of Congress NKR; page 46, Sojourner Truth, Courtesy of Schomburg Center for Research in Black Culture, Photographs and Prints Division, The New York Public Library; page 47, Coffin, public domain CC0 / Lynn Greyling; page 50, Mount Sinai, Created by AI; page 51, Truman, National Archives at College Park, public domain, via Wikimedia Commons; page 51, US Soldiers, photo courtesy of New York National Guard; page 52, Nicholas Street, Collection of the New-York Historical Society; page 53, Surrender, John Trumbull, public domain, via Wikimedia Commons; page 56, Soviet Jewry rally, © Associated Press; page 57, Sharansky, © Government Press Office / Nati Harnik; page 58, Civil rights, photo courtesy of Schomburg Center for Research in Black Culture, Photographs and Prints Division, The New York Public Library; page 58, Johnson, public domain, via Wikimedia Commons; page 60, Seder plate, RCB **, CC BY 2.0, via Wikimedia Commons; page 61, Elijah chair, Musée d'Art et d'Histoire du Judaïsme, CC BY-SA 4.0 <https://creativecommons.org/licenses/by-sa/4.0>, via

Congress, NKR; page 227, Booker T. Washington, Library of Congress, Prints & Photographs Division, photograph by Harris & Ewing; page 228, Thanksgiving, Library of Congress, NKR; page 230, Declaration of Independence, Library of Congress, NKR; page 238, Capitol ceiling, © Danita Delimont / Alamy Stock Photo; page 240, Cummings, U.S. Congress, public domain, via Wikimedia Commons; page 243, EPLACE, Obama Seder, © WDC Photos / Alamy Stock Photo; page 245, Jerusalem sunset, © Jason Busa – stock. adobe.com; page 252, Halpern, © Yeshiva University. [NKR = No Known Rights]

pages xi-x, 2, 3, 4, 5, 8, 9, 12, 13, 14–15, 16–17, 31, 32, 33, 37, 39, 30, 31, 32, 33, 37, 39, 40, 41, 42–43, 48, 49, 54–55, 59, 60, 66–67, 86, 87, 88, 90, 91, 92–93, 94, 97, 98, 99, 100, 101, 105, 106, 109, 110, 111, 112, 114–15, 116, 118–19, 122, 123, 126–27, 130, 132, 133, 134, 135–36, 127, 138, 139–40, 141, 142, 143, 146–51, 153, 154, 156–57, 158, 159, 160, 161, 162, 163, 168, 169, 172–73, 184–85, 190, 191, 194, 195, 197, 200, 218, 234, 237 – www.freepik.com

page 120, Bradford, Library of Congress NKR; page 121, Thanksgiving, Jean Leon Gerome Ferris, public domain, via Wikimedia Commons; page 122, Washing cup, http://hadadbros.com/, CC BY-SA 2.5 IL, via Wikimedia Commons; page 124, Liberated from Dachau, public domain, via Wikimedia Commons; page 125, Patton, public domain, via Wikimedia Commons; page 125, Manischewitz, © Underwood Archives, Inc. / Alamy Stock Photo; page 128, Warren, John Singleton Copley, public domain, via Wikimedia Commons; page 129, Rekhmire, Courtesy of General Research Division, The New York Public Library (1849–1856). Neues Reich. Dynastie XVIII. Theben [Thebes]: aus einem Grabe von Abu el Qurna; page 139, Soldier, Israel Defense Forces, CC BY-SA 2.0, via Wikimedia Commons; page 144, US soldiers, © History collection 2016 / Alamy Stock Photo; page 145, McNary, Henrique Medina, public domain, via Wikimedia Commons; page 152, Lazarus, T. Johnson and W. Kurtz, public domain, via Wikimedia Commons; page 155, Inauguration, Ramon de Elorriaga, public domain, via Wikimedia Commons; page 164, Civil rights, © American Photo Archive / Alamy Stock Photo; page 165, Heschel and King, Library of Congress NKR; page 165, Selma, Library of Congress NKR; page 166-67, Kotel, CC BY-SA 3.0, Willschmut; page 170, Moore, National Gallery of Ireland, public domain, via Wikimedia Commons; page 171, Songs of Joy, James Tissot, public domain, via Wikimedia Commons; page 174, Lincoln, Library of Congress NKR; page 175, Mt. Nebo, Osama Shukir Muhammed Amin FRCP (Glasg), CC BY-SA 4.0, via Wikimedia Commons; page 176, Sisera, James Tissot, public domain, via Wikimedia Commons; page 177, Sennacherib, Timo Roller, CC BY 3.0, via Wikimedia Commons; page 178, Fest, Jan Lievens, public domain, via Wikimedia Commons; page 179, Witherspoon, Courtesy of The Miriam and Ira D. Wallach Division of Art, Prints and Photographs: Print Collection, The New York Public Library (1868–1869). John Witherspoon; page 180, Abraham, James Tissot, public domain, via Wikimedia Commons; page 181, Watchmen, public domain, Wikiwand; page 182, Belshazzar, Rembrandt, public domain, via Wikimedia Commons; page 183, Jericho, public domain, Zacwill; page 186-87, Solomon, Salomon de Bray, public domain, via Wikimedia Commons; page 188, Independence Hall, Wade Dunn Jr., CC BY-SA 4.0, via Wikimedia Commons; page 189, Lincoln, Library of Congress NKR; page 190, Ten Commandments, © IanDagnall Computing / Alamy Stock Photo; page 192-93, Stained glass, CC BY-SA 3.0, Djampa; page 196, Twain, A.F. Bradley, New York, public domain, via Wikimedia Commons; page 203, Iron Dome, IDF Spokesperson's Unit; page 204, March, "US Government Photo," public domain, via Wikimedia Commons; page 206, King Jr, © Dom Slike / Alamy Stock Photo; page 208, Lee, Thomas Nast, public domain, via Wikimedia Commons; page 211, Stanton, Library of Congress NKR; page 212, Lincoln, public domain / Adam Cuerden; page 215, Freed women, Agostino Brunias, public domain, via Wikimedia Commons; page 217, Pilgrims, uncredited, public domain, via Wikimedia Commons; page 220, Touro, Kenneth C. Zirkel, CC BY-SA 4.0, via Wikimedia Commons; page 222, Jacob's funeral, public domain, Dauster; page 223, Pharaoh, James Tissot, public domain, via Wikimedia Commons; page 224, Maimonides, Lmbuga (Luis Miguel Bugallo Sánchez), CC BY-SA 4.0, via Wikimedia Commons; page 227, Tuskegee, Library of

suggested working with Rabbi Dr. Stuart Halpern. Stu, your insights, perspective and encyclopedic knowledge are reflected throughout this Haggada. You are a master educator and expert in this field from whom I have learned so much.

On behalf of my wife and myself, this Haggada is dedicated to our parents: Barbara and George Hanus, and Arlene and Moshe Kupietzky. One of the main goals of the Seder is והגדת לבנך, to teach your children. For us, our parents exemplify this *midda*. In their respective communities they have demonstrated the importance of Jewish values, education and community leadership. Through their love, devotion and dedication to our family, we have seen the blueprint on parenting and have a model for our lives. Our family has benefited in so many ways from you and love and appreciate all that you continue to teach us.

To my wife's grandmother, Mrs. Magda Hanus, your elegance and commitment to family elevates all our lives and reminds us of the miracles seen and unseen.

To our siblings, nieces and nephews, you have enhanced our Pesaḥs and enriched our lives.

To Joshua, Kayla, and Zachary, our amazing and wonderful children, this Haggada was inspired by you and created with you in mind. Your astute questions, clever interpretations, and lively debate complemented our Seders and helped identify a need. You are our greatest pride and joy. We are thankful to Hashem for each of you and love you very much.

My ultimate appreciation goes to my wife, Edy, whose love, patience, and partnership have impacted me in ways both big and small. You have made a wonderful life for us, filled with love and laughter. It is only because of your encouragement and constant support that this Haggada was able to be realized. Thank you.

Jacob Kupietzky

# ACKNOWLEDGMENTS

Pesaḥ 2020, held without additional family members due to the pandemic, created an opportunity to lead the Seder for the first time. Trying to follow the examples of our parents, who had hosted us in alternate years and led our Seders with substantial preparation, precision, and order, my wife and I endeavored to provide an interactive, discussion-oriented Seder where all could contribute and play a significant role. Recognizing our children's fascination with US history and the popularity of the musical *Hamilton*, our Seder attempted to connect the US experience to the Pesaḥ story. Through the preparation and the actual Seders an opportunity for a unique Haggada presented itself and thus became the inspiration for *The Promise of Liberty*.

Children today are exposed to a wide range of material at their fingertips, and they are used to immediate answers through the internet, social media and other mediums. The Seder by design requires a more thoughtful and deliberate experience that connects each individual Jew to a story that happened three thousand years earlier. In light of the temporal and geographic distance, for Jewish Americans, how can the story remain relevant? The last number of years have brought about a rapid increase in antisemitism across our country, prompting us to pause and take stock of our place today and more so, our part in American history. The Seder is the perfect time to reflect and recognize the integral role our faith and practice have played in inspiring America. From the colonists and the framers to civil rights leaders and modern-day government officials, the values and lessons of the Jewish story as a whole, and the Passover story in particular, have left and continue to make an indelible impression on the mosaic of American life. *The Promise of Liberty* attempts to showcase that impact and prompt new and meaningful discussions around the Seder table.

This Haggada is the result of many people who merit specific recognition. When this project was conceived, it was my close friend Rabbi Dr. Yosie Levine who helped strategize and

RABBI DR. STUART HALPERN serves as the Senior Advisor to the Provost and Deputy Director of the Straus Center for Torah and Western Thought at Yeshiva University. He has edited eighteen books, including *Proclaim Liberty Throughout the Land: The Hebrew Bible in the United States* and *Esther in America*. His writing on the Hebrew Bible's impact on the United States has appeared in *The Wall Street Journal*, *Newsweek*, *Tablet*, *Jewish Review of Books*, *First Things*, and *The Jerusalem Post*.

JACOB KUPIETZKY is a healthcare entrepreneur and advisor to hospitals and healthcare systems. His writings on healthcare have been featured in *Forbes* and *Newsweek*, among other publications. He is a Wexner Heritage Fellow and serves on the boards of multiple Chicago-based and international not-for-profit organizations.